Only in Pittsburgh

ONLY IN

PITTSBURGH

S. Trevor Hadley

Library of Congress Cataloging-in-Publication Data
Hadley, S. Trevor.
    Only in Pittsburgh / S. Trevor Hadley.
1. Pittsburgh. 2. History—urban.

ISBN: 0-9642251-0-7

The author wishes to thank the following publications in which some of the chapters, in slightly different form, have already appeared: *In Pittsburgh, Pittsburgh Magazine, Pittsburgh History,* and *Susquehanna Magazine.*

Only in Pittsburgh is available at special discounts for bulk purchases for sales promotions, premiums, fund-raising, or educational use. For details, contact:

educational publishing resources
PO Box 19942
Cincinnati, OH 45221
FAX: 513/221-8543

Desktop publishing production by educational publishing resources
Printed in the United States of America
Published July 1994
Second Printing, April 1995

To—

Elaine, for being my editor
Olive, for moral support
Pam, for publishing assistance

Table of Contents

V. The City

Appendix

Introduction

Seventy years ago as a boy living in a small Western Pennsylvania town, I anxiously anticipated my annual visit to Pittsburgh and my grandmother's house in old Allentown. After retirement, my wife, Olive—a Pittsburgh native—and I moved to Pittsburgh and my love affair with the city was renewed.

Pittsburgh is an extraordinary city. Its historical roots are central to the western growth of the United States; its ethnic groups fired the industrial furnaces that made the country an economic power; and it spawned industrial fortunes for many. Those personal fortunes comprised a philanthropic base that originated and sustains a cultural and artistic legacy that continues to prosper and benefit today's residents.

I like its people, its traditions, its cultural assets, its sports teams, its hills and rivers. I hope these historical vignettes of Pittsburgh's past will help others to appreciate this city as I do.

S. Trevor Hadley

Part I
Events

St. Clair Incline disaster on April 6, 1909

Whatever Happened to Grant's Hill and The Hump? (1758-1961)

Grant Street in downtown Pittsburgh was recently redesigned and rebuilt. It was not the first time. Through the years this urban thoroughfare has seen several reconstructions. In its earliest mention in recorded history, it was Grant's Hill. In the 18th century, when it was named The Hump, it jutted out of the Golden Triangle and effectively served as the eastern boundary of a growing city.

Actually The Hump was a gumdrop shaped hill enclosed by 4th Street, Smithfield Street, 6th Avenue, and Ross Street and it covered an area of approximately 20 acres.

One flowery writer in the 1930s declared that Grant's Hill was, "one of the Earth's immortal hills: four nations have made it so"—the Indian, the French, the English, and finally, the Americans.

Grant's Hill, less ostentatiously but more effectively referred to as The Hump by Pittsburghers, was the subject of many sessions of City Council, of innumerable public meetings and of endless business gatherings. In the early 1800s a $2 million bond issue designed to eliminate The Hump was defeated at the polls largely because taxpayers thought the project was too costly. Over the years gradual changes had been made to Grant's Hill, until in the late 1800s, only a sized-down remnant of The Hump remained.

Grant's Hill played an important role in Pittsburgh's early history. In those days if you stood on Grant's Hill, you had an unobstructed view of the forts lying at the confluence of the Allegheny and Monongahela Rivers in a natural setting unsurpassed in drama and majesty. Clumps of trees grew on its irregular surface, but there were wide open spaces as well, grassy in summer, where bushes grew in profusion. From the top of the hill you could see all the towns and villages for miles around, a view yet to be obstructed by Pittsburgh's industrial future.

At the foot of the hill was a large pond, located approximately where Kaufmann's Department Store now stands, stretching from 4th to 7th Avenues. It was named Hoggs Pond for old Granny Hogg, an early resident. According to Boucher, one of Pittsburgh's earliest historians, Hogg's Pond was a "swampy water that stood at the foot of Grant's Hill and had a narrow outlet into the Monongahela River."

Grant's Hill earned its name on September 14, 1758, when the Indians and the French soldiers stationed at Fort Duquesne near the Point were awakened by the drums and bagpipes signaling an attack by the British army under Major James Grant. Using tomahawks and scalping knives, the Indians and French routed Grant's army on the hilltop one mile east of Fort Duquesne; from that day forward, the hilltop was known as Grant's Hill.

This skirmish proved to be the high water mark of the French domination of the area, because only two months later Pittsburgh's hero, General Forbes, crossed Grant's Hill and routed the French troops from Fort Duquesne. France's threat to dominate the river routes to the West had ended.

As the city grew, Grant's Hill became a parade ground, a pleasure park, and a tavern lot. The tavern, owned by John Marie, a Frenchman, was the center of the area's social life, the headquarters of the Republican Party as well as for the officers of the militia, and the meeting place for many Pittsburghers and their visitors. Marie's Tavern stood on the northeast corner of Grant Street and Braddocksfield Road where it connected with 4th Street. It contained six acres of gravel walks and cultivated gardens. The militia's parade ground adjoined the tavern and here onlookers came to watch the colorful military parades in April and October.

Fifteen hundred citizens gathered on Grant's Hill in 1788 to celebrate the ratification of the Colonies' Federal Constitution. Thirteen huge bonfires were built, one for each of the colonies, but only nine were fired, representing the nine states that had ratified the new Constitution. Later, all thirteen fires were ignited and while youths danced around them on the

4

green, one commentator observed that, "the Indians who were present stood in amazement at the scene."

Just beyond Grant's Hill was a hunter's paradise. The buffalo had recently disappeared, but there were many bears, wolves, panthers, and wildcats. Also in abundance were wild turkeys, pigeons, ducks, pheasants, rabbits, squirrels, deer, elk, beaver, raccoons, and fox. One fur trader from the area in 1786 recorded that he had traded over 4,000 fur pelts in one season, principally for whiskey and flour.

Grant's Hill also played a small but interesting role in the Whiskey Rebellion of 1794, when a motley army of insurgents marched through the city, threatening to burn it. Alexander Hamilton, America's first Secretary of the Treasury, in an effort to increase the nation's revenues, had just placed in effect new tariff laws and a direct excise tax on liquors. Back country farmers were furious; whiskey was their most salable product and the one easiest to transport. Only when Washington sent an army of several thousand into Pennsylvania were the armed mobs dispersed and order restored. The mob that invaded Pittsburgh was persuaded to rest on Grant's Hill, where refreshed with food and whiskey, the rebels were kept in good humor, and apparently lost their fervor for insurrection.

Despite The Hump's rich history, Pittsburghers increasingly felt that the future growth of the city depended on the removal of this awkward landmark. In fact The Hump was so steep that wagons were frequently unable to reach its top; the grade was awesome, rising over 20 feet in 100 linear feet. After much bickering and indecision, four separate projects were utilized to finally eliminate The Hump forever from the Pittsburgh scene.

In 1836 pick and shovel laborers cut 10 feet off the top of The Hump and used the dirt to fill in Hogg's Pond which disappeared forever from Pittsburgh maps. In 1844 another minor effort was made to remove several feet of the hill.

In April of 1845 a great fire destroyed much of the city, and this event initiated the removal of seven more feet from the top of The Hump in 1847. This attack on The Hump created considerable controversy because the old St. Paul's Cathedral opposite the Courthouse was left high and dry, fifteen feet above Grant Street. Parishioners had to climb twenty-six wooden steps to reach the main entrance to the church. Three years later the church burned to the ground; Henry Clay Frick bought the property, and the controversy was ended. Pittsburgh was experiencing severe growing pains; land available for downtown development had become scarce, and most agreed that The Hump had to go.

Not everyone agreed. Henry Marie Brackenridge, the son of a famed Pittsburgh judge, Hugh Henry Brackenridge, recalled in 1840, how as a lad, he had rolled over and over down the green velvet sides of Grant's Hill. Brackenridge's nostalgia for his own childhood and its idyllic play influenced both his perception of the hill's charms and his resentment toward the modernization affecting it. He declared that, "The shallow pond at its base where we used to make our first attempts at skating, has been wickedly and willfully filled up, and is now concealed by brick buildings; the croaking of the town's frogs having given place to men more noisy still than they."

It wasn't until 65 years later that the city of Pittsburgh launched its final attack on The Hump. In 1909, Public Works Director, Joseph G. Armstrong, ordered the preparation of a chart showing which property owners would be affected by the proposed cut. Major opposition to the project had finally disappeared and plans for its removal moved forward with little controversy.

However, The Hump did not disappear without one last addition to the annals of Pittsburgh history. In an effort to block the project, based largely on the project's cost to the taxpayers, Attorney A. E. Anderson of Pittsburgh filed a suit in the name of his client, Wensel Novotny of Steubenville, Ohio. The suit asked the court for a permanent injunction to stop the project, claiming that the cost would be more than the City Council had the authority to approve.

The city nonetheless moved ahead with its plans, largely ignoring the suit, and signed a contract with Booth and Flynn Construction Company to remove 143,000 cubic yards of dirt, to replace 175,000 square feet of sidewalk, to purchase 150,000 square feet of lumber for temporary sidewalks, and to lay 18,000 feet of new sewer lines. In the process 17 feet of The Hump was to be removed. The total bill for the project was $3,165,000, which included $2,400,000 in property reparations, no small project for the early 19th century. Over 159,000 cubic yards of earth and rock were removed and used to fill in low lying streets on the North Side of the city which were subject to frequent flooding.

Pittsburgh's two major daily newspapers had striking headlines on April 5, 1912. The *Pittsburgh Post* read, "Work of Cutting Troublous Hump To

Start at Last: Removal of Wart from City's Complexion To Begin This Morning." The *Pittsburgh Dispatch* countered with, "Pittsburgh's Populace Turns Out To See Puncture of Mooted Obstacle." In a town blackened by soot and grime, this landmark had lost its charm and was now seen as a barrier to the city's progress.

In prose suggesting that the city was performing a generous act of euthanasia on an ailing terminal patient, the *Pittsburgh Dispatch* on the same day declared that "one by one of the councilmen and friends of The Hump extracted some earth from the rapidly growing incision and The Hump began to feel for the first time a little of the sluggish blood, undisturbed for some decades past, beginning to ebb away."

Councilman Babcock, speaking at the ground breaking, hoped to expose Anderson, the attorney who filed the suit. He claimed his only purpose was to get publicity. Babcock stated:

He is the man who had to go outside the city of Pittsburgh and buy a client. I would not dare to say so or he would sue me in 24 hours, but the newspapers say that he bought a client to stop the great improvement in the city. He is as much use to the city as a wart on your nose. You don't need him.

The newspaper account duly reported that Attorney Anderson was present at the ground breaking and demonstrated his sense of humor when he added that, "He didn't want to get too close to the hole, or he would have been dumped in."

After the speech many of the onlookers made a mad dash to dig up paving stones as souvenirs of the big event. Some property owners were so delighted with the disappearance of The Hump that they refused property damages from the city. Fortunately by this time, steam shovels, called "steam Irishmen," were used for the heaviest work. Miles of sewer pipes, water and gas lines had to be re-installed and many buildings were demolished because their foundations did not extend below the new ground surface. Larger buildings had to spend extensive sums of money to create new entrances and new first floors that did not exist before the removal of The Hump.

Actually the final attack on The Hump did not occur until 1961. One last chunk of old Grant's Hill still stood at the corner of Webster and 7th

Avenues. When the Crosstown Boulevard was built, this last vestige of a famous hill was gone forever.

Today the most visible signs of the existence of The Hump can be found at the Frick Building and the Allegheny County Courthouse, directly opposite in Grant Street. The impressive "doubled" lobby of the Frick Building illustrates the major remodeling required when The Hump was removed. The two lobbies are easily identified. The lower lobby was created out of the original basement and was totally rebuilt in 1912 when The Hump was removed. The original lobby, now the second floor, had to be uniquely redesigned so that it now exists as a mezzanine. The two huge sculptured lions which now rise up 20 feet above the street, were originally at street level. These lions, sculpted by Alexander Phimaster Proctor, a noted sculptor of the day, were prototypes of the lions gracing the New York City Public Library.

At the Courthouse, Grant Street in 1910 stood 10 feet higher above the street than it does today. When The Hump was finally removed, the doorways to Grant Street were lengthened downwards and the entrances rebuilt. This reconstruction was accomplished with tact and with little damage to the original design of the building. Before 1910 the arched doorways led directly into the first floor; no steps were necessary.

It is doubtful whether Grant's Hill deserves to be called "one of the Earth's immortal hills," but it did play a unique role in the history of Pittsburgh. Grant Street's history for the next 200 years may prove just as exciting, although Grant's Hill and The Hump are gone forever.

Pittsburgh's Great Expositions (1875-1916)

Pittsburgh in the late 19th century was badly in need of a good press agent. Although recognized as one of America's industrial goliaths, it had become known far and wide as a dreadful place to live. In 1868 the Boston journalist, James Parton, called Pittsburgh, "Hell with the lid taken off." Willard Glazier describing Pittsburgh in 1883 said that, "Pittsburg (sic) is a smoky, dismal city at best. At her worst, nothing darker, dingier, or more dispiriting can be imagined."

Cases of typhoid fever and the incidence of industrial accidents were higher in Pittsburgh than in any other city in the world. H. L. Mencken, the most widely read journalist of his day, spared no words when writing about the city:

Here was the very heart of industrial America, the center of the most lucrative and characteristic activity, the boast and the pride of the richest and grandest nation ever seen on earth—and here was a scene so dreadfully hideous, so intolerably bleak and forlorn that it reduced the whole aspiration of man to a macabre and depressing joke. Here was wealth beyond computation, almost beyond imagination—and here were human habitations so abominable that they would have disgraced a race of alley cats. I am not speaking of mere filth. One expects steel towns to be dirty. What I allude to is the unbroken and agonizing ugliness, the sheer revolting monstrousness of every house in sight.

It became obvious to Pittsburgh's leaders in the late 19th century that the city needed a vehicle by which to do something positive about its image. Pittsburgh was oriented to manufacturing and to business, but it wanted to portray a different face to the country and to the world. An Exposition Society was formed in 1875 to promote and exhibit Pittsburgh goods, to provide its citizens with entertainment, and to boast about the city's industrial achievements. England since the 1850s had been staging successful exhibitions highlighting its industrial and technological achievements. Pittsburgh felt it was time to showcase its industrial might.

The first Expositions were held in a large hall on an island in the Allegheny River, named Smokey Island, later known as Kilbuck Island, located off South Avenue in old Allegheny, at that time a separate borough, not part of the city. The Exposition first opened its doors in 1875 and held annual exhibitions along with fireworks displays, balloon ascensions, art exhibitions, and enjoyed modest success until 1883. Those were the first in a long history of Pittsburgh Expositions.

The Expositions opened each year with huge parades and immense crowds; exhibitors were turned away due to lack of space. People did complain that the smoke and steam from the main building hid its beauty, but there was no question about the success of the annual event in the eyes of Pittsburgh's citizens. Some of the wonders first shown in the Old Exposition included the first telephone, the first arc light, and a startling demonstration of electrical current moving through a barbed wire.

Fire leveled the Exposition buildings in 1877, but they were quickly rebuilt only to experience yet another fire. On October 3, 1883, enormous crowds thronged the buildings all day and late into the evening. The city was celebrating Grand Army of the Republic Day, and all the booths were smothered in tinsel and cotton bunting; floors were highly polished. Shortly after the closing hour of 2 a.m., the whole complex went up in fire and smoke, making the "grandest display of fireworks ever seen in the city." Those were the words used by the news media the next day describing the event. One eyewitness claimed that the fire started from a hot air balloon spread out in a boiler room to dry.

Among the exhibits destroyed in the great fire were Old Arabian, a Baltimore and Ohio steam locomotive, Stephenson, one of Pittsburgh's early street cars, and over 50 engines of every variety. Also destroyed was a collection of rare coins and a display of sealskin coats worth a $1,000. Merchants lost thousands of dollars in the fire. Mary Roberts Rinehart, one of Pittsburgh's famous novelists, told how at seven years of age she watched the 600-foot long wooden structure go up in flames. Newspapers reported the fire loss at $375,000, a tidy sum in those days. Insurance coverage was almost non-existent; the loss was total.

The site on the North Side of the city was eventually sold to the Pittsburgh Baseball Club and the baseball field built there was always known as Exposition Park. The Pirates played at Exposition Park for many years and among the baseball immortals who played there were: Honus Wagner, Fred Clarke, Tommy Leach, Rube Waddell, Joe Tinker, Johnny Evers, and Frank Chance. The first World Series was played in the park in 1903 between the Pirates and the Boston Red Sox. The old park was abandoned in 1909 when the Pirates moved to Forbes Field in Oakland.

Not long after the fire a number of Pittsburgh's leading citizens were aboard a steamboat observing the dedication of the new Davis Island Dam and also viewing the ruins of the fire from the river. They vowed that the idea of an annual Exposition "might not pass out of the minds of the people," and determined that they would establish a new and permanent Exposition at a new location. Pittsburgh needed a new image; for too long it had been known as the Smoky City. Newspapers the next day quoted them as declaring in mixed metaphors and mixed motives, moral and economic: "The city must emerge into the sunlight, and like a huge elephant reposing in the dust, arouse finally to shake off the dust and cause it to fly off in all directions. It must shake off its swaddling clothes and come into its own. You cannot build a city without advertising."

The first formal meeting of this dedicated group of citizens was held in the back office of the old Bindley Hardware in downtown Pittsburgh. Each man present donated a hundred dollars as a nucleus of the half million dollars they estimated they would need to pull off the project. The president of the group, S. S. Marvin, said that the Exposition was, "floated on the back of an envelope and the stub of a pencil."

The Exposition Society was incorporated in 1885. Charter members included some of Pittsburgh's best known names, Gillespie, Burchfield, Bindley, Heinz, Rosenbaum, Buhl, and others. Fourteen hundred charter members were enrolled at a hundred dollars each. In return each member was given twenty-four 25¢ admission tickets to each annual Exposition. The Exposition in old Allegheny had been somewhat crude, resembling a county fair with horse races and amusements, but its loss had been keenly felt and a public clamor called for its renewal. The new Society began to plan for a more permanent location along with more emphasis on educational and instructional features. The Society claimed that its purpose was to "entertain, uplift, and instruct the people, not only of Pittsburgh, but of the entire surrounding area, and to give them year-by-year information on the progress of their own community in all lines from music and art to advancements in science, horticulture, agriculture, and commercial pursuits." As further evidence of their civic mindedness, the Society proclaimed that all its proceeds would be used to establish a new polytechnic school "for the coming generations of the sons and daughters of workingmen who otherwise would not be able to afford higher education for their children."

This educational objective caught Andrew Carnegie's attention and he threw considerable support behind the project. The largest single contribution reported in the press was $5,000 from Mrs. Mary Schenley. Smaller donations poured in from employees in large and small establishments, and a subscription fund in Pittsburgh newspapers raised an additional $1,500.

The Western Pennsylvania Exposition Society was chartered under the Wallace Act as a non-profit organization with no dividends to its stockholders. It was an educational enterprise, with free admission guaranteed to all school children, where they "might study the wonders of the most remarkable city in the world." Provision was made for music, not the minstrel type so common in that day, but for classical and semiclassical performances by the most famous artists, orchestras, and bands. Admission was to be 25¢ for all adults, which entitled the holder to admission to all shows and exhibits.

The Society immediately made plans to find a new site for the Exposition. It was decided that a plot of land along the Allegheny River near the Point was the best available, and the city leased the land to the Society at an annual rental of $1. The Pennsylvania Railroad Company provided $20,000 in loan certificates and promised that if the Society had to default on the loan, they would take the unfinished buildings and convert them into a freight depot.

Unfortunately, construction was delayed for some time when a suit was brought by several property owners near the site claiming that the

Exposition would interfere seriously with the boat building industry near the Point. Work on the project was delayed for one year until the State Supreme Court declared that the grant of land from the city was legal.

One of the arguments used in selecting the new site for the Exposition was that it might help clean up Pittsburgh's river banks. Until this time no attempt had ever been made to beautify the banks of Pittsburgh's three great rivers. Until then, the banks of the rivers were lined with large industrial establishments, or they were the dumping ground for refuse of every kind— old boilers, chairs, skeletons of decayed boats, and general rubbish of every variety. In the summer citizens complained of the foul odors, and the Point was notorious for its rancid smells on hot summer nights.

The main building was erected first, next to the Point; later the Music Hall was constructed. The Music Hall was unique in design, part of the audience being located in elevated seats behind the stage, with an immense seating capacity in front of the stage. Machinery Hall followed soon after, a portable building which could be dismantled and moved. Even the slate on the roof was held in place by copper nails which could be removed with little loss of slate.

Machinery Hall was designed by William Hemphill of the McIntosh– Hemphill Co., and was built by the Marshall Foundry and Construction Co. The news media reported that, "the building was begun with hardly a dollar in sight," but the Marshall Co. said that if it did not get its money, it would put a lien on the building and use it as a foundry and machine shop. Like all the other projects, the building was completed ahead of schedule, and was promptly paid for. The Exposition re-opened its doors in 1899.

It is difficult for us today to visualize life as it existed in Pittsburgh in the 1800s. The city had no public parks, no art galleries, and no serious efforts were made to promote musical activities. Many streets were unpaved and life beyond the forge, the office, and the shop was given little attention. None of the streets near the Point were paved, no street cars ran near the place, and the new site of the Exposition was decidedly unattractive. It was quite an act of faith to invest heavily at the new Exposition site. In spite of these shortcomings, over 250,000 people attended in 1899. The city's railroads made a significant contribution by running special excursion trains from all over the tri-state area, and soon Exposition Week became Pittsburgh's most important attraction.

Contemporary accounts of Pittsburgh's Expositions provide striking insight into the crucial role that they played in the social lives of Pittsburgh's citizens. Mary E. Bakewell, daughter of one of the city's best known families, writing in the *Western Pennsylvania Historical Society Magazine* in 1947, had fond memories of the early Expositions:

> In September we were permitted to go farther afield—to the Expositions at the Point. The Expos were the outgrowth of less sophisticated county fairs. They were a valuable asset for merchants and manufacturers. Twenty-five cents and we were in the midst of it—a welter of grinding or pushing or rolling machines of every description, dry goods exhibits, large variety of materials samples of pickles, jellies, butters—popcorn, most of all, once munched, never forgotten. Another twenty-five cents to enter Machinery Hall where twice a day music could be enjoyed—brought from the Land of Culture, meaning Philadelphia and New York. Usually a brass band, playing martial melodies, but notably Walter Damrosch—bringing Wagner to Pittsburgh—heard dubiously at first, but even to untrained ears something great in *Pilgrim's Chorus* and *Song of the Evening Star*—we waited patiently not then knowing how far along the road to glory *Tristan and Isolde* would take us.

Elizabeth Ledwidge, a teacher in the Pittsburgh Public Schools, wrote about attending the Exposition in 1908 which was also Pittsburgh's Sesqui-Centennial. She wrote:

> We spent Exposition Day at the Point. Large crowds had assembled to hear Mayor Guthrie and Roger Pryor's Band play compositions from Pittsburgh composers. Among other things we saw specimens of armor plate and many projectiles. The major exhibit was a model of the Sprague, the largest river steamboat in the world, towing 50,000 tons of coal in barges.

Herbert Steinbrink, a friend of the author, grew up in Pittsburgh as a young boy and spoke of some of the early Expositions at the Point which he attended:

Pittsburgh used to have wonderful Expositions. They had beautiful buildings. That's where Goldman and Sousa came with their bands; every time Sousa or Goldman came, the place was crowded. It was like a little Smithsonian Institution; they had a lot of things. They had shows and an iron building there. The New York City Fire Department had a display of saving peoples' lives in a burning building. It was all steel. They would set off a fire inside and the flames would be coming out all over the building—and the horses—regular big fire horses—would come in with the steam pumper and pump water into the windows. Then they would get the net out and people would jump into the net. One time the jumper did not wait for the proper moment and jumped before the net was ready.

Only two years after the opening of the new Exposition buildings, a third great fire figured prominently in the history of the Exposition. In the early morning of March 18, 1901, fire broke out in a large frame stable directly opposite the main building. Wind blew flaming embers across the street and soon the Exposition buildings were a mass of flames. The fire was long remembered for its intensity, and when it was out all that remained was Machinery Hall. Among the valuables lost in the fire were Stephen Collins Foster's piano and the nation's first steam locomotive. The fire was a tragedy because the Society had virtually wiped out its debts and was preparing to turn over its receipts to the long-planned-for technical school. The fire proved to be the death knell for the technical school, but not for the Exposition.

By May of 1901 a new contract was signed to replace the burned buildings. The James Stuart Co. began construction immediately with completion promised in time for the regular season of 1901. The rapid completion of the project and the fact that no interruption of the Exposition occurred, did much to animate public interest to a higher level than ever before. The Exposition season was extended to 46 days with expanded programs.

The annual show grew in size and importance. It changed over the years from a local exhibition into one of international scope. Foreign countries began to participate; the national government was a regular exhibitor, and the state of Pennsylvania became a strong supporter. No other exhibition in the United States had lived so long or prospered so abundantly, and scores of other cities began to emulate it. Most inventions by Pittsburgh men were first displayed there, and many prosperous businessmen credited their success to the exposure given their products in the Exposition. The Exposition buildings were used for other memorable events in the city's history. The International Sabbath School Association held its greatest convention there entertaining over 1,200 delegates for over a week. The famous Gypsy Smith evangelistic campaigns were staged yearly in the main building. President Theodore Roosevelt and Republican Presidential candidate Charles E. Hughes addressed vast crowds of followers there. In May of 1896 the national convention of the Prohibition Party was held in the main building. Harry Castle, delivering the keynote address, declared that, "I know of no other city with darker skies and brighter men and women, with dirtier hands and cleaner hearts, with narrower crookeder streets and broader straighter hospitality." This speech was one of the few positive highlights of the convention as the assembled delegates split over the free coinage issue, formed two separate parties, and neither ever regained much popularity.

The annual musical shows became world famous. The finest orchestras and bands from around the world were featured. Among the musical organizations that appeared were: Walter Damrosch's New York Symphony, John Philip Sousa and his world famous band, Lt. Dan Godfrey's British Guards Band from London, Banda Rosa's great Red Band from Italy, Emil Paur's renowned metropolitan orchestra from Leipzig, Germany, and the Chicago, Philadelphia, and Cincinnati symphonies.

Exceptional art exhibits were shown every year. In 1890 the renowned Bierstadt Collection of fine art was brought to Pittsburgh to be shown to the public for the first time. Every year some valuable art was brought to the city for its citizens to view and enjoy.

Each year's featured attractions give a good overview of the variety and quality of the Exposition's programs, a heterogeneous combination of high and low culture:

1889   A smokeless powder mill; a completely furnished Pullman car; a demonstration of deep sea diving equipment.

1891   A huge illustrated fountain; a diorama of the Fall of Pompeii; a demonstration of glassmaking.

1893   Demonstrations by D. W. Reaves, who invented triple tonguing of brass instruments; a great singers series featuring Black Patti, Scalchi, Materna (Wagner's favorite soprano), and Blauvelt.

1894   The first typesetting machine; a model of a beef processing plant; a machine for testing cloth, cement, iron, steel, and paper; a working model of a coke mill and a coal mine.

1895   A switchback railroad ride similar to a roller coaster which followed the river front for 1,000 yards and cost 5¢ to ride; Carnegie Steel Co. demonstrated the manufacture of armor plate; a ferris wheel; a high illuminated sign with letters four feet high.

1896   A replica of the W. M. Laird Shoe Factory showing the manufacture of shoes from animal to finished product.

1900   A merry-go-round; a gravity railroad; a wonder horse which could "read, write, spell, count, change money, and use a cash register"; replicas of an Alpine Village and a Mexican village.

1901   Dioramas of the Johnstown Flood and the San Francisco earthquake; cruises on a river steamboat with a ballyhoo man with a megaphone who promised, "On my honor, you will get your money back, if the boat sinks."

1908   A portrayal of the Rough Riders charging up San Juan Hill under fire from Spanish guns, replete with fumes of gunpowder; the sinking of the battleship Maine; American troops storming Spanish trenches.

1909   A diorama of the battle between the Monitor and the Merrimac with copious gunfire and a man with a megaphone describing the event.

1910   A great live display of a blazing fire in a tenement house complete with fireworks, flames, fire horses rushing to the fire, and a girl jumping from an upper floor into a fire net. The press reported that one night the regular girl was ill and the understudy was so eager to make good that she rushed to the window before her cue and jumped into the street with no net below. She was seriously injured.

1911   The sinking of the Titanic.

1913   Lincoln's Emancipation Proclamation was exhibited; a painting was shown of the Great Seal of the United States; a modern Gatling gun; oil paintings of Fulton, Edison, and Benjamin Franklin; the original army wagon that accompanied Sherman on his march to the sea.

It was 1916 when the Exposition finally closed, falling victim to World War I and a serious outbreak of polio in the city. The day after the Exposition opened in that year, health authorities banned all children from mingling in crowds. Parents stayed away by the thousands and the great Pittsburgh Exposition was doomed. It closed its doors deeply in debt.

The buildings stood for many years after the closing of the Exposition. The city used them for various purposes. Old Machinery Hall was used to store cars and to house the city's machine shop. Old fire trucks were dismantled; automobiles were repaired; and ladders were manufactured for use by the fire department. Forges made springs for automobiles; street signs were painted; traffic lights were repaired; and hose nozzles were manufactured. For years the old Exposition site was a dismal place until 1950 when the last remains of the Pittsburgh Exposition were torn down to make way for the new Duquesne Way traffic artery.

It took another 40 years before a concerted effort was mounted to clean up Pittsburgh's river banks and to capitalize on one of its most striking geographical advantages. Today the better use of these rivers is high on the priority list of every city planner, but it seems tragic that it has taken so long for the city's residents to realize the potential of its physical location.

Nothing remains of the Pittsburgh Exposition but memories. Once thousands of school children passed through its portals, lunch boxes in hand, waiting patiently to view the marvels displayed inside. There were souvenir pickles to take home, limitless pans of colored taffy, peep shows, roller coaster and steamboat rides. One could easily survive on the free samples passed out in the Main Hall—cheese crackers, cakes, popcorn, new cereals, pickles, and candy, not to mention free balloons.

When evening came it was time for the great concerts—Victor Herbert, Walter Damrosch, John Philip Sousa, or the Chicago Orchestra. Pianos tinkled; there was laughing and shouting from the crowds of people; there were long walks along the riverfront and romantic steamboat rides on the rivers; and up on the balconies there were fortune-telling devices, weight guessing, and little movie theatres showing the Keystone Cops, or a "Trip Through Switzerland."

Only a small number of Pittsburgh residents are still alive who have firsthand memories of the Great Pittsburgh Expositions, but they are remembered as important events in the early history and development of a great city.

3

Inclined to Disaster
(1909)

Eighty-five years ago, passengers on the St. Clair Incline on Pittsburgh's South Side took a ride to the top—and a much faster ride to the bottom.

It was 3:30 on the morning of April 6, 1909, several hours before the first gray streaks of dawn would slip over the hills lining the Monongahela River and pierce the smog over Pittsburgh's industrial South Side.

Pittsburgh had been built around its three river waterways, and had early used inclines to transport its workers to and from their homes on the hills to their working places in the river valleys.

The night shift at the D. O. Cunningham Glass Company at Jane and 22nd Streets on the South Side had just finished its turn. The workers scattered, many of them heading for the St. Clair Incline, which lifted them up the steep hillside to St. Clair Borough, where they lived. Many of the passengers were 15-, 16-, and 17-year-old boys, already part of the urban work force of the city. On most mornings there would be more than 50 men and boys on the incline, but on this particular day, many were delayed and missed the first incline trip.

On schedule, the creaky old incline began its ascent. Men and boys grasped their empty lunch pails and either dreamed of the night's sleep that lay ahead or simply stared blankly at the darkness of the night.

As the car headed toward the depot at the top of the hill, it appeared to proceed normally, though several passengers later said that the car seemed to have been moving unusually fast. With a sickening jolt, the incline hit the cement abutment at the top of the hill and rebounded away from the platform, careening back down the steep grade at a rapid rate of speed.

Screams and cries of help filled the air. Two boys, Arthur Miller, 17, and Albert Klingenberger, 16, jumped from the runaway car into the darkness of the hillside. Both were later found dead of their injuries. Frank Bredl, 17, also jumped, but made his decision earlier, before the car achieved its maximum speed. Although he received many cuts and bruises, he was not severely injured.

One of the other passengers, Herman Weidershift, was reported to be the hero of the day. Other riders said that when the car started down the incline out of control, he yelled to everyone to lie down to cushion the force of the collision. When interviewed, he said:

I can't remember what I did, but I hope what they reported is true, because it was the right thing to do. You know that when you are speeding to certain death with only a few seconds to think, you can't remember what you did. I was in an accident on the same incline several years ago, but last night was about the most thrilling experience of my life. I'm getting my nerve back a little bit today, but I'm not denying that it was about all taken out of me last night.

Later it was found that neither cable on the incline had broken, but both cables had been torn loose from their drums. This was crucial to understanding the accident, because if this had not happened, the lower car would have begun its counter-balancing upward trip and would have served as a brake on the descent of the upper car. Instead the upper car careened wildly down the inclined plane.

The crash was heard for blocks. People came running to the incline from all directions. News spread rapidly; long before daylight, frantic fathers, mothers, and wives besieged those in authority for news. The entire South Side was aroused; hundreds of sympathetic friends converged on the homes of the dead boys.

Fortunately, all the injured recovered, so that the final toll in the accident proved to be two dead and eight injured. Spectators marveled that the injury and death toll was not higher. One need only look at the picture of the accident to marvel at the low death toll. The city was in mourning. The deaths of the boys were reported to be the first fatalities on a Pittsburgh incline since the first one, the Monongahela, went into service in 1870.

The *Pittsburgh Post* headline the next morning read, "Incline Cars Smashed to Kindling Wood When Engineer Falls in Faint." Patrolman Arthur Schwalm, who was on duty at the top of the incline, claimed to have seen the entire event. He said that he saw the car moving too rapidly toward the top of the incline. He saw and heard the engineer, Jesse Burton, appear at a side window and yell, "My God, I want air," and then fall over in a faint. Burton later confirmed this observation, saying that he felt faint, went to brake the car to slow it down, and then fainted, falling against the controls, which released the brakes and resulted in the car careening down the inclined plane. Fortunately, the engineer was not seriously injured.

Burton, who had worked at the incline for more than a year, was highly regarded by his employer; no attempt was ever made to blame the engineer or the conductor at the bottom of the incline.

The two "boy workers" who were killed had been out of work for a long time and had been called back to their jobs only a few days before the accident. They were happy at the prospect of bringing money home to help their families. Mary Miller, the mother of one of the boys, reported that her son "had premonitions and did not want to go to work that day because he was afraid of being fired; when I saw him next he was a corpse."

Many official investigations followed. It was reported that the State Railroad Commission had filed a detailed report many weeks before. The report claimed that there was overcrowding on the inclines and strongly recommended that an extra operator should be present on every trip.

It was also confirmed that when the cables slipped the drums, the lower incline car remained at the bottom and may have saved many lives. It seems that the descending car rammed into the stationary one at the bottom of the rails and it was assumed that this served to cushion to some degree the impact of the crash. The picture of the accident at the beginning of this section (p. 1) was a postcard that sold widely in Pittsburgh after the accident. One can clearly observe in the picture how the one car sideswiped the other at the bottom of the incline.

Deputy Coroner George Ambrose was very critical of the incline's operation. He insisted that all inclines should have automatic stops and "a second man at the top, since any man can have a heart attack."

It was weeks before the South Side managed to talk about anything but the accident. This incident is well documented in the *Pittsburgh Post* editions of April 7, 1909. It is interesting to note, however, that the *Pittsburgh Press*, in an article appearing on May 24, 1970, said that "no human rider has ever been killed in the history of all Pittsburgh inclines." And in a feature article about Pittsburgh's inclines which appeared in *Pittsburgh Magazine* in May 1983, Pat Kiger asserted that "there have never been recorded passenger fatalities on Pittsburgh inclines."

These statements are doubly inaccurate since on October 7, 1953, a thirteen-year-old boy, Alan Schilling, who lived on Excelsior Street in Allentown, was hitching an illegal ride on the back of the old Knoxville Incline. He was returning home after a football game on the South Side, lost his hold, and was found dead the next morning by friends who went looking for him.

However, Pittsburgh's 17 famous inclines certainly played a significant role in the growth and development of a great industrial city, and over the years compiled a safety record that would be hard to match by any public transportation system.

4

The Great Pittsburgh Poetry Hoax (1916-1918)

OPUS 79

Only the wise can see me in the mist,
  For only lovers know that I am here...
After his piping, shall the organist
  Be portly and appear?

Pew after pew,
  Wave after wave...
Shall the digger dig and then undo
  His own dear grave?

Hear me in the playing
  Of a big brass band...
See me, straying
  With children in hand...

Smell me, a dead fish...
  Taste me, a rotten tree...
Someday touch me all you wish,
  In the wide sea.

    Emanuel Morgan

OPUS 118

If bathing were a virtue, not a lust,
  I would be dirtiest.

  To some, housecleaning is a holy writ.
For myself, houses would be empty
But for the golden motes dancing in sunbeams.

  Tax assessors frequently overlook valuables,
Today they noted my jade,
But my memory of you escaped them.

    Anne Knish

It was the autumn of the year 1916. Magazine editors and literary critics found on their desks a small, unpretentious volume of some 60 pages bound in gray with a black and white cover. The volume was titled SPECTRA in large black letters and beneath the title appeared the names of two authors, Emanuel Morgan and Anne Knish, two names totally unfamiliar to the literary world of the day.

The book had no dust jacket, no biographical information on the poets, thus, one would assume, would have probably gone unnoticed. Instead, it proved to be something of a literary bombshell. Many aspects of the story added to the mystery. Critics were bemused that a new form of modern poetry should spring up out of Pittsburgh, a city never identified with literary movements and certainly never considered a likely birthplace for a new literary invention.

The publicity which the volume aroused was not all favorable. The *Philadelphia Public Ledger* of March 24, 1917, said that the Spectrists would, "not disturb the world of verse in America or set any river on fire unless it be the Monongahela when it is covered with oil scum."

Nevertheless for a brief and shining period in the early 20th century it appeared that Pittsburgh would become world renowned for generating a new school of poetry, and its "Spectric" theory of composition which would "push the possibilities of poetic expression into a new region—to attain a fresh brilliance of impression by a method not so wholly different from the methods of Futurist Painting" as Anne Knish phrased it.

The early years of the 20th century saw poetry being analyzed and categorized as never before. Critics began to speak of schools of poetry, among which were, the Romanticists, the Empiricists, the Vorticists, the Imagists, the Pessimists, and the Idealists. Symposiums were held, and anthologies tried to label each of the poets as members of various schools. Therefore, the sudden appearance of a new school of Spectric Poetry seemed to be one more natural development in the literary world.

The sudden emergence of this new Spectric School of poetic expression aroused a variety of responses both in the literary world and without. *Others*, an influential little magazine of the day edited from New York by Alfred Kreymborg and backed by Walter Conrad Arensberg, one of the great patrons of modern art, devoted a special issue in January, 1919, to the Spectric School of poetry. Thomas Raymond, a Republican candidate for mayor in the city of Newark, New Jersey, included in his campaign speeches, presumably rousing readings from SPECTRA. He won the election, and in a party celebrating his victory at the polls, he read the poetry of Anne Knish. Harriet Monroe, the editor of *Poetry Magazine* (considered the voice of American poetry) accepted several of Emanuel Morgan's poems for publication.

Emanuel Morgan and Anne Knish were the two poets whose names were associated with this new school of poetry. Readers soon learned that Emanuel Morgan had just returned to his native city of Pittsburgh after 20 years in Paris. Anne Knish, it was said, was born in Budapest, but had lived in recent years in Pittsburgh. Morgan was said to have originally been a painter, but had been introduced to poetry by his good friend, Remy de Gourmont. Anne Knish was purported to be strikingly beautiful, had published one volume of poetry in Russia, and was rumored to be excessively temperamental.

One thing is certain; they quickly captured the imagination of the poetry world. Emanuel Morgan became known for his regular metrical forms and rhymes, while Anne Knish was better known for her free verse form.

Some of their lines were quoted as characteristic of the "new approach to poetry."

Knish's lines were widely recognized. In Opus 50, she said, "I think I must have been born in such a forest, or in the tangle of a Chinese screen." In Opus 67, she said, "Thank God this tea comes from the green grocer, not from Ceylon." In Opus 118, "If bathing were a virtue, not a lust, I would be dirtiest." She used whimsical images yet phrased in identifiable poetic diction; it looked like poetry.

Morgan's lines also were frequently quoted. In Opus 15, "Asparagus is feathery and tall and the hose lies rotting by the garden wall." In Opus 88, "The drunken heart finds epics on the breastbone of a chicken. And lyrics under the lettuce." And in Opus 41, "With a beaded fern you waved away a gnat and maidens hung with vivid beads of green, one of them bearing in her arms an orange cat held palms about a queen."

Such colorful phrasing seemed to bring a new element of interest to poetry. Critics began to analyze what Spectric poetry claimed to be. Anne Knish gave Emanuel Morgan credit for originating the new school, and tried to explain its purpose by saying that if a Spectric poet described a landscape, "he would not draw a map." She described Spectric poetry, somewhat obscurely, as "winged emotions, fantastic analogies, with a tinge of humor." She and Morgan finally elaborated and said that Spectric poetry had three principal characteristics:

- "a process of defraction—colored rays of light; a poem is like a prism—white light transformed into glowing, beautiful and intelligible hues."
- "reflex vibrations of physical sight—the luminous appearance seen after the exposure of the eye to intense light. The after colors of the poet's initial vision."
- "overtones, adumbrations, or 'spectres' which haunt all objects both of the seen and unseen world."

Not surprisingly, these criteria were met with varied reactions. Edgar Lee Masters, with diplomatic imprecision, said, "That it was an idea capable of great development along creative lines." Eunice Tietjens, associate editor of *Poetry Magazine*, said, "It is a real delight." *The Los Angeles Graphic* called it, "Gibberish—written only to attract attention." *The St. Louis Post Dispatch* wrote:

They have a theory of poetry all their own, but the stuff in the volume does not seem to be poetic. It is mostly a conglomeration of stuff thrown together so that stars and cheese, and female limbs and green shadows and similar combinations are catalogued in one bit called opus number so and so. Well, for those who like this sort of thing, this is the sort of thing they like.

The world of poetry waited anxiously for more Spectric poetry to appear. Critics were arguing its merits; editors were scrambling to print the next volume of Spectric poetry. Writers were arguing over the contributions of this striking new school of poetry.

Witter Bynner, one of the better known poets and critics of the day, writing in the *New Republic* in November of 1916, was strong in his praise of the "new poetry." He wrote, "There is a new school of poets, a new term to reckon with, a new theory to comprehend, a new manner to notice, a new humor to enjoy…These later comers bring to the new poetry a quality it had rather lacked; they penetrate the surface with a curious vibrancy of imagination.…Perhaps a wider experience of life and of media has made the Spectrists' ability in English verse more flexible and more potent than that of the other poets we may compare with them…I can promise that there is amusement in it and that it takes a challenging place among current literary impressionistic phenomena."

Witter Bynner lectured throughout the country about poetry, high in his praise of the Spectric poets, but was generally critical of all other "schools of poetry." An explanation of Bynner's support came a bit later when the story finally unraveled.

The mystery surrounding Ms. Knish and Mr. Morgan escalated. Reporters, critics, and aspiring poets tried to contact them in Pittsburgh, but could never find them. Sometimes they were told that they had moved on to New York, but sustained efforts to reach them proved fruitless. Knish and Morgan did respond to written enquiries. Anne Knish answered a written request to participate in a symposium saying,

> I do not know if I have a right to speak on this subject, for American poets will resent the criticism of one whose native tongue is the Russian, and who has written only one English book. These are in American poetry days only of beginning; and I think those people know nothing of European literary history who speak so much of "new, new, new."

Finally the hoax was exposed. On April 26, 1918, Witter Bynner was giving a speech before the Twentieth Century Club in Detroit, Michigan. Half way through his lecture, to his utter amazement, a young man stood up and asked, "Is it not true, Mr. Bynner, that you are Emanuel Morgan and that Arthur Davison Ficke is Anne Knish?" Mr. Bynner's answer was just as simple; it was, "Yes."

And thus the entire Spectra Hoax and the new school of poetry founded in the great industrial city of Pittsburgh was history and one of the greatest literary deceptions had ended with a quiet, yes.

It was quickly learned that Bynner and his friend, another young poet named Arthur Davison Ficke, had planned the entire set-up and had carried it off brilliantly for over two years. Bynner explained that a "direct and large lie was too much for me." So, when confronted with a direct question of authenticity, he had to confess his fabrication.

It was later revealed that Bynner on his way to visit Ficke in Davenport, Iowa, in February 1916, had stopped off in Chicago. During an intermission at the ballet, he had discussed with his friends the absurdity he sensed in some of the recent "poetry schools." He composed his first three opuses on the train the next day, and that evening he confided his scheme to Ficke and his wife. They loved the idea, and the Spectra School of Poetry was born. They visualized Morgan as a German gentlemen with a square-cut beard. Ficke, remembering that he had seen in the culinary column of the Sunday paper, a recipe for a Jewish pastry called knishes, created Mrs. Knish, a Hungarian lady of wide experience but with an open mind and a pure soul. They became so carried away with the scheme, that they retired to a hotel across the river in Moline, Illinois, and in ten days with "ten quarts of good Scotch, developed the whole Spectric philosophy."

Why had they chosen Pittsburgh? Both men had visited the steel city, but neither had lived here. They said Pittsburgh was the perfect site to maintain the hoax. "believing that their secret would be less easily discovered there, since interest in schools of poetry is not a big thing in the life of the average Pittsburgher."

Pittsburgh played one other significant role in the hoax. Bynner and Ficke, successful at thwarting all attempts to make personal contact with the mysterious poets—Morgan and Knish—had to find some way to cover their trickery. They convinced a Mrs. Helen Esquere, the wife of a Carnegie Tech chemistry professor who lived in Pittsburgh, to assume the identity of Emanuel Morgan and to answer all his correspondence. For over two years she mailed new Spectric poems to the publishers, and signed letters, E. Morgan. She succeeded admirably, but was challenged once by Harriet Monroe, editor of *Poetry Magazine*, who wrote to Emanuel Morgan. She remarked that his handwriting was remarkably feminine and asked for more biographical information.

Most literary figures of the day were deceived. Edgar Lee Masters wrote to Emanuel Morgan praising Spectric poetry as "poetry which is at the core of things." John Gould Fletcher spoke of the "vividly memorable lines." William Carlos Williams was completely taken in, not atypical for this enthusiastic experimenter. Amy Lowell, although somewhat skeptical, recommended the poetry to her Harvard students.

The chicanery took several strange turns. One was described by Ficke in an unpublished essay. One day lunching with the Fickes, Bynner purposely slipped off his chair and fell noisily to the floor, his motive being "to startle the attending waitress into violent hysterics. When order was restored and the cheese souffle cleaned up from the floor, the hostess remarked, "How terrible to entertain a lunatic." Bynner left immediately for his room where as Emanuel Morgan he wrote "Madagascar," which begins:

How terrible to entertain a lunatic!
To keep his earnestness from coming close!

Shortly before the final exposure of the hoax in 1918, Ficke, a U.S. Army captain and a judge advocate, breakfasted one morning in France with a brigadier general of the regular army, whom he knew only slightly. The general asked Ficke if he thought the Spectra poetry was genuine. Ficke answered that although some thought it genuine, he was inclined to consider it a hoax. The general congratulated him on his astuteness and said firmly that he was quite right. When asked why he was so sure, he replied, "Because I myself am Anne Knish." Ficke, amused, begged him to reveal the identity of Emanuel Morgan, but the general refused saying that he was under oath and could never reveal Morgan's identity. Ficke described the event as "one of the most deliriously happy hours I have ever spent."

As it turned out there were no Pittsburgh poets associated with the Spectra school of poetry, and the name of Pittsburgh no longer held any significance to this historical event in the world of poetic expression. For a brief two years, it appeared as though the city might lend its name to a significant new development in the world of literature, but fate was to decide otherwise.

However, a true Pittsburgher, the renowned literary critic, Malcolm Cowley, played a small role in one of the last events in the Spectra story. In 1918 Bynner, then teaching at the University of California at Berkeley, received several poems written by an Earl Roppel from Candor, New York. Bynner was impressed and felt that they demonstrated "freshness and sincerity." The prize poem was put to music and was sung by a chorus of

3,000 trained voices in San Francisco. When attempts were made to find Mr. Roppel no such person was found. Later Malcolm Cowley admitted that he and a friend, S. Foster Damon, had written the poem in less than an hour. Thus a true Pittsburgher, Malcolm Cowley, had tricked the trickster and put a finishing touch on the grand hoax.

Why do such hoaxes succeed? William Jay Smith, in his book *The Spectra Hoax* points out that the public has always been "attracted by the seeming profundity of what it cannot understand." At any rate those who derided the poems when they first appeared, rejoiced; those who were taken in by the hoax claimed that Bynner and Ficke had written better poetry than they had under their real names. Bynner and Ficke finally agreed that perhaps that was true. They were good poets to begin with, but the freedom of expression, the letting go of conscious restraints, the wit and the spontaneity had perhaps made them even better poets.

The Day the Pittsburgh Symphony Almost Went to Jail (1927-1928)

It sounds like an implausible occurrence during the "Roaring Twenties," but on Sunday, the 24th of April of 1927, the Pittsburgh Symphony almost went to jail—for playing on Sunday.

It was the only prosecution in American legal history for holding a musical concert on Sunday. It was the result of the Pennsylvania Blue Laws, of conservative members of several religious denominations, and of the zealousness of the then powerful Pittsburgh Sabbath Association.

Pennsylvania's Blue Laws became the law of the land in 1784. They declared illegal a wide variety of activities from sports events to shopping on Sundays, and for over 100 years there were few serious attempts to modify them. In fact, Pennsylvania came to pride itself as a bastion of morality and religious piety among the then-existing 48 states.

Near the end of the 19th century conflicts arose. In 1896 free organ recitals, presented on Sunday afternoons in Carnegie Music Hall, in Pittsburgh were widely attacked as sacrilegious; as were the annual Flower Shows at Phipps Conservatory, labelled by many religious groups as "unsuitable Sunday entertainment." "Safe and Sane Sabbaths" became the rallying cry for the purists, who felt that only worship services were proper social activity for the seventh day.

A few years earlier the city of Philadelphia had been challenged in the courts for violating Pennsylvania's Blue Laws with its Sesquicentennial celebration. Opponents had charged that the celebration presented a "wedge" which would eventually destroy the Blue Laws. These charges were upheld in the Dauphin County Court, and were still under appeal to the State Supreme Court. Philadelphia had for some time presented free Sunday musical concerts which were quite popular. The courts of Pennsylvania, however, had always frowned on sports events and all money-making activities on the Sabbath.

Feelings were running high in Pittsburgh. The Pittsburgh Symphony Society stated that its goal was to develop an "orchestra that would compare favorably with the best in the country." Internationally known musicians were being invited as guest conductors. Music lovers in Pittsburgh were eager to promote Pittsburgh as a cultural center, not just a heavy manufacturing city. The Symphony Society announced plans to hold the "first ever in Pittsburgh" Sunday concert at the Syria Mosque on April 24, 1927. Eugene Goosens, a composer and director of the Rochester Philharmonic, was to be the guest conductor. Josef Lhevine was to be the featured pianist.

In an attempt to avoid breaking the Blue Laws, no tickets were sold to the public. Instead they were only distributed to members of the Society. It was reported that over 4,000 tickets had been distributed even though the official capacity of Syria Mosque was only 3,200 people. Clearly the concert was going to be a success.

But the Blue Law supporters rose in righteous indignation. Opposition coalesced around the Pittsburgh Sabbath Association, which seemed anxious to play the leadership role in the fight. Robert M. Blackwood, secretary for the Sabbath Association, and Rev. J. Alvin Orr, United Presbyterian pastor from the North Side, denounced the Symphony's plans and employed Attorney William Pratt to seek legal means to stop the concert. They promised a fight to the finish in the courts and predicted that anyone attending the concert would be thrown into jail.

The Symphony Society vowed to hold the concert in spite of all opposition and employed Attorney Frank Ingersol from the prestigious law firm of Gordon, Smith, Buchanon, and Scott as its legal representative.

The lines of conflict were drawn. Both sides vowed to take the matter to the State Supreme Court if necessary. The news media enjoyed the confrontation and made it front page news for days.

The Sabbath Association first sought an injunction from City Solicitor Waldschmidt to prevent him from issuing a concert permit. This move failed when the solicitor ruled that, "A concert given on Sunday for members of an association does not offend the laws of Pennsylvania." The ruling declared that the Symphony concert was not for profit, was not open to the general public, and was really a private performance; thus, a permit was unnecessary. James Clark, Director of Public Safety for the city, then sanctioned the concert and stated that only the courts should decide the legal issues. Clark was vigorously attacked by Rev. Orr and the Sabbath Association for "taking a middle ground and leaving matters to the courts."

Tensions were rising. The community was clearly polarized and each side was determined to win.

The executive committee of the Sabbath Association met on Thursday, April 21st, in the dining room of Kaufmann and Baer's Department Store on Smithfield Street and issued a statement to the news media that they were prepared to see the matter through to "a victorious solution." They promised to arrest all of the orchestra members and spectators who attended the concert and predicted a $25 fine for everyone involved.

Everybody wanted to get into the act. Guest Conductor Goosens was quoted in the press as saying that, "If they don't get a religious fervor out of this music, then I'll miss my guess."

Rev. Dr. John Ray Evers, pastor of the East End Christian Church, was quoted in the *Pittsburgh Post Gazette*, " The Sabbath was made for man to rest and worship. There is no harm in Sunday baseball, auto rides in the country, or a game of golf, if we remember to attend worship services on the same day."

The *Post Gazette* editorialized that, "They expected the conflict to reach the State Supreme Court, but that the court would certainly rule in favor of the Symphony Society." They further said that they believed that the Sabbath Association had made a tactical error in selecting the Symphony concert as its target for action, pointing out that the chances of successful legal action would have been greater if they had selected a more commercial venture.

The Missouri Synod of the Lutheran Church, meeting in Pittsburgh for a pastoral conference, issued a statement declaring, "We condemn the Sabbath Association for foisting their religious convictions upon others. They should not try to speak for all Protestants." On Friday, April 22nd, Mrs. William Maclay Hall, president of the Symphony Society, issued a public statement assuring members that, "If they attended the concert, they would not be arrested; that all actions taken would be against the society's officers." The Sabbath Association, in turn, publicly announced that they planned to prosecute "the participants as well as all the spectators."

The *Post Gazette* on Saturday morning, April 23, reported that, "The eyes of the entire nation are focused on Pittsburgh."

On that fateful Sunday morning, April 24, 1927, most Pittsburgh area churches participated in a poll of their worshipers. It was reported that 20,443 voted against holding the concert, only 67 voted yes in support.

Local papers covered the Symphony story as they had never written about the Symphony before. Guest conductor Goosens, interviewed in his "yellow Chinese robe" in the William Penn Hotel, informed reporters that he had to leave Pittsburgh immediately after the concert to catch a boat to England. He had no time to be arrested. Pianist Lhevinne, billeted at the Hotel Schenley in Oakland, expressed his apprehension about the concert, but he strongly supported it.

By 8 p.m., the huge auditorium was filled to capacity. A half hour later, prolonged applause greeted the Pittsburgh Symphony members as they filed on to the stage.

Rev. D. C. Edwards, rector of the Protestant Episcopal Church of the Ascension, appeared and asked the audience to join him in prayer. According to the *Post Gazette*, "He asked God to overcome the conflicts of social life by a larger understanding and thanked Him for the joy brought by the power of music."

Each of the works—by Weber, Beethoven, and Tchaikovsky—were wildly applauded, demonstrating the audience's appreciation of the new symphony orchestra. The *Post Gazette*, the next day, hailed it as the "First Sunday Concert in this Blue Law century."

Its front page headline trumpeted:

3500 Attended Sunday Symphony Concert Here
No Attempt Made to Halt Program at Syria Mosque
Uniformed Police Stand Guard; Disturbance Absent

Harvey Gaul, a musical giant in the city, wrote a long review, that opened: "It was a triumph. Now we can go on and take courage. Things are not as indigo in this sterile old town as certain Blue Laws would have us believe, and last night at the Mosque it was evident." He went on to write:

> One doesn't know where to begin congratulations. Shall it be a
> salute of 21 backfiring trombones for Dick Rauh and Eddie Specter?
> Shall we say it with flowers for Mrs. Hall? No matter; it came to
> pass and the only disappointment was that 3,800 people came with
> $25 each and no one was arrested and there was no way to spend the
> money. No Black Marias, no rides to the Oakland station, no
> warrants, no nothin' and that just about ruined the evening for some
> of us.

The concert had proceeded without interruption…but one minute after midnight on the 25th of April, 10 arrest warrants were issued. Served with warrants were Concertmaster Breeskin and nine members of the Symphony Society: George Benson, Richard Rauh, Max Rothschild, Max Seifert, Israel Weinstein, Homer Oschenhart, Edward Spector, Wilmer Jacoby and Bert Floershaber.

On May 3, 1927, a hearing was held in Alderman Samuel McKinley's office on Frankstown Avenue. Over 100 people crowded into what the *Post Gazette* reported was "a ten foot square, dust-covered, unpainted office." The reporter said that the alderman perspired and listened and wished that somebody would open a window. Spectators stood on chairs to see over the crowd in front of them, and "cheered their side as it scored with hoarse whispers which carried for two blocks and greatly added to the joy and contentment of the court."

A Miss Margaret Peacock testified that she applied for membership in the Symphony Society, paid her fee of $2, was enrolled as a member in the manner declared legal by the city, and received two tickets for the Sunday concert. These she turned over to Rev. Blackwood of the Sabbath Association who in turn gave them to Mr. Edgar Ray, a paid investigator for the Sabbath Association, who then attended the concert with his wife.

Mr. Ray provided some comic relief. He admitted that the information served on the defendants had been drawn up on Sunday before midnight, but said it had not been signed until 12:01 a.m. on the 25th of April, which he felt, would make it legal. When the attorney asked Mr. Ray if "he felt any worse for having attended the concert?" He replied, "It's about an even break." When asked if he hadn't had a little worldly employment on the Lord's Day when he attended the concert, he replied jovially, "Oh, yes, you and me both." When asked how he was able to identify Mr. Goosens, the conductor, he said, "Oh, that was easy; he was the guy who went through the motions."

One week later the hearing was reconvened. Again over 100 people crowded into the same small office. When the Sabbath Association was asked why it only arrested ten people instead of everyone at the concert, Pratt responded that it was "a prosecution not a persecution." As proof of that position he said that they had not arrested any women. At one point an ugly charge surfaced that they had arrested only Jews, but it was pointed out that two of the defendants were not Jews. A Miss Martha Agnes Woolslayer, a witness for the Sabbath Association, was asked if the music had not been beautiful and inspirational, the kind one would have been better for having heard? Her reply was, "Yes." The prosecution claimed, however, that Sunday concerts "were leading to a commercialized 'Continental' Sunday." Pratt declared that, "Those who don't like our Sabbath should go back to the Old Country where they came from." Emotions were clearly running high.

After a raucous hearing Alderman McKinley declared the defendants guilty and fined each of them $25 plus costs of $8.40. Attorney Ingersol immediately appealed the summary convictions.

The *Post Gazette* headlines the next morning read, "Blue Law Advocates Win First Legal Tilt" and editorialized that, "the country needs Supreme Court clarification; the 20th century is certainly different from the 18th century when the original Blue Laws were passed."

The public quickly took sides. Col. Samuel Harden Church, president of the Carnegie Institute, wrote an indignant defense of the Symphony's position in the *Carnegie Magazine*:

Those Protestant ministers who organize their congregations' forces to restrain the masses from intellectual and spiritual enjoyment of an otherwise drab and unendurable Sunday are sinning against the liberty of the nation. Seventy per cent of the people are not church members. There is not one church in Pittsburgh where a person longing for good music can hear it on Sunday evening. What he does hear is a tune four inches long, sung over and over, depending on the number of stanzas—not music in any sense.

36

A Rev. Charles Potter was quoted as saying, "Pittsburgh is the lowest spot on the American cultural map, with the possible exception of Columbus, Ohio."

Several months later, the appeal on the matter was heard by the Allegheny County Court before Judges R. A. Kennedy and D. M. Miller. One of the chief witnesses for the Sabbath Association was Dr. Charles Heinroth, organist at Carnegie Music Hall and the Third Presbyterian Church, who testified that the supply of good music was more than adequate to meet the demand; that there were always empty seats at the concerts, and that there, "was no demand from the masses for Sunday concerts."

Attorney A. M. Imbrie and Mrs. Litchfield testified that there was no demand for Sunday concerts and that young people were not interested in symphonic music. The United Presbyterian Ministerial Association of Pittsburgh presented a resolution against Sunday concerts.

The Symphony Society countered by claiming there was a real demand for Sunday concerts, that there was no place to go on a Sunday evening, and that, "a large proportion of cultural foreigners cannot have too much good music." The Society also pointed out that Sunday was the only day of the week when the symphony musicians could be free from their other jobs.

The County Court promptly reversed the Alderman's decision and declared the defendants not guilty. As promised, the conflict was taken to the State Supreme Court, and after the usual legal delays, was finally heard by the court in July of 1928. The passage of time had smothered the fires of conflict somewhat, and when the State Supreme Court at Philadelphia quashed the indictment on technical grounds, the entire case against the Symphony Society was history.

It was over five years later at the November election in 1933, that a rider attached to a Sunday sports law finally legalized Sunday concerts in Pennsylvania. An interesting footnote to the story is that the first legal sale of a ticket to a Pittsburgh Sunday concert was ceremonially sold by George Gershwin, the famous New York composer and pianist, for $50 to a Mr. Leo Lehman. Paramount News carried the story to every movie theatre in America, and local newspapers reported that over 4,079 people attended the first "legal Sunday concert in Pittsburgh."

Once again Pittsburgh had made national news. This was the only prosecution in the courts in the history of the United States objecting to a Sunday concert.

Part II
Places

The Strip, 1992

Washington's Landing, Another Lost Opportunity? (1753-1989)

Herr's Island, now known as Washington's Landing, could it become the showplace of a great new city, the Central Park of Pittsburgh? The history of this little island is as fascinating as the history of the city of which it is a part. Pittsburgh is once again at a crucial time in its ongoing effort to become a truly Renaissance city. What it does or does not do with Herr's Island may prove to be another triumph of planning or another lost opportunity of great significance.

Herr's Island, for those who have not been introduced, is a 42–acre island, three quarters of a mile long and 600 feet wide, situated in the Allegheny River opposite the communities of Troy Hill and Millvale. The island has some unique advantages, not the least of which is a magnificent view of the Golden Triangle which lies only two miles to the southwest.

In the beginning it was an "idyllic spot," at least according to Leland Baldwin, Pittsburgh's best known historian. But in the years that followed an imaginative range of descriptive phrases have been employed to characterize it. Among these have been, "a sow's ear, smelly, urban blight, desolate, the source of 'Herr's stink,' forlorn, flatulent, and miserable."

The island's history has three easily identifiable periods. Until the middle 1800s it was largely pastoral. In the late 19th century it became industrialized and remained so for about 100 years. The third era saw the gradual decline of industrial usage, and the island became a desolate eyesore in the midst of a deteriorating heavy industrial city. Since 1935 it has been the subject of numerous negotiations, of countless plans, and of dozens of abandoned projects all in an attempt to find some publicly beneficial use for it.

Each of the three periods of its history has its own distinctive characteristics. The earliest references to the island describe an Indian trail which was a major East-West route and which passed through the old city of Allegheny, now the North Side. On its way through the Pittsburgh area, the trail went through a small Delaware Indian village, called Shannopin's Town, located at the mouth of Two Mile Run on the east bank of the Allegheny River. This little community was situated in the vicinity of what is now 40th and Butler Streets in Lawrenceville. The trail crossed the river at Herr's Island and on to the west bank of the river where it roughly followed present day Ohio Street. It then proceeded westward paralleling the Ohio River to the present location of Beaver, Pennsylvania. Since the island was somewhat isolated from the mainland, it probably was used for overnight encampments.

The Indian trail became an historic highway. Among the famous people who traveled it were Christopher Gist (1750), an early Christian missionary, George Washington (1753), Christian Post (1758), a renowned Moravian missionary, and General John Forbes (1758), a well known military figure in Pittsburgh history. There is no record of the Indians using the island for any kind of a permanent settlement; apparently it was used as a place to cross the river, particularly during periods of high water.

The 18th century history of Herr's Island is closely associated with the early history of Western Pennsylvania. George Washington first visited the Pittsburgh area in November of 1753 accompanied by Christopher Gist. He was on his way to the French Fort at LeBoeuff in what is now Venango County. There had been repeated reports that the French were planning to build a series of forts stretching from Lake Erie on the north to the Ohio River on the south. Washington was carrying a letter of protest from the Ohio Company to the French commander, Contrecouer, protesting this activity. On their way back on the trail, called the "Venango Path," severe winter weather set in. Washington and Gist lost their horses and were forced to continue on foot and by canoe.

When they reached the Allegheny River, which was swollen by fall rains, they built a crude raft which capsized. George Washington was hauled from the icy water by Gist, after what Samuel H. Church, the historian, called, "the greatest effort." Reaching Herr's Island, Washington and Gist built a fire and spent the night on the island. Historical accounts indicate that Gist had frozen hands, and the night on the island was anything but comfortable. By morning, however, the river had frozen over and they proceeded on foot to Turtle Creek, where in the home of a John Frazier, they received fresh clothes and supplies before continuing their trek to the East.

The first recorded owner of the island was a William Wilson, who obtained patent to the land on May 18, 1792. Five years later he sold the island to Benjamin Herr, who gave the island its name. For decades it was largely used for farming, but as the years passed, it became the site of many homes. Mr. Herr, the owner, began to give 90–year leases to new home-owners, but later regretted this action because the value of the land increased sharply. He somewhat humorously asserted that when the leases expired, the owners should expect large increases in their rates.

Benjamin Herr, for whom the island was named, was born in Lancaster County in Pennsylvania to a family of Swiss Mennonites. He came to Pittsburgh in 1780 and stayed in the city by pure accident. He was a mill-wright who planned to move on to Kentucky to set up a grist mill which would serve the pioneers settling the West. Arriving in Pittsburgh, he found the waters in the rivers too low to proceed by boat, and for some reason never left the city.

Benjamin Herr married Magdalena Lichte, and had 11 children, four of whom died in infancy. At least some of the children were born on a farm in what is now Millvale, but about 1828, the log homestead was moved to Herr's Island to make way for the construction of the new Pennsylvania Canal which paralleled the Allegheny River on its way to Pittsburgh.

By 1852, maps show that the island was laid out in streets and was connected to the west shore of the river by a bridge and a street, appropriately named Bridge Street. Main thoroughfares on the island were named Washington, Franklin, and Herr streets. Property owners at this time included the names of Morrison, Litch, Miller, Harvey, Warner, Mead, and Judge. As more and more homes were built on the island, farming became less and less important.

It was about 1860 that the pastoral era of the island's history ended, and the second or industrial era began. The industrial period of its history did not arrive overnight; instead it was a slow transformation. The island population of cows, chickens, and ducks began to decrease and small businesses began to appear on the island. By 1872 businesses on the island included a tube works, an oil company, and a refining and storage company. Ten years later there was another tube works, a sawmill, and two ice houses; the slow industrialization of the island had begun. The island had some economic importance because directly across the bridge from the island was a railroad station, Herr's Island Station, on the main line of the Pittsburgh, Fort Wayne, and Chicago Railroad.

By 1901 there was a complete change of property owners. Many of the original street names had disappeared, and the island was occupied by a steel company, a beef and provision company, extensive stockyards, a soap and fertilizer works, a sawmill, and a branch of the Pittsburgh Junction Railroad, which crossed the north end of the island.

By 1925 the island seems to have been taken over entirely by the stockyard and meat-packing industry, by several junk and salvage companies, and by garbage disposal companies. By this time the pastoral idyll and the "green quality" of the island described by Leland Baldwin in his early history of the city had long since disappeared. Herr's Island was now known for the foul odors which it spread over Lawrenceville to the east and Troy Hill and Millvale to the west. When the wind was right, the smells of Herr's Island could be enjoyed clear down to the Golden Triangle. The principal source of the foul odor was a rendering plant where animal fats were pressure cooked to produce tallow, an important ingredient of soaps and perfumes.

By the early 1900s Herr's Island had become Pittsburgh's stockyard and was trying to compete with Chicago's better known one. Railroad companies were using the stockyards on the island as a rest stop for cattle to comply with a federal law which required a day's rest for livestock in transit for more than 36 hours. The railroads decided that it did not make sense to have cattle from Chicago debark for 24 hours and then reboard trains for New York City; so instead, Herr's Island became a major meat packing center for the whole Pittsburgh region and a major source of pollution in the Allegheny valley. The smell was so bad at times that workmen on the 31st Street Bridge complained that, "You can't even drink your coffee when the wind blows the wrong way."

By 1910 the only green spot left was a weed-infested field in the middle of the island, and it was marred by stacks of discarded building materials and obsolete machinery. The main feature of the island was hundreds of cattle pens, which eventually sat abandoned as the meat packing industry moved elsewhere. Just as the pastoral era had slowly faded, the industrial era also began to disappear. One after another of the industries vacated the island, and by the 1960s the island was once again desolate, deserted and forgotten.

The last historical period of Herr's Island is hard to characterize. It has been a huge eyesore, begging or daring the city to do something with it. The possibilities are endless. Countless plans have been proposed, discussed, and discarded. Herr's Island even possesses a history of proposed rejuvenations. In 1935 some of the city fathers decided that it would be a perfect site for a massive incinerator plant for the city's garbage, since the smells were already there. This idea bounced around for several years until 1943 when a strike at the city incinerator in Lawrenceville prompted the City Council to buy seven acres of land on the island for $100,000. However, the strike was settled; the old incinerator was reopened; and the city's first plan for Herr's Island died. In 1965 Mayor Joseph Barr authorized a grant of $37,500 to study the possibility of filling in the island's back channel and absorbing the land into the west shore of the river bank. This plan went absolutely nowhere.

By 1969 the meat packers had abandoned the island, and the City Planning Commission began to eye it as a site for a city park. Planners spoke enthusiastically of the possibilities and pointed out how rare an opportunity it was to find a 42–acre plot, free of any significant buildings, which could be turned into a park to rival Central Park in New York City. Such a visionary project failed to excite the city authorities; once again the project stalled. Some spoke of developing a huge municipal amusement park similar to the Tivoli in Copenhagen or the Skansen in Stockholm; again there were few supporters.

Mayor Flaherty talked about converting the island into an industrial park for light industry. In 1976 he appointed the Regional Industrial Development Corporation, RIDC, to study the future of the island. The plan called for a combined industrial and recreational use for the island.

In 1981 the Reagan Administration entered the picture briefly. Efforts by the city to seek some federal funding were rebuffed by the

Administration which replied that, "We have no plans to expand the National Park System."

By 1987 the official name of the island was changed from Herr's Island to Washington's Landing, probably a wise move since the name of Herr's Island was associated in most Pittsburgher's minds with dirty cattle stalls and the stench of meat slaughter houses.

Current plans call for a three-acre park on the southern rim of the island, a pedestrian walkway circling the island and crossing the back channel to the mainland, a marina with a minimum of 200 boat slips, a development of 200 to 300 town houses and/or condominiums, a small commercial "Town Center" with shops and restaurants near a proposed new bridge, from 200,000 to 600,000 square feet of office space and light industrial development, and a corporate conference center on the northern tip of the island with 250 sleeping rooms. meeting rooms, a restaurant, and other recreational facilities. It is estimated that if the plan is carried out, some 2,500 jobs would be created.

The project will be an expensive one. Six hundred fifty thousand dollars was spent in 1978 to buy land from a meat packing firm. Eight hundred thousand dollars had been budgeted to buy land along River Road on the shore opposite the island. Over $4 million dollars is projected to build the new bridge linking the island to the mainland. About $1.5 million has been spent demolishing cattle pens and building utility lines and a spine road. Four hundred twenty thousand dollars was spent in 1979 to purchase 25 acres from the Buncher County. Over $2.3 million was spent by the State of Pennsylvania to acquire the rendering plant property which will be used for park land construction. Over $1 million is projected for the construction of the three-acre park, and over $2 to $3 million will be used for the development of a publicly funded marina. Estimates call for an expenditure of $130 million to carry out the plan.

Construction has been started on a two-story 45,000 square foot building that will accommodate up to ten tenants. The building being built by the Rubinoff Co. and the RIDC is intended for office, research and development, and light industrial uses. The architectural drawings feature trellises or arbors and special landscaping.

Washington's Landing could become many things. It could be the "Central Park" of a new Renaissance City; it could become another example of suburban blight; it might be primarily a high technology center; or it might become an up-scale residential center with rapid river transit carrying commuters to and from their downtown offices. If past history is any guide, one would have to bet that whatever happens it will fall far short of its potential.

What will be the future of Washington's Landing? As far back as 1973, Arthur Harris, then president of the Three Rivers Development Corporation, stated, "There are no political problems; everybody wants the same thing." Almost 21 years later plans are still on hold and little has been accomplished.

A visit to the island today is anything but encouraging. The cattle pens are gone, most of the old buildings have been razed, but there is little indication of a bright future. Three building are standing on the island, but none are fully occupied. The only attractive spot on the entire island is a one-story brick building near the north end of the island which is used by the Three Rivers Boat Association. The balance of the island is as desolate and forlorn as ever.

The great danger is that Pittsburgh may miss the chance to develop a new economic magnet, one more important step in the Renaissance of a great city. Washington's Landing is two miles from the Golden Triangle, only 16 miles from the major new international airport, and only a few miles from the educational and medical centers in Oakland—what a unique and fascinating opportunity for a truly innovative development plan. Pittsburgh for many reasons has never managed to utilize fully the possibilities presented by its unique three rivers location and its unlimited waterfronts.

There isn't much on the barren island to reflect all the fertile planning of the last 59 years. The Urban Redevelopment Authority says that its plans are progressing. Executive Director Paul Brophy warned in April of 1988 that, "Projects like this take time. They don't happen overnight." How true! —but let's hope they happen in this century.

Pittsburgh's Forgotten Islands (1795-1885)

Pittsburgh history is replete with stories about Indians, wars, river boats, and the growth of giant industries, but one aspect of its early history has not often been recorded or remembered. In the early days of Pittsburgh, three islands, all situated near the Point, played varying roles in the growth of the city. All of them have disappeared, long forgotten in the passage of time and the shifting sands as well as fortunes of Pittsburgh's great rivers.

The best evidence for the existence of these islands is in a 1795 map of Pittsburgh's Golden Triangle in which all three islands are clearly outlined. Two of the three islands were located in the Allegheny River channel directly opposite the Point and were first named Smoky and Nelson Islands, while the third island was situated in the Monongahela River channel. Identified only as a sand bar, it was nonetheless the largest of the three.

All three islands have disappeared in fact and memory, but their history deserves a solid footnote in the archives of Pittsburgh history.

The confluence of the Allegheny and the Monongahela Rivers that formed the "mighty" Ohio River caught the attention and admiration of early explorers. In 1749 the French explorer, Celoron, affirmed that this was "the fairest spot along La Belle Riviere," and four years later George Washington noted the strategic nature of the future site of Fort Duquesne and Pittsburgh.

The least known of the three islands was located in the Monongahela River, least known because least noticed. Early writers referred to the

Monongahela as the "islandless river," and it is true that it is most unusual for a river as long and as large as the Monongahela to be totally devoid of islands anywhere along its entire length. The Allegheny and the Ohio Rivers have many islands scattered all along their channels. The Monongahela River was not always devoid of islands. In the late 18th and early 19th centuries a large island extended for a considerable distance in the middle of the river directly opposite what is now called "The Golden Triangle."

The 1795 map referred to above shows that the island extended from very near Point State Park eastward to where Grant Street ends at the Monongahela River. Historical records show that as late as 1793 crops of buckwheat were grown on this island. Attempts to use the island for agricultural purposes were soon abandoned, however, since frequent floods destroyed the planted crops before they could be harvested. There is no evidence of any specific project to eliminate the island. Apparently it gradually disappeared due to the action of the river current and the continued dredging operations to improve navigation on the river. Whatever remains of the island has long since floated down the Ohio and is no longer recognizable.

It is interesting to speculate about the possible uses today for such an island if it still existed. Its proximity to the coal mines on Mt. Washington might have made it a prime industrial site. It could have been transformed into a municipal amusement park to attract tourists, or it might have been the perfect site for the Gateway Clipper Fleet. Its history was short; historical records gave the island no name; it was always referred to as the "sand bar."

The other two islands were located in the Allegheny River channel. They could easily be identified as sister islands judging from the 1795 map. The islands, named Smoky and Nelson, were approximately 70 yards from the north shore and with a channel of 40 to 50 yards cutting between them. Most map makers of the time represented Smoky as being the larger of the two, but at least one map of the day showed Nelson to be the larger. Smoky Island was directly opposite the Point and could have been called an Ohio River island since it did extend beyond the point where the Ohio River begins. Nelson Island lay to the east of Smoky and was approximately half as large.

50

It is almost impossible to be exact about the size of these two islands. Samuel Vaughan's journal recorded the existence of "Smoak Island," and claimed that it was 400 acres in size. When Chief Killbuck purchased the island in 1806, it was recorded as being 20 acres in size. John Boucher in his history of Pittsburgh said the island was "one fourth of a mile long and one hundred yards in width." *A History of Allegheny County* published by Warner and Co. in 1889 said that Smoky Island extended into the Ohio River and up the Allegheny River to about a square below the 6th Street Bridge." Whether these differences are due to inaccurate observations or to the changing conditions of islands in the rivers is impossible to ascertain.

Nelson Island is shown on the 1795 map as being entirely wooded, and there is no evidence of any permanent habitation on the island. Both islands were frequently used by the Indian tribes at the time, but Smoky seems to be the only one that was settled for any period of time.

In 1792, if one stood along the south bank of the Allegheny River near the Point, Fort Pitt would be at his back, and instead of the bustling North Side in front, he would be looking at untouched forest—a wild expanse that began at the river's edge and disappeared over the rolling green hills to the north. It was a scene of silent wilderness save for the smoke rising from the campfires of the Delaware Indians who made Smoky Island their home. And, in fact, the Delawares did so much smoking and campfire building on the island that white men arriving at the Point christened the island Smoky.

In 1786 Justice Hugh Henry Brackenridge, an early promoter of Pittsburgh, described Smoky Island in the *Pittsburgh Gazette*:

At a distance of about four or five hundred yards from the head of the river (Ohio) is a small island lying to the northwest side of the river at a distance of about seventy yards from the shore. It is covered with wood and at the lower point was a lofty hill, famous for the number of wild turkeys which inhabited it. The island was about one-fourth of a mile long and in breadth about one hundred yards. A small space at the upper end of it was cleared and overgrown with grass. The savages had cleared it during the Revolution, a party of them attached to the United States having placed their wigwams and raised corn there. The Ohio .....winds around the lower end of the island and disappears.

Historians record that until the French and British forces came to the area, there was little in the early history of the period to support the idea that the Indians were "savages" with a "lust for white men's scalps." Neighboring Indian tribes appeared to get along well together. Each had its own villages, its favorite hunting grounds, celebrated its own rituals and festivals, and often invited their neighbors to participate. European traders passed freely among them, exchanging guns, ammunition, and rum for furs and other merchandise. It was only after the appearance of armed troops in the area that this peaceful coexistence changed. When British and French soldiers arrived, Indians began to feel a real antipathy toward the invaders, but even then they refrained from widespread violence.

Early in the summer of 1755, the Shawnee, Delaware, and Seneca gathered at Smoky Island to hold a major gathering, probably for the edification of the white man's settlement at the Point. The braves of the various tribes held the starring roles, and squaws and children played a part as well. Some Scotch Highlander soldiers from General Braddock's army had been captured by the Indians. Historian George T. Fleming wrote that animal skin-covered drums signalled the beginning of a great Indian celebration. He described how the Indians, naked except for loin cloths, their bodies colored yellow, green, red, and black, carried tomahawks and knives and began their traditional war dances. After forcing their victims to run a gauntlet, they tied and burned them at the stake. Historian Fleming admitted that no white man was present to report on the events, but he stated that the torture processes he described were typical of Indian practices of the day. This, of course, renders the whole account suspect since it replicates most of the stereotypes of native Americans that most of us still hold today. Too much history is based on only one version of many events. At any rate, the historian recorded that across the river at the Point, French sentries were obliged to hear the sounds of the violence they were powerless to prevent.

It is clear that Smoky Island was one of the Indians' favorite camping grounds from the time that the first fort was built at the Point until after the War for Independence. The early presence of Indians on Smoky Island probably explains the reluctance of the early white settlers to move to the north shore of the Allegheny, too far removed from help and constantly subject to Indian attacks.

The north bank of the Allegheny River and the convenient location of Smoky Island directly opposite Fort Pitt made it the perfect spot for attacks on the fort. The fort was frequently under siege from the island, with Indians firing a continual rain of burning arrows into the fort in an attempt to burn the fort's buildings. Time after time small groups of Indian raiders would cross the river at night and take pot shots at sentries from under the very walls of the Fort. It was not until 1796 that General "Mad" Anthony Wayne and his "clean-up" troops drove the last of the organized Indian tribes westward into Ohio country, and thus included Pittsburgh in the long, tragic history of the European conflict with Native Americans.

Throughout the years Smoky Island made its way into Pittsburgh history. In 1748 Celeron, the French explorer, sailed down the Allegheny River planting "plates" at various places claiming the territory for the French. William M. Stevenson recorded the strange fact that "Celeron did not see the Point, although he passed it and entered the Ohio River, because he passed behind Smoky Island and missed seeing the confluence of the rivers."

In 1753 George Washington along with his guide, Christopher Gist, crossed the Allegheny River near the Point and passed between Smoky and Nelson Islands on his way to the north shore of the river. In 1827 Stephen Collins Foster and his family sold their "White Cottage" in Lawrenceville and moved to the banks of the Allegheny River directly opposite Smoky Island. When the Indian threat finally ended, industrialists saw the advantage of locating their plants near downtown Pittsburgh, removed from city traffic and subject to lower taxes.

The Island was renamed, Killbuck Island, for a Delaware Indian chief, who became a friend of the European settlers; his name still survives as Kilbuck township. European tradition has it that Chief Killbuck risked his life many times to help the white settlers in their fight with the "hostile" Indians and proved so helpful to the Americans during the Revolutionary War, that Col. John Gibson, then in command of Fort Pitt, made the chief a present of Smoky Island. Killbuck took up permanent residence on the island and made his home there until 1802, when he sold the island to a man named Abner Barker for the munificent sum of $200.

Trouble followed however, since Chief Killbuck did not understand the European laws and never managed to get a clear title to the land. Records in the courts of Allegheny County show that over the next 20 years, one person after another tried to lay claim to the island, but no clear title ever surfaced. As a result, Abner Barker finally decided it would be foolhardy to invest any more money in the land, and gave it up for non-payment of taxes. Ownership reverted to the city.

For the next 50 years, people argued in the courts over the ownership of the island, and while the legal squabbling went on, the shape of the island was changing. As the years went by, the wooded areas of the island disappeared and the hill described by Judge Brackenridge in 1786 had ceased to exist.

The great flood of 1832 almost washed Killbuck Island away, eroding it to not much more than a sand bar. The flood became known as the "Pumpkin Flood" because at its height thousands of bobbing pumpkins washed down the river and showed up opposite the Point. The narrow channel between the remaining island and the mainland also began to disappear. Floods were partly responsible, but the people in Old Allegheny were doing a lot of excavating as they built their town, and much of this fill went into the channel between the mainland and the island. Judge Hugh Henry Brackenridge writing about the island said that, "Alluvial accretion and the refuse of the town was dumped there until it became part of the mainland." By 1850 a survey showed that the upper end of the island was now attached to the mainland, and soon the entire island was simply absorbed by the north shore and the city of Old Allegheny.

In 1860 a local resident of Old Allegheny described the scene as follows:

Ridge Avenue and Allegheny Avenue were only paths, then lanes impassable for teams. Their lower ends terminated in gravel banks and swamps. When the river overflowed, this low ground filled with water and made a good place for boys' rafts and skating. South Avenue was lined with a row of large sycamore trees from Allegheny Avenue to School St. making a pleasant walk to town. This was the bank of the river and the residents living along it were among the finest in town.

Smoky Island lay just in front, and when the river was high, a strong current ran between it and South Avenue; when the water fell in winter, there was good skating in the back channel. Stockton

Avenue was one of the choicest residential streets; it was known as Second Bank which meant it was the second rise or terrace above the river. The Pennsylvania Canal ran just in front of it, where the railroad now runs.

Pittsburgh was now a booming industrial giant with iron furnaces and foundries, and with businessmen anxious to display their wares and to further the image of the city as the manufacturing center of the West. Looking for a place to hold an industrial exhibition, they settled on Killbuck Island. A fine large exhibition building was erected and tradesmen of every variety were invited to show their wares. Eventually the exhibition added musical concerts, amusement rides, and other attractions to draw crowds of people. The grand opening was held on October 7, 1875, with prizes totalling over $50,000. Inventions of every variety were demonstrated, the arts of the time were exhibited, the nation's best known bands were booked, and the Exhibition soon became one of the city's best known attractions.

This era of Smoky Island's history lasted until 1883 when a fire destroyed the entire exhibition site including the buildings. Again Smoky Island, now Killbuck Island, lay deserted for a few years until Pittsburgh's big league baseball team, The Pirates, built their new ball park on this site and called the field, Exposition Park, where they continued to play until moving to Forbes Field in Oakland in 1909.

The land once called Smoky Island became the basis for a long drawn-out legal battle between the Pittsburgh and Western Railroad Company and the Equitable Gas Real Estate Company, each claiming title to the land along the river. For eight years the lawyers for the two sides researched and argued over the various deeds to the land before title to it was finally won by the railroad. By this time it was the right of way for the railroad lines which followed the river beds.

Smoky Island played a number of contrasting roles over the years—from a primeval forest, to an Indian encampment, to an industrial site, to the setting for a major industrial exposition, to a professional baseball field, and finally to a modern riverfront park, and a new science center.

Smoky Island stands as a sort of archeological record of Pittsburgh history; its vicissitudes reflect that of the city at large. In the 1950s, if you stood on the south bank of the Allegheny near the Point and looked over toward what once was Smoky Island, you would have seen huge piles of rusted scrap iron, old warehouses, the notorious Zubic junk fleet, a railroad yard, and the north ramp of the Manchester Bridge.

In the 1990s if you stand at the same spot, you will see no reminders of Old Smoky Island, but you will see Three Rivers Stadium, Roberto Clemente Park, and the new Carnegie Science Center with its Nautilus submarine located in the river just about where Smoky Island once played an important role in the history of a great city.

The Strip and
Its Colorful Personalities
(1811-1990)

If you were to ask one hundred Pittsburghers what section of the city is most distinctive and representative of historical Pittsburgh, it is probable that the popular answer would be The Strip.

Many names for the area have disappeared including Bayardstown, O'Haraville, Northern Liberties, and Denny's Bottom. Today the area is known as The Strip, but no one is sure when that descriptive name was attached to it. Yes, the names for The Strip have changed, but the names of the people who graced its streets remain alive in its history.

Urban areas do not become unique for their geographic locations but for the colorful personalities that are identified with them. From its earliest history The Strip was known for the unusual, the distinctive, the inimitable characters who either lived or plied their trades within it.

The Strip is composed of a narrow band of land bordered on the south by Bigelow Boulevard, on the north by the Allegheny River, on the west by the Convention Center, and on the east by 33rd Street. It is an area that has gone through dramatic changes, from a lovely wooded riverbank, to a densely populated residential area, to a manufacturing center that fostered a number of the giant corporations active today, and then finally to a produce, seafood, and meat retailing and wholesaling area that in recent years has become trendy and popular as a shopping center for a wide variety of Pittsburghers.

The first personality associated with the area was James O'Hara, an early Indian trader, one time Quartermaster General of the United States

Army, pioneer industrialist, and a large landowner in Pittsburgh in the early nineteenth century. In 1811, James O'Hara purchased from a Thomas Smallman land known as The Springfield Plantation, consisting of over 400 acres along the Allegheny River. Until the time of the Civil War in the 1860s, this land was considered to be quite a distance from the city.

James O'Hara was a notable figure. He and Major Isaac Craig, both of whom were Revolutionary War heroes, established a window glass factory and were responsible for developing the first Pittsburgh industry that exported its wares to other parts of the country. General O'Hara also played an important role in the construction of the Allegheny Canal which connected the Allegheny River with the Susquehanna River and provided a waterway between Philadelphia and Pittsburgh.

The land he purchased was fertile, with many fine springs and creeks, valuable stands of oak, sugar maple, and walnut trees, and was populated with squirrels, deer, grouse, and other forms of wildlife. James O'Hara knew that he had purchased good land; it had promise. Pittsburgh would grow into it. O'Hara's married daughter, Elizabeth O'Hara Denny, later built a 20-room mansion on the land, but the house was destroyed by fire in the railroad riots of 1877, during the violent period of Pittsburgh history.

The Pittsburgh railroad riots were an important chapter in the labor movement in the United States. In June of 1877 the Pennsylvania Railroad lowered all wages by 10% and reduced the size of the crews who were operating the freight trains through the city. Feelings among the railroad workers were very intense. On July 19th, the crew scheduled to take a freight train out of Pittsburgh refused to move the train. The other railroad workers immediately declared a strike. The sheriff of Allegheny County, fearful of violence, wired Harrisburg for police assistance. Three regiments were ordered to the scene by Governor John Hartranft. Large mobs gathered at the railroad station and, when the militia tried to clear the tracks, firing began. Twenty people were killed; many were wounded, looting and burning broke out all over the city. The mob destroyed 1,600 railroad cars, 126 locomotives, and burned at least 16 buildings nearby, one of which was the Denny mansion. The riot burned itself out in a few days, but it set back the cause of unionism in Pittsburgh for many years. The Strip was in the midst of this discord.

Another of the early personalities associated with The Strip was Elizabeth Wilkinson. Elizabeth was the assistant principal of the first school in The Strip area. Pike Street School, was a three-story brick building, located on the northeast corner of Pike and 13th Streets. The Pike Street School tried to educate the children employed in the glass industry. Elizabeth had aspirations to be a writer, and like most women writers of that day, felt it was necessary to disguise her identity by using a nom-de-plume. Elizabeth became known about the city as Bessie Bramble, and, although it is almost impossible to find any surviving examples of her writing, Bessie Bramble did not lack for recognition in the city at the time.

The Strip proved to be a writer's colony of sorts. Bessie was not the only aspiring writer from the area. John Jack McKee, an eccentric character, was widely known as the "poet of Bayardstown." If you refused to buy his poetry, usually written on long strips of paper, he would become irate and castigate you as illiterate and worthless. He was a tall, Lincolnesque figure, who always wore a black slouch hat, a large black tie, and a long black frock coat. He carried a black thorn cane, which he used to retaliate against the neighborhood boys who could not resist teasing him. His head was as bald as a billiard ball, and the boys loved to sneak up behind him and push his hat from his head. One day some boys were tormenting him, and Jack picked up a frozen head of cabbage, threw it and, missing his mark, knocked over a display in front of Siebert's store and broke a window. A crowd gathered, the police were called, and Jack was threatened with arrest. After some confusion, amid the cheers of the crowd, a collection was taken up, the tub display and window were paid for and Jack was permitted to go on his way.

Joseph French also hailed from Bayardstown. He was a very large man who weighed over 300 pounds and in the 1860s was the superintendent of the city water works at the end of 12th Street on the Allegheny River. Joseph French's appetite was legendary. It was claimed that he had to pay the rates of two men at his boarding house owned by Salvador Slocum at the corner of Stevenson Alley and Penn Avenue. When in town eating at a restaurant, he would invite a friend to accompany him, and would then order two large meals. When his friend would object, indicating that he wasn't hungry, he would say, "Never mind, I'll take care of it," and he would proceed to eat both meals. Legend had it that if Joseph French ever died, the city would be without water, because no one else knew how the city's water system worked.

At the same time, Joseph Barker was a local Methodist preacher and a leader of the Know Nothing Party. The Know Nothing Party, a political phenomenon which surfaced in the 1850s, was a secret society determined to safeguard native American culture against the "poison" of "foreign influences" especially that of the Roman Catholic Church. Clean shaven, and of good appearance, he often wore a stove pipe hat, a white necktie, and a large cape. On Sunday mornings and at other times, he would preach from the old Canal bridge at Penn Avenue and 11th Streets. Any stranger who showed up at the site would be interrogated, and, if his answers were not acceptable to Barker and the Know Nothing philosophy, he would be brow-beaten, berated, and often physically assaulted.

Barker could be found in the middle of many controversies. When the first street railway was proposed for the city, businessmen widely opposed it. They argued that people would ride the trolleys past their business establishments. Handbills and large posters were posted all over the city by the trolley company to convince people that the plan was feasible. Threats were made by opponents to the plan that if it was carried out, all the tracks would be torn up, and anyone found operating one of the new trolleys would be injured. Barker was hired by the trolley company to make public speeches in support of the transit system, and he was credited with smoothing over the situation and helping to quell the disturbance.

At one point Barker was committed to jail. While an inmate at the County Jail, he was elected Mayor of Pittsburgh, an unorthodox candidate indeed. Rather than promising to be tough on crime, he became a tough criminal. Several years later while walking along the Baltimore and Ohio Railroad tracks near Hazelwood Station, he was struck by a train and killed thus ending a public career.

It was while Joseph Barker was Mayor of Pittsburgh that a German mechanic from The Strip named Jenigen, who worked in the rolling mills of Lyon Shorb and Company, invented the calliope, setting the stage for one of Mayor Barker's best monologues. The calliope became standard equipment on the steamboats which plied Pittsburgh's three rivers. In an effort to attract passengers, the riverboat owners had employed brass bands to play on deck for an hour before departure. On one of these boats, Jenigen's calliope was installed in place of the band. As soon as the brass band on a competing boat would begin to play, Jenigen would start his calliope, overwhelming the brass band. The rival boat owners were incensed at the unfair competition. The captain of the rival boat went before Mayor Barker and demanded that the calliope be restrained. Mayor Barker replied in his typically zenophobic fashion, "The calliope is an American institution, and the brass band is a damned imported Dutch institution brought over here from Germany. I am for America all the time. Get out!"

During the Civil War John Sample from The Strip was afforded wide publicity. Although a married man with small children, he was drafted for the army. Sample wanted to go to the army, but his employer, Knapp's Foundry, considered him indispensable. Sample, an expert horseman, claimed to be the only man able to handle the 24 horses needed to haul the 20-inch Columbian cannon on heavy timber wheels from the Knapp Foundry to the railroad yards. Frequently, crowds gathered to watch this master horseman handle the 24-horse team. Amid the cheers of the crowd, a purse of $300 was collected in order to procure a substitute for him in the draft—a common practice in that day.

Not all of Bayardstown's citizens were "pillars" of society. The Bayardstown Rats, as The Strip's youth gang was called, had a bad reputation as one of the city's toughest. Any strange boy who invaded their turf was liable to be browbeaten and abused. Battles with rival gangs, The Allegheny Boys from across the river and the Hill Boys up beyond Bigelow Boulevard, were common. Battles with the Allegheny Boys frequently took place on skiffs in the river or in the winter time on ice, Invasions of Allegheny Boys were not uncommon and pitched battles often ended on the old canal viaduct. The hill above the Pennsylvania Railroad tracks became a regular battleground. The Hill boys, because of their location, often held the advantage until the McCully Glasshouse Boys would finish their day's work, when superior numbers would outflank the Hill Boys and drive them to flight. On one occasion the Hill Boys took refuge in a schoolhouse, which was promptly bombarded with stones. All the windows were broken, and much damage was inflicted on furniture and books.

Gangs of boys and young men, ranging in age from the teens to the early twenties, were familiar in The Strip around the turn of the century. A brochure entitled, *The Strip*, a sociological study of the district by the Methodist Episcopal Church Union and published in 1915, described the situation as follows:

Gangs operating in The Strip resembled somewhat the famous gangs of New York's East Side. The most notorious of these is the Fourteenth Street Gang, composed of about a score of members, who loaf around poolrooms and saloons and give themselves largely to vice and crime. An investigator who spent several days with them, found them sleeping in freight cars, stealing beer and planning other crimes, particularly assaults on women. Their offenses are chiefly in the way of larceny and such assaults,...and which they go about boldly claiming political protection. There is no doubt that these gangs are virtually schools of crime, affording an environment which takes the boy of the street and makes him into a professional criminal.

Besides this sort of gang warfare, other types of crime also flourished. Murder was not uncommon in the early history of The Strip. The most sensational murder case was that of Steve and Nick Hoffman. Steve had a saloon on Penn Avenue between 12th and 13th Streets. Nick, his brother, was the bartender. One evening a gang of mill workers entered the saloon under the leadership of a young giant of a man, who began arguing with Nick, who was reputed to be a tough fighter. Suddenly the front door was closed, the lights went out and a fight began. When peace was restored, several people were hurt, and the young giant was found on the floor stabbed to death with a bread knife. Both Steve and Nick were indicted for murder. They engaged as their lawyer Pittsburgh's noted defense attorney, Thomas Marshall. He petitioned the court demanding separate trials, which were granted. Steve was the smaller and quieter man, and on account of Nick's reputation, everyone assumed that Nick was the guilty man. Steve was put on trial first and acquitted. When Nick went to trial, Steve was called to the witness stand and testified that he had actually killed the man; his testimony resulted in Nick's acquittal also. It was celebrated at the time as a classic of legal defense, since Steve's earlier acquittal made it impossible to try him again.

In the 1860s peace in often violent Strip area was maintained not by policemen, but by watchmen or constables. They were not in uniform and could be identified only by the large star badges they wore. Every three or four blocks, they had boxes where they kept extra clothing and lighting sticks. One of their tasks every evening was to light the street gas lamps with these lighting sticks. Offenders of the peace found on the street were frequently locked in these street boxes until they could be transported to the jail on Diamond Street below Smithfield. Real troublemakers were transported by police wagons called by the watchmen. Drunkards were often trundled to the jail by wheelbarrow.

Churches railed about the evils of liquor in The Strip. By 1915 there were 78 licensed saloons and wholesale liquor houses in The Strip. In addition there were ten Chartered Clubs, which were purely Sunday drinking clubs, and eight drug stores which commonly sold whiskey without prescription. Churchmen claimed that there were at least ten or fifteen "fly-by-night" speakeasies and about a dozen "dope" joints where alcohol and drugs were easily obtained. Thus there were over 100 establishments serving alcohol in the small area known as The Strip.

The Strip seemed to spawn picturesque characters. Before the days of street cars in old Bayardstown, a Mr. Naser operated a hack line from Butler and 42nd Streets to Penn and St. Clair Streets. The hacks seated 12 people and were drawn by two horses. Mr. Naser collected the fares and became famous across the city because at every cross street he blew his bugle to warn others of his coming.

Another character by the strange name of Zug owned and operated a successful iron works at the corner of 13th and Etna Streets. A horse fancier, Zug loved to drive beautifully groomed horses. One day there was a boiler explosion in his plant; sheets of iron roofing were blown high into the sky. Zug lost his plant and most of what he owned. It was reported that for years afterwards he drove around The Strip in an old buggy drawn by a homely mule with most of its hair burned off, seemingly a testament to the story of his decline.

Oldtimers in Bayardstown liked to talk about Father Garland, a large and genial Irishman who was the pastor of St. Patrick's Roman Catholic Church, one of the largest congregations in the city. He played a vital role in the railroad riots of 1877. In the worst of the rioting, a large grain elevator, the railroad depot, the 28th Street Roundhouse, and hundreds of freight cars were burned. The Pennsylvania Militia, ordered into the city to stop the rioting, fired on the mob, but were besieged and forced to take refuge in the old Roundhouse. The populace was incensed at the appearance of the militia, and attacked them at every opportunity. Father Garland was asked by Pittsburgh Mayor McCarthy to intervene and was given credit for pacifying the situation. Father Garland, constantly wielding his heavy black thorn cane, could strike anybody with impunity because no one dared to hit him.

The cartoon below published in 1915 in the *Survey* represents the public's perception of The Strip at this time.

| Material | "A CONVERTING MILL" | Product |

of which Pittsburgh cannot be proud
The Bessemer Converting Mill has long been the pride of Pittsburgh steel plants. In the "Strip" are scores of saloons and pool rooms always busy at this converting of a different kind.

(Courtesy of the Survey)

Not all The Strip's inhabitants were characters; some were ingenious businessmen. Chauncey Bostwick, a one-armed man, a constable, and water assessor, was famous for years in The Strip as "The Inventor." He claimed that he had a patent for a ditch digger, which was never completed and which no one ever saw. His plea for financial support based on the story that "he only had to finish one more wheel" was legendary. Not surprisingly, the ditch digger was never completed.

Another ingenious inventor from The Strip was a German named John Wagner who owned a modest butcher shop on Penn Avenue opposite Stevenson Alley. He supplied butchers with cleavers, knives, and saws. He invented a sausage stuffer and a meat cutter which he managed to patent. The meat cutter had four or five blades in the shape of rockers on a child's cradle. It proved superior to other devices then in use and it was sold widely in the United States and Canada. His advertising claimed that with his device "a child could do the work more easily than what was formerly done by an able-bodied man."

The Seibert family also played a prominent role in the commercial life of The Strip. The family consisted of seven brothers and three sisters. The oldest, Barthel, was in the milk business. The second boy, Wilm, was an expert shoemaker. He had a large one-story large wooden boot on wheels which sat in front of his business establishment and for many years was one of the famous landmarks of The Strip. Boys, particularly on Halloween, loved to kidnap the big boot and pull it around the streets. The third son was The Strip's principal wagon manufacturer. The fourth son, Christian, was an entrepreneur. He was a shoe and boot manufacturer, a leather finisher, a farmer, and a real estate operator. In 1867 he came into possession of the charter for the construction of the Ewalt or 43rd Street Bridge. He organized a company, sold stock, and after two years completed the bridge even though it was virtually destroyed twice by floods. Stock of this type was generally considered to be a poor investment, but Christian cleared up his bonded debt in two years and began to pay dividends to his stockholders. The bridge was eventually replaced by the present Washington Crossing Bridge.

A fifth son, William, operated a grocery at the little Strip market, and also dabbled in politics. His store became the political headquarters for The Strip. At one point he spent time in the County Jail along with other City

Council members who expressed their displeasure when a German banker defaulted on railway bonds to the city. William was the only grocery man in the city who refused to sell whiskey in his store. At that time all grocers sold whiskey, and customers when buying goods frequently expected a free drink. Friends told him that refusing to sell whiskey would cost him his business, but he replied that if he couldn't make a living without selling whiskey, he would quit the business. When his position became known, his sales were said to have improved dramatically.

Today The Strip is considerably more placid and law abiding, but characters are still plentiful. Many present day Strip customers are familiar, for instance, with Tom Rubino at the Produce Store on Smallman Street. His deep guttural holler is known throughout the area, and Tom himself is quoted as saying, "Others yell, but nobody does it better than me." Tom is now over seventy years old, but says that he has been doing what he does all his life. Not far away is Bobby Zadrozny, who, although not as loud as Tom Rubino, is equally renowned for his pitch to customers. He looks like he's having fun and claims that he truly is. He calls himself a "produce solicitor" who makes noise to attract attention. When asked about his history, he responds, "Honey, I love it. Fifty years ago I came down here when I was this high (holding his hand about knee height). I came down here with a horse and wagon and here I am today."

As recently as the 1980s "The Mayor of Penn Avenue" was renowned throughout The Strip. That is what they called Willi Hambone, Jr. Willi was a song and dance man and also a bit of a preacher. He claimed that his real name was Willi Hamm, Jr., that he was born in North Carolina and raised in Washington, D.C. Willi said his father was a full-blooded Cherokee Indian who was also a song and dance man. If you were lucky, you might have caught Willi's routine; he seemed to sway rather than really dance, but he accompanied himself with some low-down blues, which he followed up by extending his hands, palms up, for a donation. He liked to say, "I'm the ham; you talking to the ham. You got to grease these palms." Willi seems to have disappeared from The Strip for the last few years and no one is familiar with his whereabouts.

Albert "Ubbie" Cohen is one of The Strip's more recent characters. Ubbie was a veteran of over 65 years dealing in produce in The Strip. He often talked about the time when lettuce was two heads for a quarter, and wine grapes sold for about six cents a pound. Ubbie grew up in the First Ward and got plenty of training for survival in The Strip. In the March 18, 1979 edition of the *Pittsburgh Press*, Ubbie recalled:

> You had to fight your way then. I had a friend who used to hang out down by the Point, but you had to win the right to hang out there. He set up a fight for me with an athletic instructor from Grove City College. We were going at it pretty good, when my pants started falling down. I had to keep backing away from him as I tried to keep my pants up. I finally got them buckled and went on to win the fight—and the right to loaf at the Point.

Ubbie would say that the produce business will always be good because people have to eat, but he would never want his son to go into the business. The hours are too hard, overhead is high, and it is too much of a financial struggle now. He says that you really have to hustle to succeed in the produce business today.

The Strip has outlived several existences, but while others argue over the feasibility of different plans for its renovation and old time "Strippers" fight to retain its unique ambience, the characters of The Strip continue to provide color and mood to the shoppers who weekly invade The Strip. It is hard to put into a few words what gives The Strip its flavor, but those who shop The Strip on a regular basis will tell you that there is no other place quite like it and that the rather sterile, aseptic atmosphere of the modern shopping market cannot compete with it.

Today a visit to The Strip on a busy Saturday morning will flood your senses with the smells—of fish, melons, nuts, pastries, coffee, fried rice, and cheese, with the sounds—of honking automobiles, strident street vendors, delivery trucks, and the chatter of customers, and with the sights— of milling crowds, busy clerks, and make-shift counters filled with fruits, vegetables, and meats and, of course, the sense most catered to by The Strip—the sense of taste.

In between the sights, the sounds, the tastes, and the smells you can buy your favorite plant from the florist, you can visit an art gallery, you can savor "The Best Breakfast in Pittsburgh," you can browse through your favorite flea market, and you can entertain the kids with a visit to the live lobster tank in Wholey's Fish Market.

Today there is a new "Down By the Riverside" entertainment complex and the Western Pennsylvania Historical Society is busy converting an old warehouse building into an historical museum. The Strip's future appears bright, but it is doubtful that the same quality and quantity of unique personalities will brighten its modern history.

Pittsburgh's Canal
(1830-1857)

It was a hot mid-summer day in downtown Pittsburgh in the 1830s. The news of the imminent arrival of another packet boat from the East spread throughout the city. Since the Pennsylvania Canal had recently opened, canal boats were arriving from Philadelphia. This was the beginning of Pittsburgh's participation in the history of long distance canal transport in Pennsylvania, a history of great hopes and brief successes.

Half the population of the city gathered around the Stevenson Basin to welcome the new shipment. The long drawn out note of the boatman's horn, carried on whatever summer breezes existed, and signaled to the city that Lightning Fanny was ready to dock at the wharf and to unload its valuable cargo. Pat Collins, the captain of the Lightning Fanny, named his boat for his current girlfriend, and added the Lightning because he had just broken the record for speed between Philadelphia and Pittsburgh. Lightning was a pretentious name for the packet boat because the fastest speed it ever attained was eight miles per hour.

The housewives of the city lined up waiting for the gangplanks to be lowered so that they could go aboard and dicker for everything from dressed chickens to little green onions. At least three or four days each week, canal boats arrived with their loads of merchandise.

The boats had colorful names: The Gliding Jane, The Spirit of the Spray, and The Bard of Erin for example. In addition, many of them sported legends or mottos on their sides, frequently referring to the cook on board, who was recognized as a vital crew member. Among these signs were: *"Beauty and the Beast, Beauty Missed the Boat but the Cook's Aboard"; "Four Precious Souls and One Cook Aboard"; "Capacity of the Boat 120 Tons, Capacity of the Cook Two Quarts."* When the boats were finally unloaded, the passengers safely disembarked, the crowds gradually dispersed and returned to whatever activities they were engaged in before the boatman's horn had summoned them to the day's big event.

The completion of the Pennsylvania Canal in the city had brought significant changes to downtown Pittsburgh. The Stevenson Basin, the first of four basins constructed within the city, was located where the Union Station now stands. Basins were large docking areas. There the boats found the port officers; all the arrivals and departures were noted; the captains secured their clearance papers; the merchants registered their shipment of goods or receipted for the arrival of consignments; the booking officers there were all shipping companies that had their headquarters. Not all the crowd who gathered for the arrival of a packet boat were there for business purposes because the remarkable canal was relatively new and attracted many of the city's residents out of pure curiosity.

The canal basins became the chief centers for local trade and traffic. Warehouses and shipping offices lined the docks. Hotels and rooming houses for laborers appeared around the basins. The basins ranged from 30 to 70 feet in width, and for a period of about 20 years were the main business centers in downtown Pittsburgh.

Like public highways, the canals were free for the use of any man who had the money to buy or build a boat. A boat was not very expensive; a few hundred dollars would build one; wages for a few laborers were not exorbitant, and the boat owner was in business. Boats were 12 feet wide, usually 25 to 30 feet long, and most of them depended upon mules for their movement. The typical rate of speed was about three miles per hour.

It was a busy canal; in 1839 there were over 1,400 boats operating on the canal, with over 125 boats commuting between Pittsburgh and Johnstown. Their crews numbered over 900 men.

Rivalry was intense among the boat captains. Many accidents resulted from attempts to break various records. No ocean liner captain was prouder of his position or more of a czar over his ship than the canal boat captain. The canal boats hauled the government officials, the politicians, the soldiers, the wealthy merchants, and the manufacturing tycoons from place to place for business or pleasure. It was a common occurrence for a boat's crew to engage in brawls with the crews of other boats in their attempts to get to the locks first, or for no other reason than that the rival crew had boasted about its superiority. Many fights broke out over tangled tow lines since boats passed very close to each other in the narrow canals.

The canal was not all romance and roses. In fact the basins, particularly in summer, became rancid reservoirs of polluted water, and the accumulation of garbage and refuse created many problems. Water had to be pumped into and out of the basins in order to keep the areas around them reasonably livable.

The early 1800s was the high point of the canal age in America. The Erie Canal in New York State, which had been a successful forerunner of the Pennsylvania Canal, was largely responsible for the rapid building of the Pennsylvania Canal. Pennsylvania's political leaders were afraid that the Erie Canal would so destroy the commerce of Pennsylvania that they fell all over themselves trying to put the Pennsylvania Canal into operation. The Erie Canal had caused a reduction in freight rates for its total length from $100 per ton to less than $10 a ton; small wonder that the economic future seemed to be tied to canals. Robert Fulton, the father of steam navigation, wrote to the Governor of Pennsylvania saying, "The time will come when canals shall pass through every vale in our land, and every hill, and bind the whole country in one bond of social intercourse."

Freight boats were drawn by three mules, changed every eight miles. Passenger boats were drawn by horses and therefore were faster. Fifteen days was the usual time for a canal trip from Pittsburgh to Philadelphia. Since time, even in the 1800s, was a valuable commodity, many races occurred along the creeks and rivers, passengers often offering the crews extra money if they could set a new record or defeat a competing boat.

Passenger boats left Pittsburgh from the Stevenson Basin at Penn Avenue and 11th Streets. The boats contained sleeping berths which were folded up during the day so that the long boat looked like a parlor. The upper deck of the boat formed a long promenade. Trips during the summer were said to be very enjoyable. The canal was quite crooked, following the meandering streams and rivers.

A number of first-hand accounts of Pennsylvania Canal boat trips are available. A passenger, George H. Thurston, described his trip as follows:

"It was a leisurely, pleasant three day trip, and on moonlight nights with the boat gliding quietly along the still waters, through the shadows of the forests and hillsides, or amid the bright moonlight, that mode of travel had a charm peculiarly its own. It was the custom where the canal made a long curve or bend, for the helmsman to land the boat and allow the passengers to get off for a walk across the mountains or hills, around which the canal wound, meeting them again on the other side. These were pleasant rambles, and many laughable adventures were had in the scramble over rocks and through thickets, and acquaintances thus made often ripened into companionships which lasted throughout life...The captains and crews of the passenger boats were well behaved and courteous, but the crews of the freight boats were often of a rougher mold.

In 1842, Charles Dickens, the English novelist, arrived in Pittsburgh on a canal boat. He described the experience in vivid detail in his travel book, *American Notes*:

A barge with a little house on it, viewed from the outside; and a caravan at a fair, viewed from within; the gentlemen being accommodated, as the spectators usually are, in one of those locomotive museums of penny wonders; and the ladies being partitioned off by a red curtain, after the manner of the dwarfs and giants in the same establishment.

We sat here, looking silently at the row of little tables, which extended down both sides of the cabin, and listening to the rain as it dripped and pattered on the boat, and splashed with a dismal merriment in the water....A train of three horses was attached to the tow rope, the boy upon the leader smacked his whip, the rudder creaked and groaned complainingly and we had begun our journey.

The menu that evening consisted of tea, coffee, bread, butter, salmon, shad, liver, steaks, potatoes, pickles, ham, chops, black puddings, and sausages, which was repeated at breakfast the next morning, while the only variation at the noon-time meal was varied by omitting the tea and coffee.

Dickens's description of his trip is the most detailed account available of travel on the Pennsylvania Canal. The variety of food available would seem to have been more than adequate, but the amenities were clearly very primitive. He went on to relate some of them:

> By the time the meal was over, the rain which seemed to have worn itself out by coming down so fast, was nearly over too; and it became feasible to go on deck; which was a great relief, notwithstanding its being a very small deck, and being rendered still smaller by the luggage, which was heaped together in the middle under a tarpaulin covering; leaving, on either side, a path so narrow, that it became a science to walk to and fro without tumbling overboard into the canal. It was somewhat embarrassing at first, too, to have to duck nimbly every five minutes whenever the man at the helm cried "Bridge!" to lie down nearly flat.

Dickens described that he slept on "a hanging bookshelf designed apparently for volumes of the small octavo size."

His description of the canal boat trip was delightful; his talents as a writer were clearly evident as he went on to describe what he considered to be a most unique experience:

> Between five and six o'clock in the morning we got up, and some of us went on deck, to give them an opportunity to take the shelves down, while others, the morning being very cold, crowded round the rusty stove, cherishing the newly kindled fire, and filling the grate with those voluntary contributions of which they had been so liberal all night. (This was a reference to the spitting habits of the Canal boatmen as well as the passengers.) The washing accommodations were primitive. There was a tin ladle chained to the deck, which every gentlemen who thought it necessary to cleanse himself, fished the dirty water out of the canal, poured it into the tin basin, secured in like manner. There was also a

jack-towel. And, hanging up before a lookingglass in the bar, in the immediate vicinity of the bread and cheese and biscuits, were a public comb and hairbrush.

In spite of the negative observations, Dickens was moved to continue his version of the trip in very romantic and nostalgic sentences. The following paragraph seems almost poetic in its simplicity:

Even the running-up, bare-necked, at five o'clock in the morning, from the tainted cabin to the dirty deck; scooping up the icy water, plunging one's head into it, and drawing it out, all fresh and glowing with the cold, was a good thing. The fast, brisk walk upon the towing path, between that time and breakfast, when every vein and artery seemed to tingle with health, the exquisite beauty of the opening day, when light came gleaming off from everything, the lazy motion of the boat, when one lay idly on the deck, looking through, rather than at, the deep blue sky; the gliding on at night, so noiselessly, past frowning hills, sullen with dark trees, and sometimes angry in one red burning spot high up, where unseen men lay crouching around a fire; the shining out of the bright stars undisturbed by noise of wheels or steam, or any other sound than the limpid rippling of the water as the boat went on; all these were pure delight.

The actual route from Philadelphia to Pittsburgh was not entirely a canal route. From Philadelphia the traveler took the Columbia Railroad at Market St. and proceeded by train to Harrisburg. From Harrisburg the traveler took a canal boat on the eastern division of the Pennsylvania Canal to Hollidaysburg, Pennsylvania. There the traveler proceeded to Johnstown, Pennsylvania on the Allegheny Portage Railroad. The Portage Railroad was for many years considered the wonder of the civil engineering world. It had 11 levels or grade lines and 10 incline planes, 5 on each side of the mountain. From Johnstown to the summit of the mountain was over 26 miles and from the top of the mountain to Hollidaysburg slightly over 10 miles. At the Portage Railroad the horses were unhitched, the cars were fastened to a rope which passed up the middle of the track. The boats were placed on flat cars and pulled to the top of the incline by steam engine. The boats, built in sections so that they could be more easily loaded on the flat cars, were true forerunners of the containers used by railroads and motor trucks today.

Once over the mountain in Johnstown, the packet boats again took over and followed the western division of the canal arriving at Pittsburgh along the western bank of the Allegheny River. Here the canal had to cross the river to reach the downtown section of the city. Residents of Allegheny (now the North Side) were bitter opponents of this plan; they argued that it would be less expensive to continue the canal along the west bank of the river in to their city, and then transport goods across the river into the downtown on existing bridges.

After considerable controversy the construction of an aqueduct across the Allegheny River began. It was considered to be an engineering challenge, but was completed by 1829 at a cost of $100,000. The wooden structure, 1,140 feet in length, was supported by stone piers, and at each end was anchored to massive stone abutments. The stone piers rose 40 feet above the river and had to support the water course of the canal as it rushed across the wide expanse of the river. There was a towpath along one side of the aqueduct route and a footwalk on the other side. After crossing the river, the canal entered the Stevenson Basin where the Union Station now stands. The original aqueduct had a roof with pine shingles and pine weatherboards on the side, but by 1832, pictures show no roof over the aqueduct.

The *Pittsburgh Gazette*, in its edition of November 10, 1829, reported that the aqueduct had been completed, and the next day an observer in Pittsburgh wrote to a member of the legislature:

> Yesterday was probably a day of more enthusiastic feeling than Pittsburgh ever witnessed. The 10th inst. (sic) was fixed for letting the water in, to cross the aqueduct.... The men were in fine spirits, and went on cheeringly during the night of Monday and up to twelve o'clock on Tuesday. Five minutes before the appointed hour, the water touched the Pittsburgh shore. In half an hour the canal was filled to the tunnel, and three packet boats crossed in fine style, hailed by ten thousand spectators, and under a salute of 105 guns from the artillery.

Thirteen years later Charles Dickens was impressed enough by the aqueduct that he included this description of it in his book, *American Notes*:

> On the Monday evening, furnace fires and clanking hammers on the banks of the canal warned us that we approached the termination of this part of our journey. After going through another dreamy place—a long aqueduct across the Allegheny River—a vast, low wooden chamber full of water—we emerged upon that ugly confusion of backs of buildings and crazy galleries and stairs, which always abuts on water, whether it be river, sea, canal, or ditch, and were in Pittsburgh.

The aqueduct proved difficult to maintain, as evidenced by the fact that it had to be completely rebuilt in 1845.

Although the early days of the canal were clearly successful, competition from stagecoaches and railroads forced the canal owners to expand their operations in order to compete. They extended the terminus of the Pittsburgh Canal to the Monongahela River. In order to accomplish this, it was necessary to build a tunnel under Grant's Hill. This section of the Canal was never successful, since in addition to the 810–foot tunnel under Grant's Hill, it required the construction of four locks to lower the water level down to the Monongahela River level.

American tunnel techniques were still in their infancy. The Grant's Hill tunnel was one of the first of its kind attempted in the United States. Massive rock formations required drilling and blasting; black powder was the only explosive available. Considerable skill and care were necessary to avoid cave ins and loss of life. As a result the project proved much more costly than anticipated. Later another branch of the canal was extended down the west bank of the Allegheny River into the city of Allegheny (now the North Side). There were four locks and a large basin, called the Allegheny Basin, on that side of the river.

The golden age of canals was surprisingly short-lived. The first merchandise from Philadelphia had arrived in Pittsburgh via the canal on October 31, 1829. This event had cheered Western Pennsylvania, and had renewed its faith in the economic future of the region. In 1831, Neville B. Craig, editor of the *Pittsburgh Gazette*, published a map showing the city with a great maze of proposed canals radiating from it in all directions. It became known far and wide as "Craig's Spider."

Pittsburgh's prestige as the main gateway for traffic between the east and the west was temporarily preserved through the construction of the Pennsylvania Canal, but it had hardly been put into operation when it became apparent that railroads were to be the more permanent answer. When winter forced the closing of the canal for several months each year, it soon became evident that railroads were a better solution. Construction of the Pennsylvania Railroad west from Harrisburg began in 1847; this signalled the demise of the canal age.

In 1857 the entire canal was sold to the Pennsylvania Railroad for $7,500,000 and the age of the canal was history. There was much public clamor over the sale, many believing that the Pennsylvania Railroad had in fact created a transportation monopoly and that the canal should have been maintained as the Erie Canal had been in New York State. The total debt which the State had absorbed for the Canal amounted to over $40,000,000. It was a tax burden which the State of Pennsylvania shouldered for a generation.

Several times various construction projects have unearthed remnants of the old canal. In 1911 excavations near the County Jail unearthed the old tunnel under Grant's Hill. Crowds of people assembled to see the remains of the old tunnel; reporters and photographers walked about "two hundred feet into the tunnel." and marveled at its massive construction, some expressing admiration for the skill of the masons who built it. Some of the masons who viewed the old tunnel remarked that, "it appeared as if masonry was a lost art, because of the super excellence of the work on the old tunnel."

During the two weeks that the old tunnel was exposed, thousands of citizens viewed it and many entered the tunnel for short distances. Scientists from the Carnegie Museum collected several samples of stalactites and stalagmites, of which there was said to be thousands in the old tunnel. When the East Street Parkway was being built in 1989, several remnants of the old canal were discovered in the excavation required for the completion of the Parkway.

By 1857 the Canal Age was history; the country was ready for the Age of the Railroads. But old-timers who were alive in the first half of the 19th century could spin wonderful tales of the canal days. They would tell you about the skill of the canal boat captains, of how they would take aboard the mules without stopping the progress of the boats, of how once in a while a green driver would fail to adjust the proper amount of slack in his tow line so that all of his mules would be whisked into the canal, and he along with them if he happened to be riding the last mule.

The canal boats did have their colorful, even romantic, aspects, but it is hard to believe, given its discomforts, its complications and its snail's pace (Lightning Fanny's claims not withstanding) that anyone would choose this form of travel today. The Pennsylvania Canal enjoyed some minor successes, but eventually became an example of great expectations that failed. It failed, not because it did not work, but because the technology of transportation was moving so rapidly.

"What Do You Think This Is, The Monongahela House?" (1830-1935)

"What do you think this is, the Monongahela House?" This happened to be a favorite saying of my father-in-law. When someone at the dinner table complained about the food before him, this was always his standard response.

For nearly a century the Monongahela House was the epitome of stylishness and glamour in fast growing Pittsburgh, the industrial capital of the United States. When one wanted to locate the center of high society and the setting for most of Pittsburgh's major social events, the Monongahela House always came to mind. It was the classiest inn in the city.

On April 13, 1935, Harry E. Irwin of Cumberland, Maryland, prepared to move out for the last time. Mr. Irwin was the final guest at the famous hostelry. An engineer on the Baltimore and Ohio Railroad, he slept in the hotel several nights a week for the previous 30 years. C. C. Barker, a downtown hardware store owner, also moved out that day; he had the distinction of having lived in the Monongahela House for the longest time—25 years. Countless memories were lost in the debris as the old hotel was demolished on May 1, 1935. Very little of value was identified amidst the crumbling ruins. A glass goblet, found in one piece, might have been grasped by a guest, famous, infamous, or unknown, during a toast to his beloved.

Indeed its roster of famous guests was impressive. At least 12 presidents slept there, including John Quincy Adams, Andrew Jackson, Zachary Taylor, Abe Lincoln, U. S. Grant, Theodore Roosevelt, Andrew Johnson,

Rutherford B. Hayes, Benjamin Harrison, William McKinley, Grover Cleveland, and William H. Taft. Other celebrities whose names appeared on its guest ledger included: Mark Twain, the Prince of Wales, (later King Edward VII), Jenny Lind, Henry Clay, James Blaine, Prince Louis Napoleon of France, Carrie Nation, Buffalo Bill, Ethelbert Nevin, Billy Sunday, and Horace Greeley. Clearly the memories attached to the old hotel should be a part of Pittsburgh's heritage.

The site of the Monongahela House was on the western corner of Smithfield and Water Streets just at the northern end of the Smithfield Street Bridge. In the early 1900s a fine private residence occupied this corner, but in 1805 the site was chosen for the building of the "finest woolen mill" erected in Pittsburgh. Twenty years later, in 1825, the old woolen mill was remodeled and converted into a school house, the first free school in the city. It was first called the First Ward School. Later, when some political re-districting occurred, it became known as the Second Ward School.

In 1830 the first hotel, the Monongahela House, was erected on the site, operated by the firm, Lyon, Shorb, and Crossan. Next door to the old hotel lived William Wilkens, who served in the U. S, House of Representatives, the State Senate, and even briefly as Secretary of War under President Tyler. Mr. Wilkens was an important man, and many notable people who came to visit him stayed at the Monongahela House nearby.

This version of the hotel was burned to the ground in the Great Fire of April 10, 1845, when most of the city was destroyed. After the fire, a public meeting was held to begin collecting money for public relief, and a special committee was formed to carry the problem of rebuilding the city to the State Legislature in Harrisburg. The report said in part, "The magnificent hotel, erected at a vast expense, known as the Monongahela House, is a ruin." The lawmakers appropriated $50,000 for the relief of Pittsburgh, and exempted residents in the burned area from property taxes for the years 1846 to 1848.

The hotel was rebuilt in 1847, a fine 5–story edifice, with balconies overlooking the river front, and a great walnut staircase in the lobby. The hotel had 180 rooms, 12 stores on the first level, and a ballroom that could accommodate 1,500 people. It was considered to be the foremost hotel west of the Allegheny Mountains, and notable people from all walks of life stayed there. Travelers of the day would say that, "We spent a few days at the Monongahela House," instead of saying, "in Pittsburgh."

Today it is hard to picture life as it existed in Pittsburgh in the 1840s. Southern planters arrived via the Ohio River on luxurious packet boats, sipped their mint juleps on the Monongahela House balconies, and watched their cotton being unloaded on the wharves below. Business men from New York and Philadelphia traveled across the mountains by stage coach and canal boat. They conducted their business in the hotel, enjoyed the conviviality with their friends and left singing the praises of the new hostelry. They boasted of its luxury and appointments, comparing it with the Astor in New York, the St. Charles in New Orleans, and the Continental in Philadelphia. For an extra fee of 25¢ a night, guests were given wood or coal to provide warmth on a winter evening by burning it in their rooms' fireplaces. Hotel employees would light and tend the fires and were renowned for how well they catered to the needs of their guests.

A huge registration desk in the lobby was widely admired and the winding black walnut staircase leading from the lobby to the upper floors was famous. Leading orchestras of the day played in the ballroom, where with gas lamps turned low, stylishly groomed dancers bowed to leaders of state as they waltzed over hardwood floors. Guests at the hotel were traditionally awakened at 6:00 a.m. by the vigorous beating of a gong. The hotel's bar served only strong drinks; beer was left to the German beer halls, common in that day. Although common rooms were lighted by gas, guest rooms were not, and when it was time to retire, guests carried small oil lamps up the stairs to their rooms. Contemporary accounts say that the lights from the city's steel mills and coke ovens lit up the sky so that little additional lighting was needed.

All the great social events of the city ended at the Monongahela House if they did not actually begin there. Ethelbert Nevin, Pittsburgh's famous composer of "The Rosary," was married in St. Peter's Church in Pittsburgh and following the wedding, took his bride, Anne Paul, to the hotel, where the high society of the city enjoyed a huge banquet and danced to the strains of a ten piece orchestra until 11:00 p.m.

During the almost 100 years of the Monongahela House's history, notables from all walks of life enjoyed its hospitality. Although 12 presidents stayed there, certainly the best known and best documented visit was that of Abraham Lincoln who was an overnight guest on February 14, 1861.

On that Thursday, thousands of people from all over the area and from surrounding counties, poured into the city hoping for an opportunity to see the "Rail Splitter," who was now the President of his country. Most businesses in the city closed for the day and flags and bunting were hung from buildings all over the city.

The President's special train was due to arrive at the Federal Street Station on the North Side at 5:20 p.m. A great throng surrounded the station. They were disappointed, however, when it was announced that a railroad accident had occurred near Rochester, Pennsylvania., which would delay the train's arrival for at least two hours. At 5:00 p.m. the booming of military guns had mistakenly signaled the President's arrival. Even though a light rain began to fall, most of the crowd stayed to greet Lincoln's arrival in spite of the delay.

The suspension bridge across the Allegheny River which connected the North Side of the city to the downtown section was lined with masses of people, even though the newspapers had reported that the heavy rain and a strong east wind would make it a very uncomfortable viewing point. Finally at 8:00 p.m. the train puffed into the station. The crowds had grown so large that it was only with great difficulty that the militia cleared a way for the President to reach his carriage in the pouring rain and proceed to the Monongahela House. The air was filled with cries of, "Speech, Speech." Lincoln paused as he reached the carriage, thanked them for their welcome, and indicated that he planned to speak to the crowd on Friday morning from the Monongahela House. The carriage carrying the President then crossed the river and proceeded down Smithfield Street to the hotel near the river front, where thousands of people pressed close and made it almost impossible for the President and his entourage to enter the hotel lobby. The crowd was now so dense that the militia had to draw its bayonets to break a path through it. Lincoln decided to say a few words to the assembled throng, indicating that he appreciated the welcome and would speak to them at some length at 8:00 a.m. in the morning from the hotel balcony. When some members of the throng insisted that he say something about Allegheny County, Lincoln replied that he did not think that necessary since the county was already widely known as the " banner county in the state if not in the country."

The next morning Abraham Lincoln gave a short speech from the balcony of the Monongahela House and led his entourage through the city to the station where he once again entrained for Cleveland. The *Pittsburgh Gazette* editorialized the next day as follows: "In all modern history a more touchingly sublime incident is not to be found than the parting of Abraham Lincoln from his neighbors. The man, the father, the patriot, the Christian speaks. He alludes to his own sadness and to the trials that await him." The news media called him, "sincere, simple, grand, and humble."

When Lincoln arrived at the Monongahela House he was assigned to the Prince of Wales room where England's Prince of Wales, the future King Edward V11, had stayed. Naturally from that day forward the room was known as the Lincoln Room. When the hotel was finally torn down in 1935, the furnishings, the carpets, the door, the window frames, and the hexagonal square bordered oaken slabs on the floor were preserved to be displayed later in an historic museum in the city. Today no one seems to know for certain what has happened to these memorabilia.

The other presidents who stayed at the hotel were less wildly greeted and their visits to the city were not as well covered by the press. When Presidents Andrew Johnson and General Ulysses S. Grant came to Pittsburgh after the Civil War, crowds gathered outside the hotel. When the crowd threatened to mob President Grant, the General Grant reportedly told the crowd to, "Go home and mind your own business." The news media gave him credit for averting a more serious confrontation by his actions. President Theodore Roosevelt delivered a campaign speech from a balcony on the Water Street side of the hotel.

Most of the great theatre stars of the 19th century stayed at the Monongahela House. Jenny Lind, known as the "Northern Songstress," was brought to the city by the great P. T. Barnum on April 25, 1851. Amid great advance publicity, seats sold for $5 each for a gala concert to be held at the Masonic Hall on 5th Avenue opposite the Warner Theater. Ten cents from each ticket was supposed to go to charity. Following the concert, the press reported that, "Shouting and ill repressed curiosity by some young hood-lums on a shed behind the theater so upset Jenny Lind that she refused to leave the theater." The next morning's newspaper recorded that, "A drayman named Keating pried some boards off the fence behind the hall and with his dray took a roundabout trip through Virgin Alley, Cherry Alley, and Water Street until he returned Jenny Lind to the safety of the Monongahela House." Unhappy Jenny Lind left the city early the next morning. Nonetheless, the media was extraordinary in its praise of the concert, saying that:

> Jenny Lind sang as only the angels sing in the courts of Paradise; her voice is sweet as the warbling of birds. When she smiles it seems as if a flash of light from Heaven shown upon her face. She is a just offering to the noble's genius, combined with miraculous power and sweetness of voice. Whoever hears Jenny Lind not only partakes of the highest transient enjoyment, but secures a recollection that can never lose its freshness or beauty.

P.T. Barnum signed the hotel register, "The Public's Obedient Servant," canceled a scheduled appearance of his star, and hurried her out of Pittsburgh. "The experience unnerved her," he said.

Charles Dickens, the English novelist, stayed at the Monongahela House on his widely publicized visit to the United States and later in his book describing his travels spoke of the Monongahela House as, "a very comfortable hotel where I stayed." Mark Twain stayed in the hotel in 1884, and although not noted for keeping his opinions to himself, left no memorable stories or quotations for posterity.

Lawrence Barrett and Edwin Booth, renowned Shakespearean actors, stayed in the hotel on several visits to the city. George Seibel, the *Pittsburgh Sun Telegraph* drama critic, wrote that seeing Barrett and Booth, who were playing Hamlet and Cassius, walked along Smithfield Street after a matinee and stopped at a confectionery store to buy cream puffs.

Fanny Davenport, one of America's finest tragediennes, was a frequent guest. Modjeska, the famed Polish actress, exiled from her homeland because of her husband's patriotism and who became one of the most famous actresses on the American stage, stayed there many times. Maggie Mitchell, Joe Jefferson, Ellen Terry, Henry Irving, and Lily Langtry, all great names in the history of American theater, all signed the guest register at the old "Mon." Perhaps the best known singer of the time, Adelina Patti, whose golden voice earned her millions of dollars before she retired to a castle in Wales, spent one night in the hotel. Other operatic guests included Christine Nilsson, the Swedish nightingale, Emma Abbott, who sang opera in English (a rarity at the time), Minnie Hauk, and Maria Materna.

Celebrities of all varieties were guests at the Mon. Dwight L. Moody, the evangelist, Buffalo Bill, the entertainer, Bob Ingersol, the widely known agnostic lecturer, General Tom Thumb, the midget, and Chang, the Chinese giant, all signed the register in the lobby. The list of notable guests could go on for days: William Jennings Bryan, Horace Greeley, Prince Louis Napolean of France.

On October 2, 1860, a "Baron Renfrew" from England registered at the huge reception desk in the lobby. He was accompanied by Lord Lyons, Lord Bruce, the Earl of Germaines, Lord Henchenbrook, Sir Henry Holland of New Castle, England, and numerous attendants. It was quickly ascertained that "Baron Renfrew" was actually the Prince of Wales, later King Edward V11. The prince, treated as most visitors to the city today, was escorted to Mt. Washington (then called Coal Hill) for the famous view of the Smoky City. The streets of the city were decorated with U. S. and British flags. The newspapers of the day had a field day, reporting that, "The Prince was very youthful looking, dressed in light clothing with a high crowned hat, and with an easy and dignified manner. His face did not indicate a great deal of intellectuality nor the want of it. His features are good with a little cast of German in them. There was nothing to indicate that he was the heir to the British throne."

Billy Sunday, the professional baseball player and evangelist, was a frequent guest. He regularly played billiards with the desk clerk, L. D. Statler, who went off duty at 10:00 p.m. At the time Billy played with the Philadelphia Phillies baseball team and always stayed at the Mon when he was in Pittsburgh. Billy usually passed his time conversing with friends in the lobby and on one occasion was quoted in the press as saying that, "I am preparing for a bigger job." He soon retired from baseball and became a full time evangelist.

The Monongahela House burned twice, in 1845 and in 1880, both times being rebuilt and refurbished. Through the years many different arrangements were made to keep the old hotel commercially feasible. In 1852 a deal was made between Edgar Thompson, president of the Pennsylvania Railroad, and two river boat operators. The deal involved Pennsylvania Railroad travelers who would be housed overnight in the hotel and then travel the next day by river boat to Cincinnati for $6. per person. When the Baltimore and Ohio and the Pennsylvania and Lake Erie railroad depots were built near the Monongahela House, business improved, but these improvements were short lived.

In 1920 the Monongahela House got its final face lifting adding a variety of new services. Seventeen billiard tables and five bowling alleys were attached to the lobby. A cafeteria replaced the old formal dining room. The "finest fourteen chair barber shop in Pittsburgh" was installed. The priceless mahogany sills, window frames, doors, and stairways were refinished. Guest rooms were refurbished. Two historic balconies on the outside of the building were removed, because it was thought they were now unsafe, and bronze tablets were used to mark their places.

The Monongahela House finally disappeared in the late spring of 1935. Romanticists could not help but wonder how many wonderful stories disappeared with its walls. The old glass goblet found in its debris could possibly have told several of them.

One of the few remaining relics of the old hotel was a huge back bar which once graced the Monongahela House and was later installed in Christener's Cafe located on the North Side of the city in the path of the East Street Parkway. The actual date of its installation is unknown, but it was probably moved there when the hotel was last remodeled in 1920. The old back bar served the neighborhood tavern well for many years, and when the cafe was finally closed in 1969, the mirrors, uncracked, still stood in silent recognition of the brilliance of the old hotel.

The Monongahela House is gone. No longer do mustachioed swains escort debutantes in shining coaches drawn by prancing horses. No longer can Southern aristocrats sip mint juleps on the balconies while their cotton is unloaded from the river boats on the wharves below. No president will mount a balcony at the foot of Smithfield Street to deliver his message to his people, and no huge sign will grace the corner of Smithfield Street and Water Street, high up on the roof, declaring:

MONONGAHELA HOUSE AMERICAN EUROPEAN ROOMS $1 AND UPWARDS.

Central High School: Pittsburgh's First (1855-1946)

Any weekday morning it is perfectly natural to see teenagers boarding buses on their way to high school. Today, employment in our technologically advanced society virtually requires a high school diploma, but in the past, attendance was not even compulsory.

The prominent role of public secondary education in our culture tends to obscure its early history, which in Pittsburgh began over 135 years ago. In September 1855, the Board of Education in Pittsburgh opened its first high school. It rented rooms on the third and fourth floors of a building on Smithfield Street for $450 per year, and once the owner installed gas lights, the school opened. Located where the Mellon Bank building now stands across from Kaufmann's Department Store, the school had primitive facilities with rooms poorly lit, improperly ventilated, oddly arranged, and rarely warm enough.

Here old Central High School eked out a meager existence for years— very meager according to one student's account; he found it to be a colorful, although not educationally conducive, setting:

Smithfield Street in those days was paved with cobblestones, and there were no car tracks beyond Fifth Avenue. Drays were numerous and noisy; there were no railroad sidings to the mills and factories, consequently teaming was an important business. The heavy wagons hauling iron products of all sizes and shapes, massive timber wheels with unwieldy castings of many tons weight swinging from their beam and hauled by numerous horses, frequently as many as thirty, clattering omnibuses, the rattle of the mail wagons coming and going almost hourly, all the conveyances in common use combined to make Smithfield Street, a bridge street, a bedlam, and then, as now, one of the most traveled thoroughfares in the city. The pandemonium of noise necessitated closed windows and brought out their repeated admonitions from the professors, "Louder, speak more loudly, please."

Even when there occurred a lull in the traffic on the street, from one of the storewindows downstairs where "Cheap John," an auctioneer held forth, there came the reiterated cry, "I have one dollar. Who'll give the half?" And always on the street below a husker played antiquated tunes on the accordion, both wheezy and breezy, and to make matters worse his repertoire was small, hence we knew all his tunes and were full up with accordion malady.

It was a blessed relief when one or more of the predatory rats that infested the place or even some quick action mice, emboldened by hunger, would emerge from one of the numerous crannies in the old building and begin to forage for the leftovers from the lunch pails. This sort of invasion invariably led to action. Any missile in reach—a piece of chalk, a small lump of coal, an inkwell or its cover, perhaps a surreptitious bone would be hurled at the rodents, and with the resultant racket, the recitation would be interrupted.

George T. Fleming, the student quoted above, was a member of the last class to attend Central High School at its Smithfield Street location. He reminisced about the long walks that students had to take to get home, but said that most welcomed them after six hours of study in a sitting position. He also described the public transit of the day, horse-drawn and slow to exasperation. This eyewitness account of education in the old Smithfield Street school hardly engenders nostalgia for the "good old days." The first principal of the school, Reverend Jacob LaGrange McKown, a graduate of Wesleyan University, had been hired or drafted from Cooperstown, New

York, at a yearly salary of $2,000. Early faculty members included Philotus Dean (natural sciences), William Dickson (mathematics), and Mary Maitland, who was the "female assistant."

Central's first class consisted of 18 boys and 16 girls, only three of whom graduated three years later. Graduation exercises were held before a large crowd of parents and friends in Lafayette Hall, an L-shaped four-story brick building on the corner of 4th and Wood Streets used for many years for all kinds of public meetings. Miss Heppie Wilkens, the first graduate of Central High School, had the honor of receiving the first diploma because she was a girl. Later, she became Mrs. Joseph S. Hamilton and made her home in Bellevue for many years. William C. King, another graduate, founded the King Glass Company and became a successful businessman in Pittsburgh. The third graduate, Kuno Kuhn, spent his life working in the oil business in Bradford, Pennsylvania. The small size of the graduating class led the major newspaper of the day to editorialize, "The mountain has labored four long years at great expense to the city and produced only three live mice."

Thus Pittsburgh's first high school made its premiere in shoddy facilities, more than six years before the Civil War. One of the last eyewitness accounts of life in the old high school indicates that even though the student body did grow, few capital improvements were made:

There were 80 students admitted with my class, but all did not attend. We spent seven dreary months there, mostly winter months, with the grime, smoke, and murkiness characteristic of Pittsburgh in those years when the consumption of our juicy bituminous coal was universal. It was a rare day when recitations were held without having the gaslights lit. From the rear windows we looked down into the gloomy depths of Splane's Court, very much like looking into the mouth of a coal pit, as the drift entries, then common in the city, were called. This court was always dark and repressive, a real gloom provoker. We did not know what class of people were domiciled there, but we pitied them. We thought they might be some of the few descendants of Caesar's who had strayed out to Pittsburgh.

Support for public education of any kind in Pittsburgh was relatively new. It had taken more than two decades early in the 19th century to develop popular support for public elementary schools, and it took even longer to extend that support to public secondary schools. As a result, when Central High School opened, the school was unpopular with the general public. The ordinary citizen groused that he was having to support a school which primarily served the children of the rich. Economic hard times meant that most children went to work at 14 to help support their families. In fact, at one point, opposition to the high school became so strong that the alumni banded togather and passed a resolution which was published in all the city's newspapers:

> Whereas the attack lately made upon the faculty of the high school has, though unsuccessful, attained a widespread publicity and has left a prejudicial impression on the minds of some, therefore, be it Resolved:

> The Alumni Association of Pittsburgh Central High School, then whom none are in a better position to judge, do hereby express our entire confidence in the faculty as now constituted and our hearty appreciation of the marked success that has attended their earnest efforts in the cause of higher education of the people at large.

Whether this resolution changed anyone's mind is unclear, but opposition to the school appears to have died away; at least no serious attack upon the school followed.

The populist charge that Central was a rich man's school is not borne out by the records, which indicate that among the children of the first class admitted, 32 percent of the parents were involved in business, 31 percent were laborers, and only 10 percent were professionals, although how the administration defined these categories is unknown. This charge of elitism probably reflected the success of its graduates. By the early 1900s, Central's alumni included 100 attorneys, 59 physicians, 7 dentists, and 17 clergymen.

From 1861 to 1865, the Civil War seriously interfered with education and touched the lives of many students. By the end of the war, 254 men had graduated from Central High School; of that number 81 served in the Union

Army, seven were killed, ten were wounded, two died of disease, and one was a prisoner of war. Central High School boasted that 25% of its graduates had served their country, and that this percentage could not be matched by any other school in the United States.

Despite slow growth and public opposition, Central's enrollment increased to approximately 170 students and larger quarters became necessary. In 1868, the school moved to the Bank of Commerce Building at Wood Street and Sixth Avenue. The new facilities were markedly better, although not ideal. The building had five floors with long, steep stairs, but it did have light, airy rooms, steam heat, and a large chapel room. Improved conditions no doubt raised student morale, perhaps evidenced by their nicknaming of the school's custodian, Hughey Boice, as "The Professor of Dust and Ashes." Wood Street, paved with wooden blocks, proved much quieter than the Smithfield Street location. A student at the school remarked, "After lunch our pasttime was watching the boys from Rinehart's Tobacco Factory" (adjoining us) playing baseball on Wood Street. George T. Fleming, a student at the time, described the move to the school's new quarters as a move from "darkness into light; air and comfort made happier pupils and gave them a new thrill to their high school life."

The school stayed on Wood Street for only three years. Rapid enrollment growth from 169 to 370 made effective teaching almost impossible. Separate classes often had to meet in the same rooms and study space was nonexistent. In the meantime, the new principal, Philotus Dean, began almost a one-man campaign for the construction of a new building. The only effort made to recognize Philotus Dean's contributions was the establishment of a Dean's Literary Society, which remained active for several years after his death. Under pressure from several citizens' groups, the Pittsburgh School Board purchased a tract of land on the corner of Fulton Street and Bedford Avenue in what is now known as the Hill District. When construction began on the new school, a gala cornerstone-laying ceremony marked the occasion and a newspaper called it, "an epochal day in the history of education in Pittsburgh."

The gigantic celebration took place on September 29, 1869. Fully 10,000 students and friends of public education marched in a parade from Penn Avenue and Fifth Street to the new building site, just beyond where the Civic Arena now stands. The Iron City Brass Band, The Germania

Turners Brass Band, the faculty of the school, and the members of the Board of Education all marched in the parade. Four thousand school children participated and spectators thronged the streets. A beautifully decorated arch graced the entrance to the grounds and a pathway led to the platform built for the speakers. When the parade reached its destination, police opened a path for the marchers, and then permitted the crowd to gather on the hillside.

A lengthy program of speeches and music preceded the ceremony in which a variety of objects, including Bibles, directories, lists of alumni, school codes, and histories of the school were deposited under the cornerstone. Principal Dean gave a long oration; the pupils sang "America" to the accompaniment of six Etsey organs played by the city's music teachers. John Kerr, an alumnus of the school, delivered the final oration:

> We are gathered here today to hear the first sound of the hammer upon the walls of a permanent structure for free academic education. This age is progressive; we must not stand where our fathers stood. We must not wait on the portals of the future with the rust-stained key of the past. The High School approaches that true ideal of public instruction, where the schools shall be free to all, good enough for all, and attended by the children of all.

All the children wore large badges identifying their elementary schools, many carried huge banners, and girls carried bouquets of flowers. It was a foot parade; no vehicle was permitted. One newspaper noted, "The whole affair was one of the grandest and most imposing spectacles ever witnessed in the city." Central High School, built at a cost of $200,000 must have been seen as a state of the art facility when completed in 1872. Designed for 600 students, it contained 14 classrooms, a large lecture room with raised seating, 2 apparatus rooms for chemistry and physics, a drawing room, a library, a 1,000 seat auditorium, a stage with proscenium and footlights, and the requisite restrooms and offices.

The first principal of the new building, Benjamin Cutler Jillson, headed a faculty of 18 full and part-time teachers. There were 436 students enrolled the first year. The typical school day began at 8:45 a.m. and ended at 2:15 p.m.—not much different from today's schedules. There was a daily recess of 20 minutes. Two bells rang to signal a change of classes; the first bell signalled room changes for the girl students, three minutes later the boys moved to their new classes.

The man given the most credit for the creation of the new school, Philotus Dean, had tirelessly lobbied and planned for the school and had even purchased the equipment for it. However, he developed typhoid fever during the summer of 1871, and after only a ten-day illness, died at age 49, never living to see the school's opening. Dean was never properly memorialized for his contribution to public education in Pittsburgh. Many years later when Pittsburgh built its first, great, modern high school, the Board of Education chose to name it for a Captain William Harrington Schenley, a British citizen who lived in Pittsburgh for a brief period in 1863 and whose connection to education was tenuous at best.

Over the years some prominent people served on Central's faculty. Willa Cather, clearly the most famous, was one of America's major female novelists. She came to Pittsburgh from Nebraska in 1879 and spent four years working for the *Pittsburgh Leader*, a literary magazine owned by the Nevin family. Willa began to write seriously, but found that her work on the magazine left little time for her writing. She began her teaching career at Central High School in March, 1901, as a replacement for a Latin teacher, Belle Weidman. When Burkey Patterson, an English teacher, retired in 1901, Willa became a full-time English teacher the following autumn.

Norman Foerster, one of her pupils and later a renowned teacher, editor, and critic, remembers that the new school, despite its pristine beginning, was still a part of Pittsburgh's smoky past:

> The Central High School was a dismal grimy structure on a bluff looking down on the Union Station. The darkness in fog and smoke in fall and winter, the dirt of the squalid streets that led up to it, must have made Willa Cather feel that the great plains and the skies of Nebraska were very far away, as they were.

Students remembered Willa Cather as the only young teacher in a faculty of formal, grey-haired veterans. She inspired her students by what they called her "breezy, Western way with people," and folklore has it that she startled students on the first day of class by greeting them while seated on the top of her desk. She was considered to be an able English teacher and a strict disciplinarian. Cather eventually left Central High School for a new teaching position in the English Department of Allegheny High School on the North Side at an annual salary of $450. When she resigned from that position in 1906, she was earning $1,300. Willa Cather's students at Central praised her talents. They recalled her meticulous attention to detail, her forthright manner, her requirement that they write a paper every day for class—a perfectionist who often demanded too much from her students.

Another well-known faculty member at Central was Sara Soffel, also a graduate of the school. Later to become Judge Soffel, she was a good basketball player and coached the girls' basketball team at Central. She used to boast that her 1911 team was the outstanding girls' team in Western Pennsylvania. Life at Central High School was not all academics. Its budget for athletics in 1907 totalled $2,500. Central also boasted a chorus of over 100 voices, an orchestra that played for many civic events, and a school newspaper which claimed to be one of the best in the country.

To gain admission to the school, students had to pass strict examinations in arithmetic, grammar, geography, U.S. history, orthography, and algebra to quadratics. The school enforced academic standards by dismissing students regularly for "habitually neglecting their studies." Laws in those days did not require high school attendance, so permanent suspensions were not hard to enforce.

A disciplinary log from the high school provides insight into turn-of-the-century ethics. In 1901, the principal suspended a student from school for opening a note intended for his father. The log reports that he was,"suspended for two weeks, but was reinstated at the intercession of the Mayor of the city." That same year one of the students called the principal a liar. The principal replied, "I am no more a liar than you are," whereupon the student struck the principal a blow on the ear. The student was suspended for two weeks but was re-instated after one week.

Despite incidents of this kind, teachers in the early 20th century were highly esteemed, but like many of their modern counterparts were poorly paid. Beginning teachers usually started at $500 per year, with the top salary not much above $1,000. Six-room houses at the time rented for $55 and $60 per month without heat; clearly, teachers did not live very graciously.

In 1916 Central's life as a public secondary school ended. The faculty and the student body moved to the recently completed Schenley High School. From 1916 to 1933, Central's building housed what was known as the "Short Course Business High School." Many Pittsburghers learned their secretarial and business skills there and fondly remembered their school days at Central High School. After that program ended, the building was used during the depression in the 1930s as the local offices of the National Youth Administration (NYA) and the Works Progress Administration (WPA).

Central High School was the first and oldest high school building in the city. Fifth Avenue High School was the next oldest, followed by South High School, only the latter is still used as a high school building.

In 1946, Central High, by then an old landmark known for its twin towers, was torn down. Much of its building material was hauled to Mt. Lebanon and used there in the construction of that rapidly expanding suburb. In the 45 years of its existence as a high school, almost 5,000 young men and women were graduated into the professional, business, and social life of the city of Pittsburgh. That number includes nearly 1,500 teachers, most of whom taught for some time in the Pittsburgh public schools.

Long after the building had disappeared, alumni groups kept Central's spirit alive with annual class reunions. The class of 1912, for example, held regular reunions every five years until 1957, when the reunion in the Carlton House on Grant Street included alumni from as far away as Hollywood, Montreal, Dallas, and San Diego.

Controversy on the Mon—Was the Smithfield Street Bridge Too Low? (1871-1890)

The year was 1871. The Smithfield Bridge, which connected downtown Pittsburgh to the south bank of the Monongahela River, was showing signs of stress and was considered by many to be unsafe. Pittsburgh depended upon its bridges, perhaps more than any other city in the fast-growing United States. The unusual topography of the area at the junction of three sizable rivers and the city's numerous hills dividing its neighborhoods into separate little enclaves meant that bridges were essential to the development of a city which had intentions of grandeur.

One historian of the day said that, "Bridges are our life lines uniting the community into one vigorous economic and social entity." Time has not changed that reality. Today there are more than 1,500 bridges in Allegheny County; it is safe to say that the city and the county would be forced to a standstill if they suddenly lost all their bridges.

Today the Mon Valley, through which the Monongahela River flows, is considered to be one of the truly distressed areas of the United States. Unemployment is high, population is declining, heavy industry has long ago largely deserted its banks, and many of its towns are struggling for their very survival. This is in sharp contrast to its former glory.

In the early days of the 20th century, a trip up the Monongahela River from Pittsburgh was described by one historian as an "amazing experience." He wrote about the smoke and noise from 62 glass factories, of 350 coal mines, of 25 steel mills, plus hundreds of other large and small industrial enterprises lining its banks.

The Smithfield Street Bridge was built in 1845 by John A. Roebling, who later became world-renowned when he designed and built the Brooklyn Bridge in New York City. The Roebling bridge in Pittsburgh, however, was no Brooklyn Bridge. Although it continued in service for over 35 years, carrying across its eight spans heavy street traffic, eight-horse teams, wagons weighted down with heavy iron and machinery, steam rollers, and every other kind of heavy load, it was not a great favorite with the public.

Roebling had designed the bridge in a unique manner considered at the time to be revolutionary. It was a suspension-type bridge supported by 6 stone piers. On each pier stood a steel pendulum, like a truncated pyramid, $7 \frac{1}{2}$ feet square at the base and 16 feet high. From these pendulums, wire cables supported the eight separate spans of the bridge. When heavy vehicles crossed the bridge, loaded spans often settled as much as two feet with a corresponding rise of the adjoining unloaded spans.

As the bridge grew older and the wire cables supporting the spans stretched, this swaying motion became more pronounced. Newspaper accounts reported that, "The bridge's continuous swaying and creaking created anxiety among the public." Many were convinced that the bridge was unsafe. Most of the coal consumed in the city of Pittsburgh passed over the bridge in wagons drawn by four and six-horse teams; it soon became clear that the city needed a new bridge.

All the major bridges in the city at this time were toll bridges owned by private corporations and built basically as money-making businesses. The stockholders of the Smithfield Street Bridge decided to plan for a new and larger bridge, which would provide better access from the downtown of the city to the fast growing south bank of the Monongahela River. Some citizen groups were beginning to push for publicly-owned bridges, but this was still not a popular idea. The city of Pittsburgh did try to obtain the franchise for building the new bridge, but the stockholders were successful in blocking that attempt. One pundit proclaimed that, "So long as our globe continues to roll, so long will our bridges expect to take toll." In was not until 1896 that the Brady Street Bridge further up the Monongahela River gave Pittsburgh its first toll-free bridge.

The Smithfield Street Bridge stockholders commissioned a young German engineer, Gustav Lindenthal, to design a through-truss span to replace the Roebling bridge and proceeded to have plans drawn for its construction. And this is when the "Controversy on the Mon" began.

River traffic on the Mon had become a significant industry; Pittsburgh was fast becoming the largest inland port in the United States. River men, who were a crucial entity in local government, immediately objected to Lindenthal's plan, claiming that the proposed bridge did not allow enough clearance for large river boats to pass underneath. This had become a common source of controversy since many of the larger river boats had to hinge their smokestacks so that they could be lowered to a horizontal position which allowed them to pass safely under many of the bridges. And of course high water, which reduced the clearance under the bridges, often made it impossible for river traffic to move until the high waters receded.

For years Pittsburgh had objected to the bridge over the Ohio River at Wheeling, West Virginia, for exactly the same reason. Pittsburgh had long insisted that the low clearance under the Wheeling Bridge was an obstruction to river traffic and would hobble the development of Pittsburgh as a transportation center. Clearly, the height of bridges had become a political issue up and down the rivers of America.

Indeed, much has been written about the intense competition which existed among the various river towns; competition which often erupted into open antagonism. One story, repeated in several places, recalled the history of the packet boat, Valley Forge, which had been built in Pittsburgh in 1842. Naming boats and parts of boats for communities along the rivers was a common practice at the time. As part of its dedication celebration, it made a trial run to Wheeling. The staterooms and compartments on the boat were given names of different towns and cities along the Ohio River. When the boat arrived in Wheeling, a delegation of Wheeling citizens came on board to inspect the new craft. They asked to see the part of the boat named for their city. They were escorted to the back end of the boat and were shown the little room which usually had on its door, the designation, MEN. Instead, across the door was a sign with gold letters, reading, WHEELING. The visitors were stunned, but proceeded to rip the sign from the door. They were unceremoniously dumped on the wharf, where they disappeared only to return with a strong body of reinforcements intending to set fire to the Valley Forge, but by this time the boat was safely out in the middle of the river. The offending sign was removed from the door before the boat ever returned to Wheeling, but for many years, river men referred to the men's room as "the Wheeling."

It was in this contentious context that the plans for rebuilding the Smithfield Street Bridge took place. In March of 1882 the Pittsburgh city council passed a resolution which called for raising the level of the Smithfield Bridge 20 feet higher than planned for in the Lindenthal design. The city engineer insisted that a 15-foot rise was adequate; the river men wanted a minimum of 20 feet. In that same month the Steamboat Officers Protective Association, whose members were boat owners and employees on the Ohio River and its tributaries, met in secret, and although divided on the issue, put pressure on the State's Attorney General to move for an injunction to stop construction of the bridge. This effort to raise the bridge level by 20 feet met formidable opposition. The papers reported that "the best and wealthiest of Pittsburgh's business men objected, claiming that raising the bridge too high would "create a perpetual barrier to their businesses."

The controversy was joined. The river men argued that the progress and development of river traffic could only be properly supported by providing a more practical channel that would give easy access to larger and larger boats traversing the rivers. The businessmen of the city argued that starting all over with a new design for the bridge would cost a lot more money, would delay its construction, and would create such a steep grade at the point of access to the bridge from Smithfield Street that it would seriously interfere with vehicular traffic. These were the issues that the public argued about and which the news media discussed. But many observers believed that the true issue was one which was never revealed publicly, and was never considered by the courts,

Hidden agendas are not unusual in political situations. Any historian, news reporter, or commentator will tell you that the true issue behind many controversies is often not publicly acknowledged. It is sometimes politically unwise to reveal the true reasons behind disagreements. Socially acceptable reasons are often used as justification to cover up selfish or greedy ones that are best left unstated.

George T. Wiley was a primary spokesman on this issue. Mr. Wiley died in 1955 at the full age of 98. He was widely heralded as one of the leading lay historians of the Mon Valley, and spent most of the four score years of his life writing the history of the area. For most of those years he was owner and editor of the *Elizabeth Herald*, a small town newspaper published in Elizabeth, Pennsylvania, an important river town on the Monongahela River. He wrote a weekly column entitled, "Then and Now," and was the author of at least three books, *Slim Greene*, a narrative of the Whiskey Rebellion, *Elizabeth and Her Neighbors*, and *The Monongahela, the River and Its Regions*. His contributions to the history of the region have been widely recognized; Washington and Jefferson College bestowed upon him an honorary Doctor of Literature degree in 1935. His opinions and writing must be given serious consideration.

Mr. Wiley wrote that the original wood bridge and the Roebling suspension bridge which followed it were both "deliberately maintained as a known obstruction to continuous navigation through many years, the same actuated by community jealousy and fear." Pittsburgh and Brownsville were growing communities in the early 19th century. Pittsburgh was larger and more important, but in the late 19th century was fearful that a new boat building industry in Brownsville and the building of the National Pike, the first government owned highway in the United States, which terminated at Brownsville on the banks of the Monongahela River, would thrust Brownsville into a position of dominance in the river transportation industry and might seriously threaten Pittsburgh's position as the "Gateway to the West." Frequent high water often made river passage beyond Pittsburgh impossible, thus preventing the extension of river traffic up the Monongahela River. It is clear that maintaining bridges at a certain level could do much to control the future development of river traffic.

Newspaper accounts of the day recorded the actions in the courts, but none of them referred to the regulation of river traffic as a crucial reason for the controversy; not surprising, since the city could never publicly admit that this was its motivation for keeping the bridge level below a certain height. According to Mr. Wiley, the city fathers were forced to base their public arguments on the two issues of greater cost and the steepness of the approach to the new bridge.

Concern over the precipitous slope at the approach to the Smithfield Street Bridge appeared to have some substantiation. In 1884 A. W. Smith, Jr., was quoted in the *Western Pennsylvania Historical Magazine*, January 1963, as saying, "My horse did not like the Smithfield Street Bridge because she did not like the steep approach to the roadway, but once on the bridge she would trot briskly across." She must have been a remarkable horse because Mr. Smith said that when his horse reached the south end of the bridge, she would insist upon turning to the right so that she could use the mechanized incline to reach Mt. Washington, instead of turning to the left and having to climb the tortuous hill to the top of the cliff.

A search of other historical records of the event failed to provide support for Wiley's argument that the city was trying to control river traffic by keeping the Smithfield Bridge to a lower height. None of the other historians of the day refer to it, but the issue provides a fascinating insight into the politics of bridge building and river transportation. The charge cannot be dismissed too easily since George Wiley was a respected authority on the history of the Monongahela Valley. He wrote about the region for many years, and clearly had much personal knowledge about the area.

Fred Way, a former river man and considered to be one of the best informed authorities about the history of the Ohio River Valley, is now associated with the Ohio River Museum in Marietta, Ohio. A written inquiry to Mr. Way, asking if he had any information to support Mr. Wiley's claim, brought the following response, "Sorry, there are no records in my files regarding the Smithfield Street Bridge and the scheme to restrict passage up the Monongahela River above Pittsburgh."

The courts did finally accede to the river men's demands and ordered that the bridge be redesigned to the greater height. The controversy was eventually resolved at the national level when the United States government took over control of the navigation of internal waterways, and established mandatory clearances for all new bridges over navigable rivers.

The Smithfield Street Bridge has always played a crucial role in the life of Pittsburgh, and has provided us with some interesting chapters in its history. It is today the oldest bridge of the 1,500 bridges around the city and county; it is a landmark in American engineering, the nation's largest example of a lenticular truss bridge. By 1983, it carried 1,100 buses, 575 trolleys, and over 10,000 cars every day. In 1983 the city celebrated the bridges's 100th birthday, and the Smithfield Street Bridge is now scheduled for a total reconstruction in 1994. It should grace the city of Pittsburgh for many years to come.

That Fabulous Nixon Theater (1903-1950)

Grease paint and footlights—to thousands of people these words conjure up a world of beauty, of imagination, of creativity, and of pure pleasure. I grew up in a small Western Pennsylvania town, remote from a city, where the only exposure to theater was a terrible traveling vaudeville troop which came once or twice a year to the local movie house, as well as amateurish drama presented every summer by the visiting Chautauqua Society in a big tent behind the local elementary school.

I shall never forget my first exposure to real theater. My friend and I bought tickets and traveled to Pittsburgh to the Nixon Theater to see the great actress Nazimova in Henrik Ibsen's *Ghosts*. I'm sure that by that time Nazimova had seen her best days, and that this particular production was not one of the highlights of the legitimate theater that year, but to me it was overwhelming. It opened my eyes to the marvel of living theater and the magical moments that occur when the footlights come up and the curtain rises on another dramatic experience.

The history of the legitimate theater in the city of Pittsburgh is actually the history of the Nixon Theater. Called the world's "most perfect playhouse," it stood for 47 years on the site now occupied by the Alcoa Building on Sixth Avenue, between Smithfield and Grant Streets. It was the dream of Samuel F. Nixon, who built it, and it became the epitome of real theater to thousands of Pittsburghers.

Sam Nixon wanted an ideal theater, a memorial to his family name, a family which had been behind the construction of a great chain of playhouses in several cities. The building was designed by Benjamin H. Marshall, a Chicago architect, in a style termed, Modern French Renaissance. The exterior of the building was compact and solid in appearance, but it was the interior that earned the theater its pretentious nickname, "the world's most perfect playhouse."

The theater cost Mr. Nixon $1,250,000 to build in 1903. Live theater at that time was so much more important than it is today. It commanded a much broader and larger audience, since it was the chief source of entertainment during that time. There were no movie theaters and no television in 1903; as a result, the Nixon Theater stood as a symbol of live entertainment as no other place has since in the history of Pittsburgh.

The Nixon's popularity was the result of a long theater tradition stemming back to at least 1790 when soldiers presented *Cato* in the military garrison at Fort Pitt. This was the first recorded dramatic performance in the city of Pittsburgh. By 1803 there were two amateur companies active in the city—one a group of lawyers and doctors, the other of mechanics—interest in the theater was classless. The first building used for theatrical productions between 1817 and 1820 was a two-story frame structure on 3rd Avenue. The first large brick theater building was the Pittsburgh Theater, built on 5th Avenue between Smithfield and Wood Streets. Later its name was changed to the Drury Theater. Others followed in rapid order so that by the time the Nixon was built there were nine theaters in the city presenting live entertainment.

In 1903 Samuel Nixon purchased a lot on the corner of Montour Way and 6th Avenue, 122 by 172 feet, from Henry Oliver. An old church building stood on the plot of land. Construction of the new theater was not accomplished without difficulty. Ten different strikes by workmen delayed its opening. Shortly after its completion it was found that the water standpipe in the theater was two feet in diameter and that all the city's fire hoses were only one and one half feet in diameter, virtually rendering fire safety impossible. But after numerous complications and delays and the work of over 200 men, who worked day and night, seven days a week, for several weeks before the grand opening, the theater was finally ready to celebrate its birth in December of 1903.

December 7, 1903, was a bitter cold day. On that same day a seven-year-old boy, frightened by a falling pipe, jumped to his death from a moving elevator in Kaufmann's Department Store and fell from the fifth floor to the basement. A horse shied at an automobile on the 5th Avenue hill, broke free of his harness, and dashed down to Smithfield Street where he knocked over two pedestrians. The residents of Millvale petitioned the District Attorney John Haymaker to stop a Bowser-Kennedy boxing show in Millvale because they said it "would bring all manner of characters to their backyards." The 58th Congress of the United States opened its session at noon in Washington, and the Nixon Theater in Pittsburgh opened its doors to the elite carriage trade of the city that same evening.

The house was completely sold out. On that same night in other Pittsburgh theaters, E. H. Sothern starred in *The Proud Prince* at the Alvin Theater; Garrett O'Magh was featured at the Grand; Augustus Thomas starred in *Arizona* at the Duquesne; Rube Waddell, renowned professional baseball player, had top billing in *The Stain of Guilt* at the Bijou; James Hernes was featured at the Empire Theater in *Hearts of Gold*, and two traveling vaudeville companies were holding forth at the Avenue and the Academy theaters. The living theater was alive and well in Pittsburgh in the early 1900s.

Late in the afternoon of December 7, 1903, two tired men walked from the Alvin Theater in downtown Pittsburgh in the direction of the new playhouse that was to be opened that evening. Their fatigue resulted from the rush of last minute details necessary to prepare for the premiere performance in the new theater.

As they turned the corner and saw the new theater's marquee lights glow for the first time against the late afternoon haze, Mr. Nixon said to his companion, "Perhaps I made a mistake, John. This theater has cost me over a million. For one-third that much I could have rebuilt the Alvin." His companion, John Barnhart, the master electrician, answered the proud founder of the theater:

You shouldn't feel that way, Mr. Nixon. You have built just what you wanted—the finest theater in the world with the best of everything in it. You have given Pittsburgh something to be proud of, a theater that will be an everlasting memorial to your name. You wanted that, too." "Yes, John," Nixon added, "I wanted that too.

Three hours before the first performance was due to begin, thousands of people were lined up before the theater on 6th Avenue. The Nixon was one of the largest and certainly the widest theater in the country. The stage was 47 feet deep and 86 feet wide. The exterior of the building was said to be in the style of Modern French Renaissance, while its interior was in the Louis XVth style. Inside were massive imitation Parawazza marble columns capped with solid gold decorations. The side walls were paneled to look like damask silk of a delicate cerise red, framed in a molding and styling of green, gold, and red. Velvet and silk draperies added profusely to the decor.

Backstage there were 33 dressing rooms on five levels, all fireproof, with an elevator and a separate trunk lift. All the dressing rooms had built in curling irons, electricity, and gas. Two massive curtains dropped from the proscenium. The front curtain, used only at the beginning and the end of each performance, was made of asbestos, was fully fireproof, and showed a splendid panoramic view of the famous falls in Yellowstone Park. The act curtain, which was titled, *In Lover's Land* by the artist John Lewis of Chicago, was widely admired for its two prominent figures in picturesque costumes surrounded by cupids and draperies and a descriptive verse.

Backstage there were 323,000 cubic feet of space, and 80 feet above the footlights it was possible to store the scenery for at least three productions. Acoustics and visibility were considered to be the best in the theatrical world; it was said that, "you could hear ordinary conversation from the remotest corner of the house."

The large stage was widely admired. In 1905 the first production of *Ben Hur* on the Nixon stage had to accommodate four chariots and 16 horses. A later production in 1917 of the same show used 350 actors and 20 horses. In 1911, 20 Indians mounted on horses were on stage at one time for *The Round Up*. Three years later the show *Garden of Allah*, called for a herd of camels, horses, and goats and 50 camel drivers gracing the Sahara Desert. Zeigfeld in one of his *Follies* used three hugh mechanical elephants.

One of the Nixon's unique architectural features must be mentioned. On each side of the large lobby, two rising promenades, or "logelas," rose from the ground floor to the first balcony and dress circle. This enabled a patron to reach these upper levels without climbing a single step. The design was considered so unique that to highlight this feature manager, James F. Kirk, Jr., on opening night, drove a car up the promenade from the lobby and took a couple to their seats.

The opening production was an old comic opera, *Erminie*, by Jakobowski and Paulton. Francis Wilson starred in the role of the comic thief, but he found the audience "cold" and said that he had to work a full act until he was "rewarded." The coldness of the audiences at the Nixon later became legend and helped to make the Nixon a "proving ground" for many Broadway shows. On the opening night critics liked the theater but not the play or the actor. The only ovation came for Jessie Bartlett Davis's rendition of the song, "Oh, Promise Me."

The next day the *Pittsburgh Chronicle Telegraph* called the Nixon "a magnificent temple of amusement." The *Pittsburgh Press* called it "the greatest event in Pittsburgh." *The Bulletin* said that it "was an event of such brilliance, keen enjoyment, and congratulatory speeches, it will never be forgotten by those present." *The Dispatch* said Pittsburgh now had "a genuine metropolitan playhouse with beautiful architecture, with beautiful design and decorations, a temple devoted to the best arts of the theater." It especially praised the use of the electrical marquee, pointing out how superior that was to the usual loud megaphone in the hands of a barker.

Newspapers reported that the audience was "stunned by the grandeur of the new theater." In the boxes that night were nearly all of the top Pittsburgh society and business figures as well as most of the important New York City producers. Mr. and Mrs. H. C. McChesney of Baden, Pennsylvania, were present for the opening performance. Later it was reported that Mr. and Mrs. McChesney, with only six exceptions, had attended every performance at the Nixon until it was torn down.

Every effort was made to make a theater visit to the Nixon an unusual experience. Between acts boys passed cups of water to the patrons in the orchestra seats and this tradition was maintained until World War II. Ushers were bedecked in full dress suits with huge red bands across their shirt fronts with the letters, "Nixon," emblazoned there. No peanuts or popcorn were permitted in the theater. Between acts on opening night, Mr. Nixon made a prophetic speech and ended it by saying, "The Nixon Theater is finished—the babe is born—we now submit it to the tender care of the people of Pittsburgh."

The second play at the Nixon, *Dubarry*, featured the flaming red head, Mrs. Leslie Carter. Before arriving in Pittsburgh, Mrs. Carter said, "I have an overwhelming desire to play in the splendid Nixon which is the talk of the theatrical world." She certainly had an astute press agent who found out that a long neglected city ordinance banned the transportation of theater equipment on Sunday. Under this challenge, he arranged to have the trappings and props transported from the Union Station to the Nixon in full view on Sunday with a special opportunity for the curious crowds to view the guillotine used to behead the King's mistress in the play. As a result, the press agent spent 12 hours in the local jail, but the news media loved it, and the box office at the Nixon reported standing room only.

It is hard to capture in words the attraction that the Nixon Theater held for many Pittsburghers. Harold Cohan, drama critic for the *Post Gazette*, put it best when he said that it was, "more than red plush and marble pillars. It was a civic pride and a community heartbeat." For 47 years, the people of Pittsburgh looked on the Nixon as a prized jewel.

The first period in the history of the Nixon Theater has been referred to as, The Grand Opera Era. Grand opera was very popular during the early years of the 20th century. The first opera that played the Nixon was Wagner's *Tristan and Isolde*. The second, Mozart's *Magic Flute*. In 1905 the renowned Enrico Caruso appeared on the Nixon stage and in 1906 Arturo Toscanini conducted there. Grand opera slowly lost its mass appeal and more popular forms of theater quickly filled in the gaps.

Popular drama with the leading stars of the day lighted up the marquee for many years. Practically every name in the American theater played the Nixon: Lillian Russell, Helen Hayes, John and Lionel Barrymore, Marilyn Miller, Will Rogers, Otis Skinner, Cole Porter, George Gershwin, Irving Berlin all played at the Nixon. Walter Houston said, "When I begin a tour, I think immediately of the Nixon and my face lights up. It's always like coming home again." E. H. Sothern left a picture and signed it, "My salute to the finest theater in the country." The first premiere play ever presented at the Nixon, was *Cousin Kate*, featuring the young Ethel Barrymore.

Pittsburgh was noted for its discriminating audiences. Flo Ziegfeld liked the Nixon for its excellent stage and cold audiences. He usually premiered his *Follies* in Pittsburgh and used to say, "If the show goes over here, it could go anywhere." His *Follies* always did well in Pittsburgh.

Benefit shows were very popular. The all-time champion for benefit performance was *Out There* on June 1, 1918, which offered an outlet for patriotic fervor during World War I. Gate receipts totaled $138,000; no other city in the war effort came close to that figure. The second top benefit performance came on October 17, 1942, during World War II and featured Irving Berlin.

The top draw musical show was Al Jolson's *Sonny* in 1927. The top drama was *Victoria Regina* during the last week of November in 1937. The top straight comedy show was *Mister Roberts* in the third week of October, 1949, and the over-all champion was *Tobacco Road* during nine different outings from 1936 to 1948.

Not all shows were successful. In January of 1931 Lillian Foster in *With the Tide*, played to six people and the drama died a sudden death. Ballet had a tough time in Pittsburgh; Nijinsky, in Diaghilff's *Ballet Russe* sold few tickets, the first floor seats were practically empty.

Sometimes plays were attacked as being immoral. Eugene O'Neill's *Moon for the Misbegotten* and a racy *School for Brides* got the hottest blasts from civic and church leaders in 1947. In 1936 when "Tobacco Road" first opened in Pittsburgh, a group of citizens appealed to Public Safety Director Thomas A. Dunn to close the show, claiming a harmful influence. Director Dunn sent Police Inspector Samuel Wheeler to view the performance and pass on its suitability. The inspector also interviewed many patrons at intermission and determined that it was a true picture of life in Georgia's tobacco country and was not therefore a "naughty show." His filed report stated that, "It is not a great or even memorable play, but it is certainly not immoral or lewd despite the sex mores and the dishonesty of its people."

Other memorable events were recorded. In 1904 Maude Adams made her debut on the Nixon stage in *The Pretty Sister of Jose*. In 1905 McIntyre and Heath's *The Ham Tree* was the feature of Thanksgiving week and almost unnoticed in the small print was the name of W. C. Fields as a tramp juggler. George M. Cohan, the greatest song and dance man of them all, was described as "loud and boisterous" by local drama critics. A youthful Alfred Lunt made his debut on the American stage in Booth Tarkington's *A County Cousin* in 1918 at the Nixon.

On September 16, 1948, Uta Hagen in the second act of Tennessee Williams' *A Streetcar Named Desire* was explaining her love troubles when a man with heart trouble fainted in the balcony. At the same time the audience, smelling smoke, thought the theater was on fire and a near-panic resulted, stopping the show. Calmer heads finally prevailed. Smoke was traced to burning charcoal dumped in adjoining Montour Alley by a restaurant, and the show resumed.

It was during the St. Patrick's Day Flood of 1936 that Alfred and Lynn Fontaine, who had opened in Robert Sherwood's *Idiot's Delight*, became alarmed by the rising water and left the city precipitously even though the Nixon was considered well above the flood water line. Several show business figures chose the Nixon as the scene of their last performances. Among these were: Will Rogers, Maude Adams, and Adele Astaire. Ed Wynn's first broadcast as the *Texaco Fire Chief* was made in the Nixon as part of a Community Fund benefit. All time favorites of the Nixon stage-hands were George M. Cohan, Ed Wynn, Al Jolson, and Frank Fay. Wynn always got the nod as favorite comedian because he was "the cleanest and never told a smutty or off-color joke."

It is interesting that in 1912 for some reason a survey was made of a Nixon audience. The press reported that out of every 100 patrons, 28 owned automobiles, of which 18 were men and 10 were women.

For many years the Nixon was the only theater in Pittsburgh which offered consistently a high type of theatrical entertainment. But not all shows were of this quality. In 1923 Lenore Ulric appeared in a production of *Lulu Belle*. We know little about the play today, but the newspapers the day after the show panned it describing the "bedroom meeting of the star with her diamond encrusted playmate when she jabs him in the back with a morphine needle, frisks him for money, jewelry, and a gold-filled tooth."

Writers whose plays were most often booked at the Nixon were: Shakespeare with 20, Maxwell Anderson with 13, J. M. Barrie with 12, and George Bernard Shaw with 11.

In the late 1930s and the advent of World War II, audiences at the Nixon began to shrink. High salaries, expensive sets, and taxes made it more and more difficult to make ends meet. In 1945 the 45¢ tax on second balcony seats was almost double the Nixon's beginning admission price of 25¢. In an effort to increase attendance, less concern was given to quality. Female impersonators, vaudeville type variety shows, and "girlie shows" failed to turn the tide. The Nixon's days were numbered.

It is perhaps appropriate that the last show booked into the Nixon was Mae West's production of *Diamond Lil*. Mae West blew taps over an era. Mae West had never been lauded by Pittsburgh's drama critics. Karl Krug's review of her next-to-last show in Pittsburgh in 1945, *Catherine the Great* said:

What a piece of stuff like this is doing traipsing all over the country and taking up not only stage space but railroad and hotel room is beyond my ken—It is a pity that such eye-filling trapping have been wasted on such tedious trips as this exploration and exploitation of Catherine of Russia's royal bed chamber. Mae heaves, huffs, hips, and has so many amours they become monotonous and repetitious.

Diamond Lil fared no better. Mae West's most memorable line in the play was said to be in response to a question, "Aren't you afraid someone will come here and take all those diamonds?" Mae responded, "They wouldn't touch anything in this room but me." Critics said the exit production at the Nixon was not appropriate, but it was "noisy." Karl Krug, the *Pittsburgh Sun Telegraph* drama critic, called Mae West the "gal with the triple-hinged chassis."

On the night of the final performance, Karl Krug sat with his head in his hands and unabashedly wept when the audience sang "Auld Lang Syne." Not everyone regarded the old theater as romantically as the drama critics and the actors who played there. An editorial in the *Pittsburgh Sun Telegraph* the day after the final curtain, listed some of the old theater's shortcomings.

- Art critics never proclaimed the old Fontainebleau scene on the curtain as a work of art, even tho it "thrilled Karl Krug."
- The general interior decor never caused a New Yorker to "oh-h or ah-h."
- In the summer an orchestra seat in the Nixon was the hottest place in Pennsylvania.
- The smell of fried onions, sizzling steaks, and garlic salad dressings came up through the floor from Conforti's Grill below.
- The high curbstone on the hillside entrance made it difficult for motor cars or taxicabs to discharge passengers.
- The building, though not the stage, was obsolete.

The following morning, after the last performance, the *Sun Telegraph* editorialized that, "It was progress that gave Pittsburgh the Nixon Theater; it is progress that takes it away." How true that, "Beauty is in the eye of the beholder." It was April of 1950 that the Nixon was sold to the Aluminum Company of America, and the old theater came down to make way for a modern skyscraper.

Eulogies for the old theater poured in from many directions. Katherine Hepburn who had appeared that year at the Nixon in *As You Like It*, wrote:

> I'm infuriated. The ghosts of all the great personalities that once appeared on this stage, along with the fond memories of those in the audience, must resent it. Those responsible for destroying one of the most beautiful and romantic theaters in all America have shown no imagination. Why couldn't they have made plans to encase a legitimate playhouse in the new skyscraper? I believe in city planning, but the Nixon certainly lends a flavor to this city which no other institution can replace. The new skyscraper will be just another building—maybe fascinating, but not glamorous.

Miss Hepburn requested that some relic from the old theater be sent to her as a memento. It was reported that the hooks from the back of the star's dressing room were sent to her. Rex Harrison said that, "Only two or three theaters in Europe match the Nixon's theatrical atmosphere; I love this old house."

Gilbert Miller, a producer of several shows at the Nixon, turned to a staff person, working with a road show at the Nixon, and said, "Remember this theater, my boy. There is no other like it in America nor will there ever be another like it again." Harold V. Cohan, *Sun Telegraph* drama critic, wrote on May 8, 1950:

> So long as anybody lives who remembers the Nixon, the sounds of curtain calls will echo through the corridors of the skyscraper that will one day stand here. Nobody ever came near it, on either side of the footlights, who didn't find beauty and sanctuary there. The spell of the Nixon was not in its plush or spangles, but in some mysterious magic that hung suspended in the wings and in the flies and drifted out over the spacious auditorium whenever the lights went down and the curtain rang up.

After the demise of the Nixon Theater, show business never really revived in Pittsburgh in quite the same fashion. It is true that nostalgia probably helps us forget all disadvantages and shortcomings, but the Nixon will always be a symbol of theater at its greatest in the city of Pittsburgh. The Alcoa Building is impressive and very contemporary. I can stand before it and marvel at the modern technology which makes such a monument to American industry possible, but the romantic atmosphere of the old Nixon can never be replaced. I, for one, will never forget Nazimova's emoting before a packed house as I sat enthralled way at the top of the second balcony.

14

The Wabash Tunnel—
To Nowhere or to Somewhere?
(1900-1992)

The Wabash Tunnel—Is it a construction nightmare, a planning disaster, a lost traffic opportunity, or a monumental political boondoggle? Or will it prove to be a solution to Pittsburgh's worst traffic problem in history?

No tunnel anywhere in the world could have a more varied and striking history. Over the years it was successively:

- the key to the George Jay Gould's effort to challenge the monopoly held by the Pennsylvania Railroad;

- a home to thousands of bats, rodents, and stray animals of every variety;

- a furniture warehouse;

- reopened, refurbished at a cost of six million dollars and a part of Pittsburgh's ill-fated Skybus;

- used as storage shed for unused PAT buses;

- sought after by entrepreneurs who wanted to convert it into a mushroom plantation or a cocktail lounge to be named, "The Cave"; and

- the place which almost made it into the *Guinness Book of Records*.

Now it is being hailed as a possible solution to Pittsburgh's approaching traffic nightmare. No fiction writer could possibly come up with a more unique or fascinating sequence of events. Pittsburgh seems to have an affinity for projects going "nowhere." For years it was the infamous "bridge to nowhere" and now it is the "tunnel to nowhere."

It was at the turn of the century that George Jay Gould made his decision to challenge the Vanderbilts, J. Pierpont Morgan, and the Pennsylvania Railroad and to grab a share of the largest freight tonnage in the world. In the early 1900s Pittsburgh's tonnage shipped by rail was greater than the total of New York City's, Philadelphia's, and Chicago's combined.

The Congress of the United States played a strange role in the country's greatest railroad war. In 1901 an innocent looking piece of legislation was introduced which revived an old act authorizing a railroad bridge across the Monongahela River at Pittsburgh. The original bill was intended to permit the construction of a bridge for a proposed trolley line between Pittsburgh and Carnegie. No one paid much attention to the bill and it passed Congress with no dissenting voice. Frank Spearman, one of the writers of the day, said, "Behind the innocent words lay a tremendous sting in its tail." That bill proved to be George Jay Gould's ticket into Pittsburgh and permitted him to connect twelve western rail lines, which he already controlled, with the Eastern traffic corridors.

Gould was determined to break the virtual monopoly enjoyed by the Pennsylvania Railroad, which at the time was shipping 75,000 tons daily out of Pittsburgh. It was a daunting challenge. To build a competing rail line, Gould had to construct the Wabash Tunnel through Mt. Washington, referred to by engineers at the time as "the toughest couple of miles in railroad history." It also required the construction of a major bridge connecting the tunnel to downtown Pittsburgh, a new terminal in the middle of the city, and a vital 60-mile rail link from Pittsburgh to Jewett, Ohio, requiring 22 smaller tunnels, 88 bridges, and 50 land fills.

Gould's dream was an effort to open up transportation channels to and from the city of Pittsburgh, and to capitalize on Pittsburgh's industrial development. The city was enjoying the greatest industrial growth of any area in the nation, but geography had encircled it with hills and growth had been largely confined to the narrow river valleys. The time was ripe; Pittsburgh's freight system was facing collapse, unable to meet the needs of industrial expansion. Factory and mill owners, unable to get raw materials or to ship products promptly were cancelling orders, losing contracts, and closing plants. High freight rates on the Pennsylvania Railroad, due to the lack of competition, were driving many plants to friendlier locations. Skilled workers were being laid off. Gould had no trouble finding willing investors, among them John D. Rockefeller and Andrew Carnegie.

The grand scheme took an enormous toll. The over-all cost of $60 million—no one is sure of the exact cost—was only a part of the fairy tale venture. The eastern end of the new bridge collapsed while under construction, killing 42 workers. There were several costly mine cave ins in the tunnel, which resulted in delays and unexpected costs. There were strikes and injunctions, epidemics of smallpox among the workers, and a bloody riot on the South Side. The riot occurred when the Wabash Railroad tried to build an extension line into the South Side. It resulted in a pitched battle with the workers from the Pittsburgh and Lake Erie Railroad, which was an ally of the Pennsylvania Railroad. One of Pittsburgh's papers reported the next day that, "One warehouse, two omnibuses, one ice wagon, spikes, rails, rammers, and a thousand muttering foreigners allied with the Pennsylvania Railroad were the weapons used by the Goulds and the Vanderbilts in the fight for the South Side."

Money was never the problem. George Jay Gould had inherited a $72–million fortune from his father and was imbued with his dream of a transcontinental railroad empire which would push the hated Vanderbilts and the Pennsylvania Railroad into a secondary position. But Gould faced enemies at every turn. The Pennsylvania Railroad threw its immense resources into the fray and one costly roadblock after another appeared. It wasn't until February 4, 1903, three years later, that the Pittsburgh City Council finally passed a bill permitting the Wabash Pittsburgh Terminal Railway to enter the Golden Triangle and to build its lavish Palace Terminal at Liberty Avenue and Ferry Street. The Pittsburgh City Council had earlier refused such permission. Approval came only after the public clamored for an end to the freight tie-up that was paralyzing business and causing unemployment. The voters trooped to the polls and voted out the old council members who for years had refused permission for the Wabash Railroad to enter Pittsburgh.

Stories of graft and collusion were rampant. Rumors had it that one selectman, as council members were then called, had received a bribe of $30,000 to change his vote. Two others were reported to have received

$15,000 "under the table." Several years later, in 1917, the Wabash Railroad in a report to The Interstate Commerce Commission admitted that it had paid $87,000 to three "politicians" between 1902 and 1904. Later news stories reported that several Pittsburgh councilmen purchased large blocks of Wabash Railroad stock and on the following day passed the resolution giving George Jay Gould permission to enter the city.

It was July 2, 1904, when the first train pulled out of the Palace Depot in downtown Pittsburgh loaded with dignitaries, puffed its way across the new Monongahela Bridge, through the new Wabash Tunnel, and headed west. A band played "Meet Me in St. Louis" while thousands of watchers on Mt. Washington cheered, and steamboats on the Monongahela River joined in with their whistles and horns.

Within four years, the Gould dream turned into a nightmare and the Wabash Pittsburgh Terminal Railway was history. There were many contributing factors—shortages of railway rolling stock, internal dissension, large freight rate reductions by the Pennsylvania Railroad, and the unexpected sale of Andrew Carnegie's steel interests to J. P. Morgan. Andrew Carnegie, a Gould ally, had pledged all of his freight tonnage to the Wabash line for the next 20 years. The loss of this tonnage was a serious blow to Gould's plans.

George Jay Gould had spent over $2 million on the Wabash Station and the railroad had cost over $380,000 per mile to build. The financial panic of 1907 followed and by 1908 the Wabash Railroad was declared insolvent. In the March 1912 issue of *McClure's Magazine*, the editor described the collapse of the Gould empire and blamed the debacle on George Jay Gould's life of idleness and luxury. The article described in detail the millions of dollars spent on Gould's estate at Lakewood, New Jersey, and on his elaborate entertainments, yachts, and hunting preserves in England. The article also blamed the debacle on Gould's proclivity to spend all his time in England rather than looking over his business interests at home.

The Wabash Tunnel marked the first serious attempt to give Pittsburgh much needed breathing space. Years later other tunnels followed— the Mt. Washington street car tunnel, the Armstrong Tubes, the Liberty Tubes, the Squirrel Hill tunnels, and the Fort Pitt tunnels. The once proud Wabash tunnel became the property of the Pittsburgh and Western Railroad and was deserted and forgotten, but it had served one purpose—it proved that the hills which hemmed in the city did not need to serve as barriers to future growth. It was possible to go through them.

During the next period of history, pigeons and animals became the tunnel's principal occupants. Thousands of them made it their home, and quite a home it was for the lowly pigeons. They corrupted its cut stone, its marble, bronze, and Giammartini designs. It is doubtful that pigeons anywhere had fancier quarters. The few visitors to the tunnel reported that bats, rodents, and all types of stray animals were quick to join the pigeons in recognizing the merits of an expensive home. For over 20 years birds and animals were the only regular visitors to the Wabash Tunnel.

On December 29, 1965, at about 8:30 a.m. smoke was seen pouring from the cracks around the sealed up entrances to the tunnel. City firemen were called and spent the next six hours trying to get the flames under control. Firemen worked their way into the south end of the tunnel for a distance of 200 feet, but were driven back by the intense smoke. They then tried to work their way in from the north end on Carson Street. They complained about the fact that the tunnel served as a perfect chimney for the fire and made putting the fire out very difficult. About two o'clock in the afternoon 15 firemen worked their way about 2,000 feet into the tunnel from Carson Street and determined that the source of the fire was piles of shoring timbers stored about the middle of the tunnel. They finally decided that the best solution was to let the fire burn itself out, which they proceeded to do. Their only explanation for the fire was that it probably was started by children with matches who were exploring the tunnel. We have no record of how many of the inhabitants of the tunnel lost their lives, but certainly no firemen were hurt by the conflagration.

For some period after the fire the south end of the tunnel was utilized by the Hahn Furniture Company as a storehouse for excess stocks of furniture. City records seem to be devoid of any reference to this, so we know little about the extent or the fees charged for this purpose.

The next chapter in the tunnel's history is probably its most fascinating. In December of 1971 the Port Authority of the City of Pittsburgh began its renovation of the Wabash Tunnel even though Mayor Pete Flaherty and other Skybus dissidents told them that the Skybus would never cross the Monongahela River. The Skybus project, which for some time appeared to be the accepted transportation project for better access to the South Hills, was the center of great political controversy. Mayor Flaherty who always maintained that the whole proposal was a waste of time, money and effort, even went so far as to barricade the old tunnel's southern entrance.

Opposition to the Skybus project was bitter. Every excuse was taken to put obstacles in the way of its development. Back in 1959 the Philadelphia, Baltimore, and Washington Railroad, the forerunner of the Penn Central, sold 60 acres of vertical land fronting the Mt. Washington bluff to the city for one dollar. The bill of sale stipulated that the land could only be used for park purposes. Mayor Flaherty seized upon this old bill of sale to refuse permission for the Skybus project to use a strip of land 23 by 60 feet for an easement needed to construct an aerial ramp to the entrance to the north portal of the tunnel.

It is noteworthy to remember the time and money spent to build the prototype of the Skybus at South Park in an effort to sell the public on its practicality. But the Port Authority persisted and spent $6 million to reconstruct the entire Wabash tunnel. When they finished the job, the Wabash tunnel was, in the words of the *Pittsburgh Post Gazette*, "an attractive tunnel, sturdily constructed, excellently lighted and ventilated— as good a tunnel as has ever been bored through Mt. Washington—those who designed and rebuilt it should be proud of their efforts." Yet while the tunnel was being renovated, the Skybus's chance of being completed grew more bleak by the day. In October of 1974, County Commissioner Thomas Foerster, who had been one of the Skybus's major supporters, withdrew his support, and the entire Skybus project was history.

The 3,450 foot tunnel was now equipped with two elevated roadways rising 30 inches off its floor. The roadways are steel-reinforced concrete platforms a half mile long. The *Post Gazette* sarcastically said that the tunnel "could accommodate only two types of vehicles—a Skybus or a golf cart."

Edwin Beachler, PAT's Director of Marketing and Communications, sadly reported that, "There is no valid question about the technology. Skybuses are being built by more than a dozen companies around the world. Political jobs and times change. The tragedy of Pittsburgh is that it has already cost over $6,000,000 and the cost will only increase in the future." When asked why the Port Authority had gone ahead with the construction of the tunnel even while opposition to the project mounted, he added, "It was no gamble. We built then because waiting until later would mean spending more money. This tunnel will be used for the Skybus someday." Perhaps his prediction will still come true.

Whether the rubber-wheeled Skybus, as designed, was the proper answer to Pittsburgh's traffic problems will be left to traffic experts. The tragedy is that so much taxpayer money was spent with so little to show for it, and the project will always serve as a source of public embarrassment for the Port Authority.

The following chapters in its history are even more bizarre. Some cynics maintained that the most valid use for the tunnel was as a massive mushroom plantation which would make the city of Pittsburgh famous as the mushroom capital of the world. At one point some interested investors offered to open it to the public as a massive cocktail lounge and even went so far as it suggest that it be named, "The Cave."

The *Pittsburgh Post Gazette* reported in its edition of October 3, 1974, that an individual had contacted Port Authority officials for permission to open the tunnel and allow him to roll a bowling ball the length of the tunnel. His goal was to have *The Guinness Book of Records* verify that he had rolled the longest strike in bowling history. The paper reported that his request was not treated seriously. Fortunately for many people, the old tunnel was almost invisible. Its entrances have been bricked up for decades and thus few people were even aware of its existence. If it had been as visible as the famous Fort Pitt Bridge "to nowhere" it would certainly have been the subject of numerous cartoons and would have been a much maligned example of political boondoggles.

And now finally it appears that the latest chapter in the tunnel's history is upon us. Every resident of Pittsburgh has been told over and over that the city faces the most monumental traffic tie-ups in its history. The Fort Pitt Bridge is badly in need of renovation and must be closed to traffic for prolonged periods of time. It carries the bulk of traffic to the South Hills of the city and the heavy traffic to the airport. Estimates of the time needed to complete the job range up to two years. Without some alternate routes or new traffic patterns, the city fears that many of its parkways will become little more than parking lots.

One of the alternative solutions to the traffic nightmare is to reopen the Wabash tunnel and create a new traffic pattern toward the southern suburbs of the city. Legislation has already been introduced in Harrisburg that in effect will fund the construction of a new bridge across the Monongahela River into the mouth of the abandoned tunnel. Support seems to be growing for this solution to the problem. The Pennsylvania Highway Department has indicated that it will be willing to delay renovation of the Fort Pitt Bridge until this new bridge and highway can be opened.

It is not a simple decision. Complicated new ramps and approaches must be built at the south end of the old tunnel and also at the north end of the new bridge in the Golden Triangle. The old Wabash Tunnel, while still in relatively good condition, was not constructed to be an automobile roadway, and the entire length of the tunnel will have to be rebuilt as a highway.

Admittedly, the reuse of the old Wabash tunnel is far from a reality, but it does appear as though the "tunnel to nowhere" might still become the "tunnel to somewhere." A new chapter in the history of the old Wabash tunnel may yet be written.

Part III
Personalities

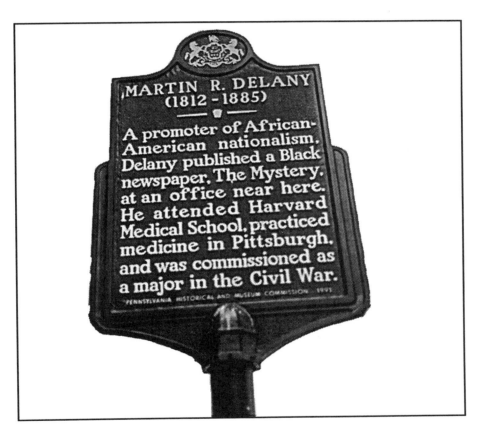

Historical Marker, PPG Place

John Ormsby:
Pittsburgh's First Aristocrat
(1720-1805)

John Ormsby was widely referred to as an "aristocrat." *The Oxford American Dictionary* defines an aristocrat as "a member of the nobility, the upper classes of a country; someone noble in style; a member of the group who ruled a country." John Ormsby certainly fit some parts of that definition, if not all.

Anyone familiar with daily life in Pittsburgh in the 1700s might find it hard to identify a true aristocrat. The sociological structure of Pittsburgh was decidedly different in the late 1700s than it was 100 years later. In the 1700s it was a staunchly classed society. "Aristocrats" did not mix with the "common man." It was recorded that when Dr. Nathaniel Bedford, John Ormsby's son-in-law, entered a tavern or a public eating place and wanted a seat, the "common" man would be thrown out of the place even though he might be only half through his meal.

United States citizens were told again and again that the new world created a revolutionary change in the way that the "common man" was able to assert his rights, and that was certainly the end result. It was only natural that members of the European nobility or aristocracy who came to this new world would assume that most of the customs of the old world would follow them here. It was never easy to give up the customs and privileges that seemed to naturally belong to them and had been their birthright for generations.

Certainly John Ormsby and his son-in-law, Dr. Nathaniel Bedford, were referred to as aristocratic. John Ormsby was considered a handsome man, and he accumulated considerable wealth. As far as is known, no portrait exists of John Ormsby, but there are several descriptions of the man. *The Pittsburgh Dispatch* edition of Sunday, August 9, 1708, describes him as: "a gentleman of the old school, aristocratic, fastidious of dress, whether in civil life or on parade, wearing his good sword, 'Sweet Lips,' and ready on instant to measure his skill with it should any mortal be rash enough to insult him."

Barbara Anna (Winebiddle) Negley, mother of Mrs. Thomas Mellon, one of his contemporaries, said John Ormsby " was a fine looking man of aristocratic and military bearing, a gentleman of the old school, noted for his immaculate breast and sleeve ruffles, the brightness of his shoe and knee buckles, and especially for his dress sword at his side."

John Ormsby's "nobility" was not of recent origin. The first known mention of the Ormsby name is in the celebrated Harleian manuscript in the British Museum where it states that "Sir Richard D. Ormesby (sic), Knight, held the lands of Ormesby(sic) in County Lincolnshire, England." The King gave him all the lands that he owned before the Norman Conquest in 1066. The "nobility" of the Ormsby family goes back over 900 years.

The Ormsby Coat of Arms shows an armored knight's arm brandishing an armored leg. The Latin inscription reads, "More Courage than Prudence." The story is that one of Erin's sons, an ancestor of John Ormsby, lost his leg in the war in Flanders, and having found his leg amputated, picked it up and used it as a war club in the ensuing battle.

When John Ormsby walked the streets of his frontier city, he always carried with him "Sweet Lips," his polished sword, which he could use very well. He learned to use it in the army in the British Isles before he came to America. After arriving in the New World, he taught dancing and the art of handling a sword in his school in Philadelphia. He prided himself as a noble gentleman of polish and refinement in the rough element of the new frontier.

John Ormsby was not a typical pioneer. He was the son of an Irish gentleman of distinguished lineage. He was born in 1720, was educated at Trinity College, University of Dublin, but for some undisclosed reason, chose to seek his fortune in the New World. It is easy to imagine how confident he must have been of success in his new country and eager for the fame and fortune he hoped to gain in his adopted homeland. In 1752, at the age of 32, we find John Ormsby in the city of Philadelphia, at that time the most populous city in the colonies and a center of colonial aristocracy. He had a wide circle of friends and associates and enjoyed a reasonable income from the school he established in Philadelphia.

In 1755 General Braddock landed his forces in Virginia ready to start his historic march across the mountains to ensure the British hold on the western frontier. John Ormsby, who had served as a young officer in the British army, was offered a captain's commission and the opportunity to act as adjutant to one of the regiments recruited by Benjamin Franklin to resist the French aggression in the West. He accepted the commission, but unfortunately a violent fever destroyed his dream of a military career.

It was three years later, in 1758, when he again had the opportunity to serve militarily. He was unable to accept an active commission but did agree to serve as Commissary of Provisions in the army of General Forbes in his march to Fort Duquesne. When the French burned and exited Fort Duquesne, Ormsby moved into the fort at the Point with the British troops. John Ormsby saw the "lilies of France" lowered, to be replaced by the "cross of St. George."

John Ormsby's memoirs describe Fort Duquesne on that memorable day as, "in truth a wretched place, as the whole of what buildings and other improvements the French had made burned to the ground. We had neither flour, flesh meat, or liquor in store; the only relief offered for the present was plenty of bear meat and venison which our hunters brought in, and which our men devoured without bread or salt." For the next three years John Ormsby lived with the small garrison at the newly named Fort Pitt. It was a hard perilous life, exposed continually to attacks from the Indians and to privation and want when supplies grew short.

When Fort Pitt was finally rebuilt and strengthened to the point where the English felt that they were now secure from a new attack from the French, John Ormsby decided to strike out on his own to make his fortune. In 1760 John Ormsby began to trade with the Indians. After at least two attempts to resign his army commission, his request was finally approved and he left his army career for the last time.

Ormsby's trade with the Indians went well for a few years, but in 1763 Pontiac and his cohorts attacked the Western forts in a valiant attempt to hold back the invasion of the white soldiers on to Indian lands. Ormsby had trading posts at Salt Licks, Gichago, and Fort Pitt, but the Indians descended on all three of these posts, seized his goods and horses, and tomahawked his employees. Ormsby described this setback in his own words:

> I had accumulated a handsome sum of money since coming to Western Pennsylvania, which to my sorrow I laid out for large quantities of Indian goods and pack horses, in which trade I had good success until 1763, when the savages murdered my clerks and people and robbed me of all my goods to a considerable value, and what was more grievous left me in debt above £1,500 to Philadelphia merchants.

Other accounts indicate that the actual debt amounted to £3,500 in the currency of Pennsylvania. Deeply in debt, John Ormsby bought a tract of land near Bedford, Pennsylvania, opened a general store, and married Anne McAllister, 17 years younger his junior, and fathered three children. But his biographers insisted that his heart was always in Pittsburgh, and 6 years later in 1770, he and his family returned to Pittsburgh. The grateful British crown, recognizing John Ormsby's contribution to the defense of Fort Pitt, presented him with a strip of land along the Monongahela River, south of the city of Pittsburgh. In addition John Ormsby bought a large tract of land adjacent to his gift from the British Crown. His land holdings extended from the southern end of the Smithfield Street Bridge to Six Mile Ferry near Homestead and back about 2 miles into the countryside. He owned close to 3,000 acres. However, John and his family lived on Water Street in downtown Pittsburgh and for several years operated a small tavern.

Tavern keeping in the late 1770s was not what it is today. Historians said that people opened taverns if they had anything over and above what they needed. John Ormsby's tavern received high ratings among the inns of Pittsburgh, but that says little for it. Schoepf, a business traveler said, "In Pittsburgh (sic) we were directed to the best inn, a small wooden cabin set askew by the Monongahela, its exterior promising little, but seeing several well dressed men and ladies adorned, we were not discouraged." That inn was John Ormsby's.

Many important meetings were held in Ormsby's tavern. The men of the city met there regularly to talk of politics, business, and social affairs.

Pittsburgh Academy's Board of Trustees held early meetings there. In 1785 a Methodist missionary, Rev. Wilson Lee, preached at the Ormsby Inn. We know that men such as John Neville, Hugh Brackenridge, Isaac Craig, James Ross, Richard and William Butler, James O'Hara, Henry Baldwin, Tarleton Bates, Michael Huffnagle, Joseph Aston, and many other prominent Pittsburghers were frequent patrons of John Ormsby's tavern.

In 1770 Pittsburgh was a rural community. The Point was covered with heavy foliage. Grassy banks sloped down to the river banks in all directions. Stiff, gabled houses were scattered along narrow streets; a typical village church nestled among the trees, and in every direction heavily wooded hills sloped to the distant skyline. Pittsburgh was a sleepy village in a now peaceful valley.

In 1773 John Ormsby was authorized by the William Penn family to operate a ferry across the Monongahela River to the strip of land he owned on the South Side of the river. Travelers going west over the Brownsville Pike Road were transported across the river to continue their journey. By 1784 there were 18 families living on the "South Side," all of them renting land from John Ormsby at a price of one third of their annual harvest. He called the small community, "Homestead Farms." By 1785 John Ormsby had sold off his Bedford County lands, and some of his "South Side" properties, and had paid off all his debtors. The property he had not sold off eventually went to his daughters, Jane and Sidney. The Ormsby family is still recognized on the South Side by several principal thoroughfares named for members of his family—Jane, Sidney, Sarah, Josephine, Mary, and Wharton. At one point efforts were made to change the name of Carson Street to Ormsby Street, but although such an ordinance was passed, it was never fully implemented. Several other South Side streets carried Ormsby names but were eliminated when north-south streets were given numbers instead of proper names.

John Ormsby was always the entrepreneur. For some years Ormsby operated a small boat yard on the south side of the Monongahela River. Several hundred yards up the river he owned a brickyard where brick was manufactured. In the meantime he leased out his land holdings for pasture land to livestock owners. He was one of the original trustees and founders of Trinity Church, the first Protestant Episcopal house of worship in Pittsburgh. In several 1786 editions of the old *Pittsburgh Gazette*, several advertisements were inserted in the paper by John Ormsby trying to dispose of more of his land.

John Ormsby was unique. He was probably the first permanent settler in the Pittsburgh area who had studied within the walls of an institution of higher education as a permanent resident. After his return for 35 years until his death, he:

> lived, an honored citizen of the city, always looked up to with reverence and respect, doing more than his share in the work of civic construction, a brave defender, a wise counselor, a courteous and obliging friend, and an active agent in everything that pertained to the city's prosperity and development.

He was called "a just and honest man and to his friends and family exceedingly kind and considerate." John Ormsby considered himself an aristocrat and all his life tried to live up to the demands of that rank. He wrote no books or pamphlets, but his intellectual influence was clearly felt by the people with whom he came in contact.

John Ormsby's family continued to play a significant role in the history of Pittsburgh for many years. His daughter, Jane Ormsby married Dr. Nathanial Bedford, Pittsburgh's first physician and the man who donated the land for Market Square to the city. Jane inherited all the land between 6th and 7th Streets on the South Side, then called Birmingham. Dr. Bedford in 1811 laid out the plans for Birmingham, and named it for his native city of Birmingham, England. It was later incorporated into the city as the South Side. Dr. Bedford was one of the founders of the Pittsburgh Academy which later became the University of Pittsburgh.

The borough of Mt. Oliver was named for Oliver Ormsby, John's son. Oliver became a very successful businessman, and it was said that he inherited his father's good looks. Oliver Ormsby had 10 children. He developed his father's interests until he owned a line of trading stores which extended from as far north as Erie and Niagara and as far west as Cincinnati. Oliver Ormsby's store provided large supplies for Commodore Perry's fleet on Lake Erie. Oliver owned a cotton factory, a rope factory at Chillicothe, a steam flour mill at Cincinnati, grist and saw mills, and a forge and charcoal iron furnace at Beaver Falls. He was director of the United

States Branch Bank of Pittsburgh, was a board manager of the Monongahela Bridge Company which owned what is now the Smithfield Bridge, and held a seat on Pittsburgh's town council.

All of the Ormsbys had magnificent mansions on the South Side of Pittsburgh. Their first homestead, an old colonial house, was the home of Josephine Ormsby, who married Commandant Edward Madison Yard, U.S.N. The Yard house was remembered for its 5 huge pillars at the entrance. Originally it stood majestically on a large plot of land that sloped gently down to the Monongahela River's edge, but by the time it was demolished in the 1920s, railroad tracks cut it off from the river front and the new 22nd Street Bridge practically abutted its eastern wall. In its final days it was occupied by Mrs. Yard's sister, Mrs. Clifton Wharton. The Ormsby Manor at 26th and 27th Street had disappeared much earlier, but it boasted its own private race track for the gentlemen of the day.

In his later years John Ormsby became a familiar figure on the streets of Pittsburgh. He certainly cast a pompous figure. He continued to wear breast and sleeve ruffles and shiny knee buckles. His brightly polished sword always hung at his side, probably the last vestige of his once promising military career.

The remains of John Ormsby and his wife, Jane McAllister, lie in the old church yard of Trinity Cathedral on 6th Avenue in downtown Pittsburgh. Their tombstones are clearly marked.

The different periods of growth in old Birmingham can be traced in the width of the streets. Streets in the original section planned by Dr. Bedford are more narrow and end at 17th Street. Even today the wider streets east of 17th Street are still apparent. The area east of 28th Street was originally known as Ormsby. As the population grew, the South Side became divided into four boroughs—South Pittsburgh, Birmingham, East Birmingham, and Ormsby. Each had it own governing body, but in time all became part of the greater city of Pittsburgh.

John Ormsby was a colorful personality, an aristocrat in a wild frontier town, a man who although totally committed to life in the New World, found it very difficult to leave behind the customs and traditions of the Old World. It is obvious, however, that although he wore his ruffles and his sword, that in most ways he adopted the mores of his new world and everyone remembered him as a successful citizen, whose family left its indelible mark on a growing city.

16

Anne Royall: America's First Feminist (1769-1854)

On The University of Pennsylvania—

A den of ignoramuses, about as enlightened as the inmates of the State prison…."University," the greatest burlesque on the word in the world. The best thing the city could do for its youth would be to clap a coal to it and burn it down—it is worse than Columbia College in New York and that is saying something.

On literary critics—"not that I regard literary critics more than I would a snarling cur, an animal which they resemble in anything but shape."

On Baltimore—"the more illiterate, proud, and ignorant city, excepting Richmond, in the Union, nor was I backward in exposing them."

These quotations direct from Anne Royall's published writings are typical of her acerbic tongue. Was Anne an infidel, a blackmailer, and a shrill-tongued charlatan who managed to alienate almost everyone with her caustic and unkind pen? Or was she a figure of historical importance in early America (her life span extended from George Washington to Abraham Lincoln), a pioneer woman journalist who took strong stands on many important issues, and whose strong personality always made her a fascinating figure? Debates aside, history seems to affirm her role as a reporter of her times.

Since her death, she has been forgotten. Her books have long been out of print; copies of the originals are extremely difficult to find. She was not a great writer, her books were never considered good literature. Her published material was noteworthy only because of its acerbic tone.

While alive, she was the most widely known woman of her day. She encured ridicule, injustice, and persecution. She had the unfortunate, but perhaps intentional, habit of supporting what in her day were extremely unpopular causes. Not the least of which was her almost fanatic antagonism toward all brands of evangelical religion, and this at a time when this conservative theology was rampant. To her credit, she never waffled in her beliefs and in her outspoken support of the causes she embraced. Although not always wise in the style of her attacks on her enemies, she sometimes exuded refreshing common sense, and exhibited uncommon cunning in controversy.

Anne Newport (her maiden name) was not a native Pennsylvanian. She was born in Maryland, but at the age of three, moved with her family to Hannahstown, a primitive home near Greensburg, Pennsylvania. Hannahstown was the first town west of the Allegheny Mountains where the white man lived under written laws. Her Pennsylvania residence dates from 1772. Anne claimed that she taught herself to read and had almost no formal schooling. Hannahstown in the 1770s was a pioneer settlement. The town was totally destroyed by the Indians in 1782 when Anne was 13 years old. Families who survived the attack were saved when they sought shelter in a nearby fort.

When Anne was 28 years old she met and married Captain William Royall, an officer in the American Army during the Revolutionary War. He was a Virginia gentlemen of some wealth, who came from an important family. Captain William Royall was well known; he carried a letter dated during the Revolutionary War, handwritten by General Lafayette, asserting that he had served with distinction and which identified him as a certified war hero. For 16 years Anne Royall lived the life of a genteel Southern woman. She was active in Virginia society entertaining widely.

It was only when her husband died in 1813, leaving her in the midst of a financial dispute, that Anne Royall's career as an obstreperous journalist commenced. When Royall died, he left most of his estate to Anne, but family members immediately went to the courts to challenge the will and claimed that his estate belonged to them. Ten years of litigation followed and finally, in 1823, the courts decided against Anne Royall's claim. Losing all hope of gain from her husband's estate, she began to write as a means of supporting herself.

She had her first book published in Alexandria, Virginia, in 1823. That year she petitioned the U.S. Government for a widow's pension. Countless legislative efforts were made to secure what was clearly hers, but it was many years until a minor recognition was given to her claim. All official records of her husband's war service were lost in a fire in Richmond, Virginia, and later Anne's myriad enemies managed to sidetrack all her attempts to have her pension approved.

In 1834 she went to Washington, D.C. determined to fight for her pension rights. For the rest of her life, she made Washington her center of operations. She was now 51 years of age, with no visible means of support, but she had an observant eye and a blistering pen and proceeded to carve herself a place as one of America's first woman journalists.

Anne decided to travel and record her experiences. This was no small cultural or physical feat for a woman at this time. There were no telegraph poles; candles were the chief source of light; natural gas was only being talked about. The Erie Canal was the pride of the country; steam locomotives were just being introduced in isolated places; not a single steam passenger ship crossed the Atlantic Ocean regularly. Most of Anne's travels were made by stage coach over horrible roads, and she stayed in country inns which were anything but comfortable or safe.

Her writing was recognized as the first real travel writing in America. Her caustic pen and vitriolic attacks on institutions and places, soon attracted wide attention in a day when the printed word had very limited circulation. To truly appreciate the power of her pen, one needs to see some specific quotations from her writing about places:

Philadelphia—

...of all the cities and towns I have ever been in, it is the most unfeeling, inhospitable, and uncharitable toward strangers in distress. I am astonished at the young men of Philadelphia particularly when they look back at their noble race of great men and find themselves at least a century in the rear.

Richmond—

…inhabited by the most ignorant rabble of any city in the United
States. There are men in the world, and women too, in this
enlightened country—in Virginia—that although in the shape of
human beings, professing the religion of Jesus Christ, were more
savage and unfeeling than any of the savage tribes, or even brutes.

Troy, N.Y.—"…inhabited by a narrow-minded bigoted people, the
refuse of New England."

Utica, N.Y.—"…its gross bigotry and ignorance—the most
blackguard place I ever put foot in the United States."

Buffalo, N.Y.—"Its young men are the most conceited ignoramuses,
(except Utica) of any town or village I have ever visited."

It was not only cities which became the object of her attacks;
institutions were also fair targets:

Quakers—

…had the proprietor, Pool, been anything but a brute, he would have
procured me a conveyance, but being a Quaker, he had neither the
politeness to offer his services or to purchase a book. The more I see
of these Quakers, the more I am disgusted with them.

Presbyterians—

It is useless to reject a fact too well known that these Presbyterians,
glutted with women and money, have become not only beastly
wicked, but are in every part of the United States arming to
overthrow our government and establish a reign of terror—if ever
the matter is decided by arms, (and there seems to be no other
remedy) my opinion is that every Presbyterian hostile to our liberty,
will be exterminated, as there is no safety where they are.

Christian Religion—"The Christian religion has become a name, a byword, a cloak to conceal, or countenance rather, not only every knave, but every class of fraud and oppression."

Religious Seminaries—"The day will come when the American people will see the impropriety of suffering priests to have anything to do with their seminaries of learning."

Navy Department—"I can never hit it. We have so much gunpowder between us—we are always sure to have an explosion whenever we come within earshot."

During her active years she wrote 11 books and traveled over the entire United States as it then existed. Her books described many important villages, towns, and cities. Although her attacks on places and institutions were often unkind, she provided capsule histories of every place she visited; her facts and descriptions were strikingly apt. She wrote with remarkable clarity using a sharp vocabulary; she made detailed observations with insight, although she often included too much detail. Her honest conviction and patriotism could not be questioned, and she exhibited a rigid intolerance of bigotry. She was abusive and too ready to reveal the objects of her scorn (she never left any doubt about whom she was writing). Royall was undoubtedly guilty of hasty judgments not always based on fact, and constantly exaggerated her praise of those she liked.

Why have her books ceased to attract readers? There are several reasons. Clearly her books were written for the living, not the dead. They were extremely topical, and she was unfortunate enough to write at a time when the Civil War blotted out a great volume of American writing. Her vitriolic opposition to churches and the theology of the day inevitably meant that strong forces opposed her beliefs and therefore her writing. Some of the causes which Anne Royall championed were:

- Entire separation of Church and State
- Exposure and punishment of corrupt officials
- Public schools everywhere, totally free of religious bias or control
- Freemasonry
- Justice to the Indians

- Liberal immigration laws
- Transportation for Sunday mail
- Territorial expansion
- Liberal support for scientific experimentation;
- Just tariff laws;
- States' rights on the slavery question;
- Abolition of flogging in the Navy;
- Better conditions for the working man;
- Free thought, free speech, and free press
- Good works instead of long prayers

Today this list would come close to an American Civil Liberties Union platform. It is surprisingly liberal and forward-looking, but in her day, many of these causes were presumed extremely radical. They aroused violent opposition and produced many powerful enemies, such as evangelical ministers, the politicians who were afraid of losing evangelical support, the Anti-Masons, a real force in that day, the United States Bank, which she fought interminably, and the temperance and anti-slavery groups in the country. No one could fault her for being cautious; she took on most of the influential forces of her day.

Her attacks on individuals, both famous and unknown, were equally vitriolic. She spared no names and asked for no quarter. Upon meeting the governor of Ohio on shipboard, she said, "He was as great a clown as we had on board. If the people of Ohio have no more taste, you would expect others to have."

She constantly railed against the bureaucracy which she saw developing in Washington. She saw no justification for government employees, not elected by the people, who she said would come to see their jobs as lifetime sinecures. She defined the problem as follows:

Even our President and members of Congress are elected at short periods from the mass of the people, and upon the same principle, all the subordinate officers ought to be often changed. The best of men, we find from history, never have been proof against corruption, and to guard against this evil, the framers of our Constitution wisely provided frequent rotation in office. It is essential to the evidence of republics, and the only security of the liberties of the people. I know that it will be said that it requires practice to do the business of a clerk. No such thing; enough can always be found who understand bookkeeping, which is sufficient, and the measure itself will act as a stimulus to qualifications, where offices and places are open to all. What incentive has the youth of our country, if offices and emoluments are to be perpetual?

She railed against the political appointments in Washington. She said, "We are paying a librarian $1,500 per year to take care of the National Library, and the books are molding on the shelves. We pay $1,500 to a doorkeeper, who is not nor has he been, able to attend to his duties for over two years." If Anne visited Washington today and could see the burgeoning bureaucracy, her reactions would be hilarious.

She constantly fought against intolerance in the realm of religious thought, in a time when fire and brimstone were being preached from pulpits all over America, when intense pressure was used to promote the establishment of a state religion, and when those who refused to espouse the popular religious beliefs of the day were often ostracized. She railed against what she saw as the injustices committed against women and Indians by organized religions of her day.

For some paradoxical reason, given her opposition to most organized religions, she became a champion of Free Masonry and bitterly castigated the Anti-Masonry movement. Anyone who attacked the Masonic lodge became her lifelong enemy.

Of special interest to Pittsburghers is the fact that she visited Pittsburgh in 1828 and wrote voluminously about her observations and experiences. She was uncharacteristicly kind in her judgments of the city in contrast to those written about other cities on the same trip.

She was much impressed by Pittsburgh and Pennsylvania, perhaps biased by her early childhood near Greensburg, Pennsylvania. She wrote that Pennsylvania was "blessed with more resources of wealth, ease, and comfort than any other State in the Union." What seemed to impress Anne most were Pittsburgh's flourishing industries. She rhapsodized about the politeness, the chasteness, and the gentlemanly deportment of Pittsburgh's working men. In fact, she claimed that they excelled those of any other city in America, "or perhaps the world." The detail and completeness of her descriptions of the plants and their workers is most unusual for a travel writer of any age.

Although Anne usually characterized industrial employees "as more or less depraved." she was highly complimentary of the representatives of the trades in Pittsburgh. She said, "I did not find it so in Pittsburgh." She wrote:

> I spent thirteen days in the houses and foundries of the city,…and never saw or heard the most distant indelicate look or word among the whole of them. I was treated with marked and gentlemanly respect; I was more astonished at this than anything else in the wonder-working city. Why Pittsburgh should differ so widely in this respect from all other manufacturing towns I am unqualified to say, but it is a well known fact here and in Europe that these manufacturing houses exhibit a most lamentable picture of low, vicious manners. On the whole of my visit to Pittsburgh I never saw an instance of intoxication.

She could not miss the pollution and the dirt, however. She wrote:

> Most of the houses are brick, and some of them are lofty, fine buildings; but all of the houses are colored quite black with the smoke. The interiors of the houses are still worse, carpets, chairs, walls, furniture—all black with smoke; no such thing as wearing white; the ladies mostly dress in black, and a cap or white ruff put on clean in the morning is tinged quite black by bedtime. Meantime the smoke, particularly in the absence of the sun, is quite annoying to the eyes of strangers, and everything has a very gloomy, doleful appearance at first, excepting always the interior of the workshops. But in a few days the stranger becomes so familiar to it that the novelty of the thing is completely worn off, and your walks and rambles through the city are pursued with the same pleasure common to others.

Anne was delighted to find a university in the city, but was much disturbed to find that most of the professors were clergymen. She summed up her visit to the city as follows:

Of all the towns in our country, Pittsburgh excites most astonishment. Everything pursued in other towns is thrown into the shade by Pittsburgh, even in the building of steamboats she excels, by a long way, our great city, New York. You see nothing but columns of smoke rolling our of these manufactories in every part of the city and in every street. Go to the river Monongahela, and you see nothing but steamboats, two stories high most of them, and two tiers of windows, precisely like a house with gable ends.

In 1830 when Anne Royall was 61 years old she was involved in an altercation in a Pittsburgh bookstore. The event attracted wide attention in the city and the press since Anne was by then a nationally known author. Court records for October 21, 1830, indicate that she was allegedly "attacked by a male clerk in a bookstore with a cow skin." The newspapers carried extensive accounts of the incidents, but did not give the name of the assailant.

During the latter part of her journalistic career, Anne published two papers in Washington, D.C. The first one was *Paul Pry* and was published over the course of several trying years. Although widely read, financial support was sporadic. It became a gadfly among the huge papers becoming popular in the city. Later she published *The Huntress*, a sprightly and readable paper, in which she seemed to tone down her rancor.

Over the years her long-standing and unsuccessful battle for a war pension became a standing joke in the U.S. Congress. Her career hit its final low point when in 1829 she was arrested, tried, and convicted of being a "common scold." Charges had been brought by two clergymen as the result of a neighborhood confrontation. Anne was accused of talking abusively and swearing at members of a congregation who met in an engine house next to her residence in Washington, D.C. The punishment for such charges was usually a public dunking. Although the jury found her guilty of being a "common nuisance and a common brawler," she was released from jail. By then she had been labeled as a malcontent and never regained the esteem she formerly held in many people's minds.

Anne died on October 1, 1854, and lies in an unmarked grave in the Congressional Cemetery in Washington, D.C. For more than 30 years Anne

Royall was a strident voice in our national consciousness. Her biographer, Sarah Harvey Porter, wrote:

> She was a child of her time—a period of national swagger—but she visited the sick and prisoners, fed the hungry and clothed the naked out of her meager pittance, gave shelter to the widow and orphan, and gave succor to the outcast.

Perhaps that epitaph outranks those of far greater fame.

Martin R. Delaney:
Pittsburgh's First Human Rights Hero
(1812-1885)

On 3rd Avenue at PPG Place, only a few steps from Ruth's Chris Steak House in downtown Pittsburgh, there stands an historical marker which reads, in part:

Martin R. Delaney
1812–1885

Thousands of Pittsburgh's citizens pass this marker every day without a glance, and you can be sure that if you asked several of the noon-time pedestrians who walk past it, most of them could not tell you who Martin R. Delaney was, even though the marker informs us:

A Promoter of African-American Nationalism. Delaney published a Black Newspaper, *The Mystery*, at an office near here. He attended Harvard Medical School, practiced medicine in Pittsburgh and was commissioned a major in the Civil War.

Martin Robison Delaney deserves a better historical fate. His life and his accomplishments should be recognized. Delaney was an essayist, an author, and a newspaper publisher. He was also a practicing physician who helped put down a cholera epidemic in Pittsburgh, a tireless worker for civil rights before the term was popular, one of the earliest theorists and advocates of black empowerment, and one of the first black commissioned officers in the United States Army. Despite Delaney's contributions to society, Oliver Wendell Holmes, the renowned scholar and judge, once expelled him from Harvard University because he was black.

These accomplishments are not half the story of his life. At various times he was an unsuccessful political candidate, an amateur scientist who led an expedition to the Niger River Valley of Africa, a public lecturer, and, before the Civil War, a Lieutenant Governor of one of the South's most southern states. Excluded from several institutions of higher learning and prevented from furthering his chosen career, Delaney nonetheless succeeded in living a notable life.

Martin Robison Delaney's ancestors were Mandingos from West Africa. Captured and sold as slaves, Delaney's grandparents were transported to America. Somehow, although the details are not clear, Martin's maternal grandparents earned their freedom. His mother was a freed slave while his father was still legally a slave. His parents lived in Charlestown, Virginia, which later became part of West Virginia. There, Martin, the last of five children, was born on May 6, 1812.

Delaney's biographer, Dorothy Sterling, reports that Martin thirsted for learning, but being black, was not permitted to attend the local schools. According to this biographer, Martin owned his first book when Jonathan Dwight, an itinerant peddler from Connecticut, gave him a New York primer and story book in exchange for some bent spoons and blunt knives. Whatever the authenticity of that story, Martin taught himself to read and started a pattern of learning that benefitted him throughout his life.

Because it was illegal in the early 1800s to teach a black man to read, the local Charlestown authorities threatened to put Martin's mother in jail. Demonstrating her independence and initiative, Martin's mother bundled up her children, left her husband temporarily behind, and fled across state lines to Chambersburg, Pennsylvania. Martin was now eight years old. In 1820 Chambersburg was a thriving community, with eight churches and three weekly newspapers, and was an important stopping off place on the major travel route between Philadelphia and Pittsburgh.

Later his father joined the family and went to work in a paper mill. Martin was permitted to attend elementary school in Chambersburg, but the only high school in the city was expensive and exclusive and thus off limits to a poor black boy. After his formal schooling had ended, Martin worked at several jobs, including one stint helping to build the Pennsylvania Canal. His biographer said that Martin's big ambition was to gain admission to Dickinson College at Carlisle, Pennsylvania, but this was a goal he never achieved.

At the age of 19, Martin packed his few personal belongings, and on July 29, 1831, said good-by to his parents and set out on a 150–mile journey to Pittsburgh. When he reached Bedford, Pennsylvania, his money ran out and he was forced to take a job helping a farmer bring in the fall harvest. After some delay, he managed to reach the growing, bustling city of Pittsburgh, where he hoped to find employment and further his educational objectives.

Martin was penniless; he knew no one in the city, and he needed a place to stay and a place to eat. As he walked along Water Street, he was fascinated by the heavy river traffic, and by the hustle and bustle of a thriving frontier town. On 3rd Street he spotted a barber pole and a shop operated by a black man. Knowing that barbering was one of the few trades open to black men, principally because white barbers did not want to cut black men's hair, Martin decided to try his luck there. The shop owner, John B. Vashon, son of a black man and a white woman, took an interest in Martin, and invited him to lodge temporarily with his family where he shared a bed with Vashon's son, George.

While living with the Vashons, Martin read *The Liberator*, a new anti-slavery paper edited by William Lloyd Garrison, and this publication seemed to energize Martin. He threw all his efforts behind a new organization being formed in Pittsburgh, called the African Education Society. At the same time Martin joined temperance societies, Bible groups, and anti-slavery associations.

By day Martin worked on the Pittsburgh waterfront, loading coal and pig iron on barges, and by night he attended classes at Lewis Woodson's school in the basement of the African Methodist Church, a few blocks from Market Square. Martin said that it was at this time that he decided to become a doctor. It is hard to imagine a more unrealistic goal for a young black man in Pittsburgh in the early 1800s. Trained, licensed black doctors were unheard of.

As a first step toward his medical career, Martin knocked on the door of Dr. Andrew McDonald's dispensary and tried to convince him to take him on as an apprentice. We know little about the details or how much resistance Dr. McDonald gave to the idea, but such a relationship between a white doctor and a black assistant was not a common arrangement in the city. Martin's principal duties were blood-letting and applying leeches, two very common medical procedures of the day. At any rate, he soon became confident enough of his skill because he opened his own business. The 1837 Pittsburgh Business Directory lists—"Delaney, Martin R., Cupping, Leeching, and Bleeding."

Delaney continued with his activities in the black community, and in 1836, he and Lewis Woodson were elected as Pittsburgh's delegates to the "Annual Convention of Colored Men in New York City." Martin was a vigorous opponent of the various colonization societies that promoted the shipment of freed and escaped slaves to Africa to form their own countries. But in the meantime he became increasingly frustrated by the lack of opportunities for black people in the United States.

Searching for a new outlet for his energies and goals, Martin determined to visit the South and the Southwest to personally evaluate the opportunities for black people in parts of the United States he had never seen. He shipped out on a river boat headed down the Ohio River from Pittsburgh, and stopped off at most of the river ports on the Ohio and Mississippi Rivers. Eventually he visited the states of Mississippi, Louisiana, and Texas, and returned home disturbed by the treatment of black people in much of the United States. It took initiative and courage for a young black man in the late 1830s to set off alone to experience the life of black people in the pre-Civil War South.

In 1840 Martin returned to Pittsburgh and threw himself into the gubernatorial campaign of Francis J. LeMoyne, a member of the Liberty Party, an abolitionist, and a medical doctor from Washington, Pennsylvania. LeMoyne's candidacy went nowhere, but Martin continually sought ways of promoting the welfare of black people in the city of Pittsburgh.

The Colored Freemen of Pennsylvania, one of the many black organizations which had sprung up to further the welfare of blacks, held its convention in Pittsburgh in late August of 1840. Martin was a very active participant. That year, *The Colored American*, the only black newspaper in the United States, had been published in New York City, and the delegates to the convention passed a resolution calling for the publication of a black newspaper in Pennsylvania. Martin saw this as a great challenge and decided to meet it.

1843 was a banner year in Delaney's life. On March 15th, he married Catherine Richards, the daughter of a well-to-do black family in Pittsburgh.

On August 30th, Delaney published the first edition of his black Pittsburgh newspaper, *The Mystery*. He chose for its motto, a verse from the Bible— "And Moses was learned in all the wisdom of the Egyptians." A four-page paper, its purpose was, "to aim at the moral elevation of the Africo-American race—civically, politically, and spiritually."

The Mystery railed against slavery, the treatment of black women, the lack of proper schooling for blacks of both sexes, minstrel shows, which Martin said denigrated all blacks, freak shows at circuses and carnivals, slave catchers, and colonization societies which encouraged the emigration of blacks to Africa. Martin's paper had many solid issues to fight for, but a black newspaper anywhere in the United States in the 1840s was a precarious endeavor. He did manage to get some advertisements from black businessmen, but white support was non-existent. Black community groups tried to keep the newspaper solvent by holding festivals, picnics, and "soirees," but these proved to be only temporary solutions, and it became clear that it could not succeed as a business proposition.

In 1847 William Douglas came to Pittsburgh to address some anti-slavery meetings and made a point of meeting this young man who had become a black leader in the city. Douglas wanted to start a black newspaper in Rochester, New York, and thought that Delaney was the perfect man to start it. Douglas and Delaney were incensed that there were 60,000 black families in the North, but over two thirds of them could not read.

The new newspaper in Rochester, *The North Star*, was financially backed by William Douglas with Martin Delaney as it first editor. Once again, Martin found himself away from his home and family, a situation which seemed commonplace to the Delaney family. Seeking support for his new paper, Martin and Charles Langston, a Virginian who had graduated form Oberlin College in Ohio, toured the West giving anti-slavery speeches and seeking new subscribers to the paper.

Efforts to make the paper solvent proved fruitless, and faced with the necessity of ceasing publication, having been away from his family for over six months, Martin returned to Pittsburgh and renewed his career as a cupper and bleeder. For almost two years he carried on his medical practice, but became bored and frustrated by the limitations placed on his attempts to practice some kind of medicine. The only solution seemed to be admission to a medical school and thus achieve his ambition to be a licensed medical doctor. In 1850 he began to apply to medical schools all over America.

By this time several American medical schools were admitting black applicants, but only if they agreed upon graduation to leave for Africa and practice medicine there. Liberia, in West Africa, had been founded as a haven for freed slaves and boat loads of black emigrants were being shipped there to form a new black democratic nation. Martin had no intention of leaving for Africa; he wanted to practice medicine in the United States, but he was too far ahead of his time. No medical school would accept a black man who said that his goal was to be a doctor in the United States.

Pittsfield Medical College in western Massachusetts admitted blacks, but when Martin refused to agree to go to Liberia, he was refused admission again. Martin then applied to Harvard University, recognized as the best medical school in the country. Oliver Wendell Holmes, was dean of the medical school, and was the one who had to pass on Martin's application. Holmes abhorred slavery, but he had never played an active role in the issue and did not belong to Abolitionist societies. Holmes approved Martin's application due largely to the strong recommendations which came in support of his application. Two other black candidates were admitted at the same time, but they signed agreements to go to Liberia after graduation.

Oliver Wendell Holmes had mixed feelings about discriminatory practices; for instance, he always insisted upon having separate anatomy classes for men and women in the medical school. Holmes' approval of the application proved to be short-lived. The Harvard medical school students submitted a strongly worded petition against admitting blacks and women to Harvard medical school, and forced Holmes to inform both blacks and women that they must withdraw from the school. The letter of expulsion was worded, "At a meeting of the faculty, it was voted that the Dean be instructed respectfully to inform the gentlemen acting as agents for the Colonization Society that this faculty deem it inexpedient to admit colored students to the medical lectures."

This precipitant action at Harvard was not covered by the press, was not alluded to in the biographies of Oliver Wendell Holmes, was ignored by the Abolitionists, and never appeared in any history book. The other two black medical students expelled from Harvard, finished their work at Dartmouth College and left for Liberia as licensed physicians.

Martin Delaney was despondent. He submitted a petition asking Harvard to reconsider its decision, but no action was taken, and once again Martin unhappily returned to Pittsburgh. In those days it was still possible for him to practice some kind of medicine, since no strict licensing laws existed, but Delaney wanted to be recognized as a fully qualified physician, and he hated having to return home without fulfilling his ambition.

He practiced medicine in Pittsburgh, but without a license. Not long after his return, the city was hit by a cholera epidemic, and in the public turmoil that prevailed, for the first time Martin found himself able to serve white patients. When the epidemic was over, the Pittsburgh Board of Health and the City Council presented Martin with a parchment scroll testifying to his skill as a doctor. Martin proudly displayed the scroll on his office wall, but continued to serve only black patients, and often made less than he had as a cupper and bleeder.

For a time Martin supplemented his income by serving as principal of a black school. Always an activist, he became worshipful master of his Masonic Lodge, published a short history of black Freemasonry, attended state conventions of black organizations, and drew up petitions seeking voting rights for black voters. He also played a role in the Underground Railroad and helped to shelter fugitive slaves who were later shipped off to Canada and freedom. Delaney could never be accused of losing his zeal for his many causes.

One of his biographers claimed that on one occasion Martin was informed by letter that a slave owner with a kidnapped black boy was due to arrive in Pittsburgh by train. Martin met the train and forced the slave owner to free the boy.

Delaney's continuous frustration over the treatment of blacks grew and festered. In 1852, another side of Martin Delaney surfaced when he tried to patent a device which he claimed would enable the locomotives on the Pennsylvania Railroad to cross the Allegheny mountains without resorting to the famous Portage Railroad near Holidaysburg, Pennsylvania. Imagine his feelings of futility when the United States Patent Office informed him that as a black man he could not be a citizen and therefore could not be granted a patent.

That same year in May of 1852, Martin published a booklet, "The Condition, Elevation, Emigration, and Destiny of the Colored People of the United States," which strongly supported the development of a powerful and respected negro nation in the Western Hemisphere. He believed that black people had to change their attitudes of subservience to whites and take the lead in their own ventures. This was published when slavery was still the accepted norm and this idea was considered wildly revolutionary to most citizens in the country.

Between 1854 and 1858, Martin Delaney, working with J. Theodore Holly, another black activist who was formerly a shoemaker, began to soften his opposition to black emigration to Africa and other lands. This reflected his growing dissatisfaction with black opportunities in his own country and the slow change in white-black relationships. By 1854 Martin Delaney was taking an active role in the Cleveland Emigration Convention, which now strongly supported the plan to form a black empire somewhere in the American tropics.

His sense of frustration growing and his inability to find adequate educational opportunities for his children, resulted in Delaney's packing up his family and their belongings and moving them to Chatham, Canada, where he continued to support his emigration objectives. Another of America's great historical figures now sought his help. John Brown visited him in Canada and tried to get him to support his plan to set up armed black camps in Appalachia, and to induce runaway black slaves to join them. We know little about what influence John Brown may have had on him, but we do know that Martin was never sold on the idea of armed camps and never gave him public support.

Delaney's obsessional desire to accomplish some of his objectives led to the Convention of the Oppressed People of America, a gathering held in Martin's adopted home of Chatham, Canada. On the agenda was the formation of a Niger Valley exploration which would go to Africa and search out the plausibility of establishing a black nation. This was the final step in Martin's total conversion from opposing emigration to supporting such a plan actively. Martin insisted that the expedition should be black organized, black financed, and that its purpose should be, "the moral, social, and political elevation of ourselves and the regeneration of Africa."

In the meantime, Martin had been working on his only novel, *Blake, or the Huts of America*. His novel was never published in book form until long after his death in 1870, although it did appear serially in two black periodicals in his lifetime. Despite its relevance to the problems of the day, it was generally ignored. Martin had worked on the novel for six or seven years and again felt he had been treated unfairly .

Because it represented personal first-hand observations and experiences, *Blake* was a more valid rendering of the black experience in the United States than Harriet Beecher Stowe's *Uncle Tom's Cabin*. Harriet Beecher Stowe was never south of Kentucky, never saw a slave cabin, and her descriptions of slave life and traditions were highly idealized. Martin, on the other hand, had slept in slave cabins, described them realistically, and devoted 80 chapters of his novel to personal experiences he had in the South. Martin wanted his novel to be the black answer to *Uncle Tom's Cabin*. Delaney's increasing militancy shows up in the novel, when he has Blake, his principal character, declare, "I am for war—war upon the whites." Delaney stressed self-reliance by blacks and urged them to lead their own rebellions and avoid dependence on whites.

On May 24, 1859, Martin and his companions sailed for Africa on the bark, Mendl. Ironically, they first landed in Monrovia, the capital of Liberia, the country he had railed against early in his career because of his opposition to black emigration. His reputation had preceded him, because he had to spend some time convincing Liberians that he was not now opposed to their nation. Martin fell ill of a tropical disorder, but did finally reach Lagos, Nigeria, where the expedition would begin its six-day trip up the Orgon River to Abbeokuta. Delaney was very critical of the practice of American missionaries giving Americanized names to native Africans.

The expedition seemed to prove very little; not much seems to have resulted from the journey, but Delaney had little to say about it and subsequently did not pursue the idea with much fervor. Leaving Africa in May of 1859, Delaney reached London, England. By coincidence the International Statistical Congress was holding its annual meeting there, and Martin Delaney, newly arrived from Africa, was asked to report on the sickness and health of Africans. The meeting was held at Kings College in London and attracted many official dignitaries. The meeting was chaired by Prince Albert, the husband of Queen Victoria, with George Mifflin Dallas, the American ambassador in attendance. A Lord Broughman, temporarily chairing the meeting and introducing the notables, turned to Ambassador Dallas and observed, "I want my friend, Mr. Dallas, to observe that there is in the assemblage before us a negro, and I hope that will not affect his scruples." This was intended to be an obvious taunt about the continued support of slavery in the United States.

Martin Delaney immediately rose to his feet and said, "I pray your Royal Highness will allow me to thank his Lordship for the observation he has made. I assure your Royal Highness and his Lordship that I am a man." This brief speech made Martin something of an instant celebrity and led to a diplomatic exchange between the two nations involved. In September a few months after Martin Delaney returned home Abraham Lincoln issued his Emancipation Proclamation.

By now Martin had brought his family back to the United States. Martin was credited with helping to convince Lincoln to use black troops in the Northern Army in the Civil War, and Martin himself was later commissioned as a major in the United States Army, although he never engaged in any active duty.

After the war Delaney settled in South Carolina and became active politically in the Republican Party. He tried in vain to get his family to move to South Carolina, but they resisted and insisted that he join them in Ohio. Martin Delaney tried to get President Grant to appoint him ambassador to Liberia, but Grant passed him over for a younger man. Martin went to work for the state government of South Carolina, served one term as the state's lieutenant governor, and at one point was considered as a possible candidate for governor.

One event marred Delaney's career. In February of 1876 Martin was arrested on a charge of breach of trust and larceny. A black man claimed that five years previously Martin had taken $212 from the John Wesley Church and had used the money for his own personal gain. A jury found him guilty and sentenced him to 12 months in the state penitentiary, but before serving any time in jail, Delaney was pardoned by the governor who later re-appointed him as a trial justice. Delaney's health was failing and he finally joined his family in Wilberforce, Ohio, where he died on January 24, 1885.

Martin Robison Delaney was clearly a man ahead of his time. He strongly believed that black people had to demonstrate their independence and initiative. He was afraid that religion might undermine the independence and self-reliance of blacks. He was a determined and forceful spokesman against slavery of any variety. Martin Delaney was an extraordinary American, who devoted most of his energy to the improvement of his race and to further his goal of making the United States a color-blind society. He deserves recognition and his role in the early black nationalism movement cannot be over-emphasized.

In one lifetime, Martin Delaney published books and pamphlets, met most of the great men, both black and white, of his generation, forced one of America's great universities to examine its practices toward minorities, traveled internationally in England and Africa, became a self-taught physician, published several newspapers, lectured all across the United States, was commissioned as one of the first black officers in the nation's army, led a scientific expedition into the heart of Africa, and tried to be the first black man to hold a patent in the United States. What a career—few men can match it.

John Brashear: Pittsburgh's Forgotten Hero (1840-1920)

John Brashear, scientist, humanitarian, educator, is one of Pittsburgh's unsung heroes. "Uncle John," as he was known to thousands of his neighbors and friends, was born of humble parents, had a third grade formal education, but became Chancellor of the Western University of Pennsylvania (later the University of Pittsburgh), and was a trusted friend and valued business associate of America's richest and most influential industrialists. In 1915 he was named the "greatest Pennsylvanian" by the governor of the state, and his 75th birthday celebration was attended by such eminent people as Charles Schwab, Rear Admiral Perry, Alexander Graham Bell, and Henry Clay Frick.

The city of Pittsburgh is in transition from a heavy manufacturing center to a service-oriented economy. But cities, much like children, need heroes. John A. Brashear would appear to be a perfect symbol for the city of Pittsburgh. Although public schools have been named for him, little else has been done to recognize his gifts to society and to his beloved city. Not a man of wealth, he made contributions to science unequaled by any other citizen of Pittsburgh, but in addition, he played an important role in the education of its youth. He lived a simple, humble existence, never accumulated wealth, yet was one of the most loved citizens in the history of this great city. As Pittsburgh celebrates the opening of a new Science Center on the North Shore, it is important that this man's role in the early science of astronomy becomes more visible and appreciated.

John Brashear's scientific accomplishments have been well documented and his own autobiography has given us the details of his long and productive life. He was born in Brownsville, Pennsylvania, of French Huguenot ancestry. His grandfather owned and operated an inn on the Old National Pike Road; his father was a saddler. "Uncle John" claimed that he first became fascinated by the stars when his grandfather took him at the age of nine to look through a telescope which Squire Wampler had made from a piece of flint glass fire-hardened in the flames of the Great Pittsburgh Fire of 1845.

His autobiography described this experience as the turning point in his life. John Brashear spent only three years in the public schools of Brownsville, but later in life he did spend one term at Duff's Business College in Pittsburgh studying bookkeeping. It took him only a few weeks to decide that this was not his calling. At one point he did play the bass drum for the Brownsville Brass Band, and must have been proficient because the band played for the commencement exercises at Jefferson College, today known as Washington and Jefferson College.

John Brashear worked in a grocery store, delivered newspapers, worked briefly as a pattern maker and, during the Civil War, took a full-time job in the steel mill on the South Side of Pittsburgh. When his salary was raised from $10 to $25 per week, he married his sweetheart, Phoebe Stewart, and moved into his grandfather's house on the North Side.

His family had always wanted him to be a preacher, and John Brashear was a faithful church member. One Sunday when his pastor was away, John was asked to deliver the sermon. He worked hard on it, basing it on the first verses of Genesis dealing with the creation. Unfortunately, he presented it in a scientific perspective which did not sit well with the conservative Methodist church members of that day. The pastor was outraged; the congregation was cold and disapproving. John Brashear was so hurt and humiliated that he never again considered the ministry as a possible vocation. During his life he was asked many times to speak at churches all over the country, but he never again attempted to preach a sermon. Instead, he always spoke with reverence about the wonders of the earth and the stars.

By now John Brashear had become one of the most skilled millwrights in the city. He and his wife bought a small tract of land on the hillside overlooking the South Side mill where he worked. They built their first home almost without help. They did enlist some of John's friends in the mill to help haul some of the heavy timbers up the hillside to No. 3 Holt Street, where Uncle John and Phoebe began a lifelong task of exploring the heavens. In the backyard, he built a "coal shed" which actually became his laboratory, and it was here that "Uncle John" began his "pathway to the stars." Above the door to their new home they placed this apt quotation,

"Somewhere beneath the stars is work which you alone were meant to do. Never rest until you have found it."

John Brashear would finish his 12-hour shift in the mill and then trudge home to spend what hours he could grinding down his first 5-inch telescopic lens. In his autobiography, John Brashear relates that he would get up at 5:30 a.m. to work his shift in the mill, return home after 6:00 p.m. to find the "steam in the coal shed raised, the shop immaculately clean, everything in order for the night's work, and a good supper on the table."

That first winter was not an easy one, however. Uncle John reported that, "The house took some hard licks. It had no plaster on it, and I had to go to bed more than once to get warm. The winds got a fair blow at it."

For 10 years John Brashear had been studying the stars with his naked eyes. He spent many hours in an old rowboat on the Monongahela River, because there he could see the stars more clearly than from the crowded streets and industrial pollution of his neighborhood.

For the next two years he and Phoebe worked every evening on that first five-inch lens—quite a task for a man who had never read a book on astronomical physics. When almost finished, he held the lens up to the light only to have it slip from his fingers and break at his feet. A kind friend replaced the glass necessary to rebuild the lens because John lacked the money to purchase it. Three years later the lens was finished. He mounted it in the hallway of his home, and neighbors were called in to see the wonders of the heavens as they had never seen them before. John Brashear was beginning to fulfill his dream of bringing the stars to men.

John Brashear's scientific accomplishments have been well documented. During his lifetime this humble millwright became a figure of international importance. He was wined and dined by the most renowned scientists of his age. He was widely recognized as "the master instrument maker of the world." He was given honorary degrees by West Point, Cambridge, Yale, Pennsylvania, Indiana, Illinois, Michigan, Swarthmore, and Princeton universities and was an honorary member of 36 scientific organizations. Among his contributions to the science of astronomy were the following:

- built the first bolemeter to measure radiant energy;
- was the first to successfully grind prisms from rock salt;
- was the first scientist to build stellar spectroscopes;
- built the finest spectrographic telescope in the world with an accuracy of 1/500,000th of an inch;
- built the interferometer used by the United States Bureau of Weights and Measures;
- designed a rotating mirror with four equiangular faces with no deviation in surface (This was later used as a basis for Einstein's theory of Relativity.);
- designed and built the Mills Spectroscope for the Lick Observatory in California;
- invented the instruments with which Flagstaff Observatory in Arizona ascertained there was no vapor on Mars;
- was one of the pioneers in experimenting with color photography; and
- designed and build much of the equipment used by Samuel Langley in his flying machine experiments.

The primary focus of this paper, however, is to emphasize the human qualities of the man and his little known love and respect for public education. How do you best illustrate the human qualities of this great man? Do you describe how he taught himself ventriloquism so that he could entertain the children in his neighborhood? Do you describe how he bought a can of aluminum paint, painted the flower boxes in his front yard, and finding that he had some paint left over, proceeded to paint his neighbor's flower boxes, the mail boxes on the corner, and the police call box? The Post Office sent him an eight-page letter accusing him of "tampering with federal property." Impressive sheets of printed rules were franked through from Washington, and John, looking out through his Nottingham lace curtains was abashed to see a stern policeman repainting his artistic efforts with the customary coats of dull green. Phoebe, his wife, was reported to have said to him, "John, remember what you always say, 'Somewhere beneath the stars is a work that you alone are meant to do.' You're no painter, John, just stick to your beloved stars."

When asked what honorary degree he would prefer, Uncle John replied, "I wish you could make me a Doctor of Humanity." He never understood why he was so frequently honored. He told one of his friends, "Sometimes I lie in bed and wonder what I have done to deserve them all. I really don't know, but if I have sent out sunshine, if I have done anything to make folks happier, I am content." John Brashear was always embarrassed by flowery introductions. He said that the best one he ever had was given by an old Quaker who said, "We have with us tonight John Brashear. John's going to tell us about the telescope. John, go ahead."

During the early 1890s a little street car left 6th and Smithfield streets in downtown Pittsburgh heading for West View and passing the Western University of Pennsylvania which was then located on Observatory Hill. It was always crowded with students, and although most people avoided the car at busy times, "Uncle John" loved to mingle with students. It was Washington's Birthday and, as was the custom, students would shout in unison, "Who was George Washington?" With a stamping of feet, they would reply in unison, "First in War, First in Peace, and First in the Hearts of Their Countrymen." On this particular holiday they persisted so long that the motorman threatened to eject all of them from the car, but Uncle John interceded and the ride went on uninterrupted.

One of the most famous stories about John Brashear concerned his first visit to Europe several years before World War I. John Brashear was on his way to Sweden to deliver a lens he had made for a Swedish Observatory. By reputation, John knew of an important man in Munich, Germany, who was interested in lenses. He assumed that the man would like to see the lens he had just ground. A man by the name of Leisser was with Brashear as an interpreter. He and John Brashear were not formally dressed; they had on soft hats, and although "there was no mud on their shoes, they were not shined." They walked to the man's home, rang the doorbell, and asked for "Herr So and So." After a long wait, a large blustering fellow, well polished and very polite, appeared at the door. He was very condescending, told them that his master was not interested in the lens since he already had the most "perfect lens in the world." John Brashear asked if he might see this "perfect lens." The man acted bored, but wanting to get rid of them, agreed to let them see it. He brought it out displayed triumphantly in a velvet lined case. Uncle John picked it up, turned it over, and printed on the back was this inscription, "Made by John Brashear, Allegheny, Pa. USA."

While visiting Andrew Carnegie at Skibo Castle, in Scotland, John Brashear met David Lloyd George, the English Prime Minister. Later David Lloyd George spoke warmly of the Pittsburgh scientist and quoted him in several talks he gave in England. A marked clipping, referring to these quotations, was sent to Uncle John in Pittsburgh. John Brashear read them, smiled, and said, "Well, that was awfully nice of that fellow to remember a greasy old mechanic like me."

John Brashear never took his honors too seriously He loved to tell the story of a Dutch army officer who appeared in public with his breast covered with medals. "Where did you get all those medals, Colonel?" a friend asked him. "Did you win some big battles?" The Dutch officer pointed to the biggest brightest medal of them all. "That's the first one," he said, "I got that one by mistake, and I got all the other ones because I had that one."

Frank Vittor, the famous sculptor, who was commissioned to make a statue of Uncle John and who had him pose for 22 days, said of him, "I've known many people in my life, but none like John Brashear. He was always thinking of other people, never of himself." John Brashear defined his own philosophy of life as follows:

> If there is anything in my life uncommon it is because from the time I was a boy, no matter what I had to do, I tried to do it a little bit better than it had ever been done before. If a workman in the rolling mill broke a hammer handle, and I set out to make him another one, I tried to make him the best hammer handle he ever had.

John Brashear's commitment to public education was less well known. Next to his beloved astronomy, public education became the driving purpose in his life. John Brashear was a master teacher and a lifelong supporter of public education. He said, "I am convinced that there is no greater field for building up the cardinal principles of our great Republic than the public school education of our boys and girls—the future hopes of our beloved country." His favorite theme in speeches he gave to large and small groups all across the country was:

> Let us take better care of our teachers, pay them a living wage, and, my word for it, the day will come and that right soon for it is partly here already, when our own and the entire world will know the true meaning of liberty, equality, fraternity, love of country, a love that abideth forever.

John Brashear was a consummate teacher, whether he was instructing the neighbor children or slyly spreading his gospel of the heavens to adult groups everywhere. He liked to point out that:

> We do not have to go roaming in space to find wonderful things. The lover of the beautiful finds in the colors of the rose the same light waves that stream from the stars; he finds a kinship between the rushing locomotive and the motion of the stellar worlds through space. The more we study familiar things the more beauty we find. Some folks declare that science robs us of the pleasing sense of awe and mystery. Ah, no! Science merely replaces one mystery with another of a greater and grander order.

In a 1916 article John Brashear wrote for *American Magazine*, he wrote:

> Dirt is only matter in the wrong place. Here on the table beside me are five bottles containing sand, lime, soda, potash, and sodium nitrate—all common enough substances. The housewife would sweep them up as dirt if she found them on the carpet. But if you put them in the alembic of the furnace they come out pure glass. Give this into the skilled hands of the optician, and that which was a little while ago dirt becomes lenses and prisms by which we are able to solve the secrets of the suns and stars, or determine the accuracy of measurements to the one half-millionth of an inch.

How effective John Brashear would have been in the classroom! He was a born teacher and liked nothing better than the opportunity to pass on his knowledge to others.

John Brashear would have gloried in the modern space age; it would have seemed to bring his life's work to a dramatic level of achievement. He had a phenomenal knack of converting scientific knowledge into common everyday insights of simplicity and beauty. He said, for example,

> Imagine you are watching a log floating near the seashore and that it strikes against a pier as it rises and falls with the waves, say once very six seconds. In order to correspond to the number of light waves in one tenth of a second, that log would have to beat against that pier for more than two million years.

That was the way that Uncle John described what it means when a ray of violet light impinges on a photographic negative.

He only attended the third grade, yet educational honors were bestowed upon him all over the world. He served two and one half years as Acting Chancellor of the Western University of Pennsylvania (now Pitt); he was one of the founders of Carnegie Institute of Technology (now Carnegie Mellon). Yet he was a man who never worried about protecting his personal assets. He rarely protected his inventions by seeking protective patents from the United States Patent Office. Often unable to adequately take care of his own family, he was most concerned about sharing his skill and knowledge with mankind.

On the 28th of July, 1909, John Brashear was summoned to Pride's Crossing, Massachusetts, the summer home of Henry Clay Frick, the Pittsburgh industrialist. Uncle John had no idea why he was being invited there. In his autobiography, he described the experience, as follows, "I was ushered into a living room as big as the whole lower floor of my Muskoko cottage, walls of silk damask, beds of mahogany, covered with the finest down, windows opening out to the sea. I could hear waves and the sound of children playing croquet. The house was built into solid rock."

Henry Clay Frick informed John Brashear that he was setting up a trust fund, later to be known as the Frick Educational Foundation. Mr. Frick had been trying to decide what he might do to improve the schools in Pittsburgh. That July evening in 1909 was the beginning of one of the oldest Pittsburgh foundations and to this day is the only foundation any- where devoted to the improvement of public education. Uncle John was given the sole responsibility of determining how the income from the trust fund, which later was worth several million dollars, would be spent. Dr. William Davidson, then Superintendent of Schools in Pittsburgh, said that, "It was the strongest and most helpful influence in the practical workings of schools that he had ever seen."

John Brashear immediately assembled a board to help him administer the fund. It consisted of two judges, two members of the Pittsburgh Board of Education, and two manufacturing engineers. Uncle John was elected president on October 2, 1909, and spent the last years of his life administering this trust fund which played a significant role in the betterment of the public schools of the city of Pittsburgh. Research projects were funded, hundreds of Pittsburgh teachers were given scholarship money to further their educations, and the Frick Training School for Teachers became famous for its innovative methods in preparing teachers. John Brashear liked to say that, "The best way to teach the child is by teaching the teacher."

By 1915 John Brashear was world renowned. In September of that year Brashear Day was celebrated at the Panama Pacific Exposition for his achievements in manufacturing and science. He was widely celebrated in the state of California for having made the lenses for their great astronomical observatories. Five public dinners were held in his honor in one week and newspapers carried his picture on their front pages in goggles and aviator's helmet referring to his work with Langley in aviation. Eastern newspapers reported that thousands of tourists came to see the famous scientist.

On Uncle John's 76th birthday in 1916, a gala celebration was held in the city of Pittsburgh, which the newspapers called the most pretentious civic function ever held in Pittsburgh. The *Pittsburgh Post Gazette* of November 24, 1916 reported:

The crowds loved it when John Brashear and Mrs. Enoch Rauh waltzed, that over $4,000 was raised at the party, and that John Brashear had a lame finger after the handshaking at the reception. All the department stores in the city had special window displays; most of the city's hotels had Uncle John's picture on their restaurant menus, and over 5,000 guests showed up in the lobby of the Frick Building on Grant Street to show their personal respects. A 500 pound cake, lit by 76 electric candles, highlighted the occasion; the

Pitt band played the Pitt Alma Mater, conducted by John Brashear himself. Guests proceeded up one of the lobby stairways to the balcony, greeted the honored guest, and went down the other stairway to the street level. News reporters were amused by several newsboys who managed to go through the receiving line three times to pay their respects to the beloved scientist.

A great banquet was held in Soldiers and Sailors Memorial Hall in Oakland, Pittsburgh, which could not hold over 700 people in attendance. Congratulatory messages came from the Governor of the State, from Thomas A. Edison, from Alexander Graham Bell, from President Woodrow Wilson, and from all the associations to which he belonged. A fund of $50,000 was presented as an acknowledgement of the numerous unpaid lectures Uncle John had given for decades in schools and observatories from the Atlantic Seaboard to the Mississippi River. Charles Schwab, who sat most of the evening with his arm around Uncle John, told reporters, "The gathering was a spontaneous outburst of love and affection for the greatest man I ever knew."

Three years later, John Brashear was too ill to host a special birthday observance, but on his 79th birthday in 1919, he received over 30,000 cards and promised to read every one of them. One year later, Uncle John passed away, somewhat unexpectedly, willing his limited estate of books and personal belongings to his family. Three pear trees were planted on the property on Holt Street on the South Side in his memory. John Brashear wrote his own epitaph. It was taken from an anonymous poem , "An Old Astronomer (Galileo) to His Pupil."

We have loved the stars too fondly to be fearful of the night.

Hervey Allen, one of Pittsburgh's best known writers, memorialized Uncle John with the poem. John Brashear, printed in the *Gazette Times* of April 25, 1920:

That was no casual bell.
That rang the great man's passing knell.
No! It was the grief of a great city.
He is gone!
The right, keen brain, the war, hot heart,
Knowledge and great pity,
The wise man all men knew as "Uncle John."

164

John Brashear has been honored in several ways. The Brownsville, Pennsylvania, school district, where he was born, named its high school, "John A. Brashear High School," and in the 1980s Pittsburgh named its newest high school in his memory. Twenty years after Uncle John's death, on the occasion of his 100th birthday in 1929, crowds gathered in the Hotel William Penn in downtown Pittsburgh and at the Soldiers and Sailors Memorial Hall in Oakland to commemorate his memory. Victor Saudek played a solo on an old flute once owned by Uncle John. Eminent scientists from around the world came to celebrate the occasion. Speakers included the president of the Westinghouse Manufacturing Company, the designer of the Mt. Palomar telescope, the man who cast the lens for the Palomar Observatory, and the top astro-physicist from the Smithsonian Institution in Washington, D.C. Since 1929 Pittsburgh has given little attention and less recognition to one of its greatest citizens.

After John Brashear's death, Mrs. John Phillips, president of the Carrick Women's Club and long-time resident of the South Side, initiated a campaign to raise money to purchase John Brashear's home and workshop on Holt Street to preserve it for posterity. In a letter appealing for funds which she mailed to Andrew Carnegie, she said that the house was occupied by two families who were renting it for $19 per month. John Brashear's workshop was being rented to another family for $12 a month.

Mrs. Phillips told Andrew Carnegie that she thought the property could be purchased for $6,000 and that in her judgment this house, "represents Americanism better than any building in our country with the exception of Lincoln's cabin." This was indeed high praise but it illustrates the place held by John Brashear in the minds of his peers. She wanted Uncle John's old telescope there as well as a more modern one so that the children of Pittsburgh could enjoy the stars and pay homage to its greatest citizen.

Plans were made to employ one trained worker at $100 a month, and a caretaker at $85 a month, and to teach neighborhood children homemaking skills, care of the sick, how to mend their own shoes, how to wash dishes properly, and how to keep a house tidy. The money was raised, the property was purchased, and the Brashear Settlement House became a reality. The Brashear Settlement was loved and respected by the entire neighborhood. An elderly resident, who lives next door to the old settlement house, told me that, "Half the kids on Holt Street would be in jail today if it hadn't been for the Brashear Settlement."

Later, Edgar and Henry Kaufmann, owners of the Kaufmann Department Store, and the Kaufmann Foundation built a new building on Sarah Street in the South Side and the Settlement House moved to its more satisfactory location. All the remaining memorabilia and scientific apparatus available were moved to the new location and a Brashear Museum was established. The old Brashear home and workshop on Holt Street were allowed to deteriorate. In 1967 John Brashear's old home was destroyed by fire. Part of the old workshop still stands, but it is unmarked and is unknown to the public.

The Brashear Museum part of the new Brashear Settlement Building on the corner of Sarah and 23rd Streets still stands. It has Uncle John's first telescope, many of the prisms and lenses from his old workshop, and valuable letters and photographs from eminent people. Few Pittsburghers today know that the Museum exists and even fewer would know where to find it if they tried.

Pittsburgh has not properly honored one of its most famous people; John Brashear deserves a special and prominent place in the new Science Center now open on the North Side of Pittsburgh near Three Rivers Stadium. No one should have a more honored place when the story of science and the city of Pittsburgh are honored together.

Billy Sunday: Professional Baseball Player and Evangelist (1862-1935)

His 1935 obituary in *The New York Times* described Billy Sunday as "the greatest high-pressure, mass-conversion evangelist the world has ever known." He had the perfect name for an evangelist. He had the charisma, a major league baseball background, media coverage—he had everything but television. It is likely that had he lived 40 or 50 years later, he would have out shown the current TV evangelists.

He was flamboyant, highly theatrical, totally unrestrained in his delivery. One moment he would be sitting on top of the pulpit with coat and tie discarded; the next moment he would be storming up and down the platform, striking the pulpit, twisting and turning his body in a frenzy that astounded his listeners. His vocal resources were just as unpredictable. He violated every rule of dignity and reverence in worship. One moment he seemed to be a clown and a mountebank; the next, he impressed his audience as an earnest, serious-minded deeply spiritual leader.

Using the idiom of the saloon, the gutter, and the yellow newspaper, he attracted the largest revival meetings ever held in any country. He claimed to have preached to over a 100,000,000 people and to have converted over a 1,000,000 people.

He liked to say:

> I was bred and born in old Iowa. I am a rube of the rubes. I am a hayseed of the hayseeds, and the odors of the barnyard are on me

yet, and it beats Pinaud and Colgate too. I have greased my hair with goose grease and blacked my boots with stove blacking. I have wiped my old proboscis with a gunnysack towel: I have drunk my coffee out of my saucer; and I have eaten with my knife. I have said "done it" when I should have said "did it," and I have "saw" when I should have "seen," and I expect to go to Heaven just the same. I have crept and crawled out from the university of poverty and hard knocks, and have taken post graduate courses.

He played his audiences like a master violinist. He demanded perfect silence when he spoke; he would stop in the middle of a sentence to wait for a coughing spell to cease or a late comer to find a seat. Local ministers did all the advance work and would then invite him to their particular cities, yet in his meetings he would call them "mutts, deadheads, stiffs, and many other opprobrious names" before the eyes and ears of the community.

Billy Sunday would stand before an audience of thousands and say, "How many of you will give a dollar? Please stand up." Just then his pianist would break into *The Star Spangled Banner*. Everyone would stand up, break into laughter, and give dollars.

In Philadelphia Sunday stopped short in his sermon and pointed his finger at a woman who had shouted, "Amen." "Just a minute, Sister," he shouted. "Hold your sparker back and save a little gasoline." One of his favorite stories was of the sinner trying to get into Heaven as if he were sliding into home plate, only to be called "Out" by God, the "umpire."

He was obsessed with the liquor problem. Billy Sunday had a drinking problem before his conversion. As an evangelist, he proposed to make this nation "so dry that a man will have to be primed before he can spit." He preached that, "Many of you have a second rate booze joint at your home and then you wonder why the world wasn't saved." In Pittsburgh he preached that, "Pennsylvania is one of the worst whiskey soaked states under the stars and stripes. Whiskey interests have a stranglehold on your politicians; it's time decent people broke it." *The Literary Digest* reported that when "Sunday preached, Old King Booze got a solar plexus punch."

His witty sayings became very popular. Examples were: "Do you know what a decollete gown is? It's a dress with a collar around your waist." "Solomon carried on in a way that would make a baseball fan at a World

Series game look like a wooden dummy in a clothing store." "It was not until the Prodigal Son got tired of living among the hogs, that he got homesick for mother and father."

Billy Sunday called Goliath "an old stiff who went strutting up and down blowing about his height and his bravery. David called his bluff, soaked the giant in his coco between the lamps. He then took his sword chopped off his block. The guy skiddooed."

Billy Sunday was born on November 19, 1862, near Ames, Iowa, the son of a Civil War veteran. His baseball proficiency with a local team in Marshalltown, Iowa, led him to a career in professional baseball. He played the outfield for the Chicago White Sox, the Philadelphia Phillies, and the Pittsburgh Pirates for 8 years from 1883 to 1890. He was a ballplayer of some repute. In fact, it was claimed that he was one of the first men in the country to run 100 yards in 10 seconds, and that he was the first man ever to run around the bases in 14 seconds. Never noted for his hitting, in his last three seasons with the Pirates, he batted .236, .240. and 257. He was one of those few baseball players who went directly to the major leagues without any minor league experience.

He claimed to have been converted to Christianity in 1887, when he was 25 years old, at a sidewalk mission in Chicago, Illinois. In 1890 he decided to retire from baseball and "hit the sawdust trail for God." He joined the Jefferson Park Presbyterian Church in Chicago, became a YMCA secretary, and began working with Rev. J. Wilbur Chapman, a revivalist evangelist. Billy Sunday held his first revival meeting in Garner, Iowa, in 1895, substituting for Rev. Chapman. He began his career in small Midwestern towns and gradually, as his fame grew, began to hold meetings in the country's larger cities. In the early days he held his meetings in tents, but after a snowstorm collapsed his tent tabernacle in Salida, California, he turned to wooden structures.

He eventually developed a personal staff of women workers, Bible study experts, physical trainers, pianists, choristers, trained directors for special satellite meetings, and personal secretaries. Before initiating his revival meetings in a particular city, his advisory staff would appear in a city two years before the actual start of the meetings. Sponsoring churches had to agree to close their doors while Sunday was conducting his meetings in their cities. Advance backers had to build a large wooden tabernacle, seating 10- to 20,000 people, before Billy Sunday would agree to appear. Hundreds of volunteers were recruited and a chorus of 500 to 1,000 voices was assembled.

When Billy finally hit a city all was in readiness for him. He encountered some difficulty in Pittsburgh, however, where local opponents of his ministry asked for an injunction to prevent the building of a tabernacle in a zone where wooden buildings were prohibited. Sunday was asked why he could not use the Exhibition Hall already available in Pittsburgh. A well- known evangelist, Gypsy Smith, had held a successful revival there previously. Sunday answered that the $20,000 being asked for rent, heat, and light was exorbitant. The hall would hold only 4,000 people. He threatened to move his revival meetings to Scranton unless Pittsburgh met his demands. City Council passed a bill and waived the fire ordinance; Joseph Spiece, Sunday's architect, built a wooden tabernacle on land near the Carnegie Music Hall in Oakland, adjacent to the present site of Heinz Chapel on the University of Pittsburgh campus. The land was donated by Henry Clay Frick.

Billy Sunday held a 10-week revival in Pittsburgh. A chorus of 1,600 voices and a band of 16 musicians from the University of Pittsburgh performed at his meetings. On January 12, 1815, the *Pittsburgh Post* reported that 30,000 men had to be turned away from an all-male meeting at the tabernacle due to lack of space, and that Forbes Street was "black with men reaching back to the Hotel Schenley." Some of the over-flow crowd was shuffled into Soldier and Sailors Memorial Hall. This all-male meeting was called a great success. Over 600 men were converted to Christianity as they "hit the sawdust trail."

On the 15th of January, it was reported in the press that 18 robust men had fainted during Billy Sunday's sermon. Every night 3 or 4 had to be transported to neighboring hospitals. *The Pittsburgh Dispatch*, in its edition of January 16, 1914, said that 22 women had fainted at the meeting and had to be given emergency treatment. When a member of his audience passed out, Billy Sunday railed, "Don't crane your necks when someone is taken out; that's the way they do in the country towns."

On the 17th of January, 1,800 men attended in masse from the Edgar Thompson Steel Works, 500 from the South Side Mill, and the entire student body from the Blind School. Delegations were present from Boggs and Buhl's Department Store, from the Pittsburgh Stogie Company, and from the Lincoln Laundry. As usual, Billy Sunday was flamboyant and direct. He said, for example, "You can't make no more impression on some people than you can by shooting green peas against Gibralter with a popgun." He shouted that, "If you drive the churches out of Pittsburgh, your real estate won't be worth 10¢ by the Fourth of July." And, "We've got thousands of university graduates going to Hell so fast, you can't see them for the dust."

After listening to one of Billy Sunday's sermons, H. J. Heinz was quoted in the *Pittsburgh Press* as saying with moist eyes, "I never saw anything like it." At one meeting on the 15th of January, Billy Sunday ranted against drinking, screamed, rushed to the end of the platform, and leaped into the reporters' benches. He faced the assembled clergymen and shouted, "If you preachers and church members do not hate the saloons, for God's sake get out of the church and quit labelling yourselves as Christians." He also said:

> It is the saloon that cocks the highwayman's pistol; the saloon that puts the rope in the hands of the mob. It is the anarchist of the world, and its dirty red flag is dyed with the blood of women and children. It sent the bullet through the body of Lincoln. It nerved the arm of the assassins who struck down Garfield and McKinley.

Pittsburgh newspapers reported that 60,000 men attended the 3 meetings on January 25th, and that 40,000 took the pledge not to drink alcohol as Sunday and his choirmaster, Homer Rodeheaver, led the singing of the song, "Brewers' Big Horses Can't Run Over Me."

It is difficult to evaluate what permanent effect Billy Sunday had on a city. Nine Pittsburgh department stores began holding 8:00 a.m. prayer meetings for their employees. Pittsburgh's First Presbyterian Church claimed to have 419 new members as a result of Billy Sunday's revival meetings. Several Pittsburgh poker clubs claimed to have renounced the game. The Pittsburgh City Council presented Billy with a resolution recognizing his contribution to the life of the city. The Cambria Steel Company in Johnstown established a religious department, the first of its kind in America, and employed a full-time minister. Many social critics gave Billy

Sunday partial credit for the political defeat of the Penrose forces in Pennsylvania at the polls. Sunday had linked Penrose with the liquor interests in Pennsylvania.

During his revival meetings in Pittsburgh, Billy Sunday held 124 meetings, preached to 1,576,000 people, and had 26,601 conversions. Three hundred Pittsburgh area churches were listed as sponsors, but the Lutherans and the Episcopalians did not cooperate, nor did Catholics or Jews. The Catholic Church frowned on Billy Sunday's evangelistic meetings and called him a "blasphemous heretic." Most Lutherans believed that Billy Sunday did harm to the dignity of the Christian religion.

Billy Sunday clearly had an anti-Catholic bias, but he tried to carefully hide it and never voiced it publicly. The official Catholic Church never supported him, but some Catholic lay organizations cooperated with his revival meetings. Billy Sunday was more open in his distaste for Jews. He said that they "had a high place in the Bible, but they were too interested in money." He called them, "Christ killers." He claimed that black people were equal with whites before God, but he was unwilling to accept their equality among men.

Billy Sunday appeared on the religious scene when the organized church, especially in its officialdom, was in a critical mood. New liberal theologies had shaken the assurance of multitudes of ministers. Billy Sunday's favorite targets were liquor, card playing, evolutionists, "the German Kaiser," free thinkers, short skirts, smoking, and dancing. He believed that it was a sin to dance, to play cards, or to attend plays. Unbelievers, Christian Scientists, and Universalists he relegated to Hell.

He preached, "Only Christians should be allowed to teach in the public schools." He was a staunch Republican and an outspoken opponent of Alfred E. Smith, the Democratic presidential candidate, whom he called "the mouthpiece of the liquor interests." Sunday was widely vilified by union leaders as a strike breaker. Rabbi Wise, perhaps the best known Hebrew scholar of the day, violently opposed him.

Dr. Gladden, a famed Congregationalist, said, "Scenes at a Spanish bullfight are less horrible than a Billy Sunday revival meeting." Billy Sunday was denounced from many Protestant pulpits as a "preacher of antiquated theology and of a department store kind of religion." Labor unions attacked him for using non-union labor to build his tabernacles.

At times Sunday could be personally vindictive and almost sacrilegious. In Toledo, Ohio, a Dr. Rev. Wallace remonstrated with him privately following one of his revival meetings. The next day from the platform, Sunday turned to the minister and said, "Stand up there, you bastard evolutionist. Stand up with the atheists, the infidels, the whore mongers, the adulterers and go to Hell." The local newspapers said that it would be impossible to describe the "venom present in the crowd." In Philadelphia Billy Sunday turned to the assembled ministers from the city and told them, "If I fought the Devil the way you do, I'd look like a spiked cannon in an abandoned fort with a bird's nest in the end of it."

He was a man with strong and often irrational beliefs. He called dancing "kindergartening for Hell." He liked the game of golf, but called tennis "too sissified." Baseball, he called a noble sport; but horse racing, card playing, and theaters were the work of the Devil.

Despite his controversial opinions, Billy Sunday had many powerful friends. John D. Rockefeller was a staunch supporter. H. J. Heinz, Henry Clay Frick, John Wanamaker, Theodore Roosevelt, and S. S. Kresge were numbered among his avid backers. *American Magazine* in 1914 listed him as eighth in a list of the greatest men in America. President Woodrow Wilson received him in the White House and was quoted as saying, "God bless you and your work."

Billy Sunday's heyday was in 1917 and 1918. During his 10-week revival in New York City, over 100,000 people "hit the sawdust trail." In Chicago over 1,000,000 people turned out to listen to his preaching. By then Billy Sunday was a millionaire, thanks to numerous "free will offerings" which were used for his earthly support. He was frequently charged with using what his critics called, "polite blackmail" in collecting his free will offerings; however, no serious improprieties ever surfaced. Apparently his private life was clean, although he was openly criticized for his wearing of ostentatious diamonds and for living the "good life."

The end of World War I found the United States in a new era. After his New York City successes, there seemed to be nowhere for him to go but down. The 18th Amendment to the Constitution stole much of his anti-drinking thunder. Overnight Billy Sunday seemed out-of-date. He became an instant anachronism, overshadowed by the movies, the radio, and the automobile.

He spent the last 15 years of his life tent-preaching in the same back country farm towns where his ministry had begun. In 1932 he returned to Pittsburgh for the last time in a 3-week revival meeting at the First United Presbyterian Church on the North Side. He was troubled with laryngitis and was visibly trembling in the pulpit. He was only a shadow of his former greatness. Billy Sunday died of a heart attack in 1935. By then he was virtually forgotten.

There is a Billy Sunday exhibit at Wheaton College in Wheaton, Illinois, where an inscription reads, "As no other evangelist before him, he captured America's fancy. For a generation, he was evangelism."

Part IV
Odds and Ends

A typical plank road

Deep Waters Run Still:
The Underground River
(Glacier Age-Present)

The Monongahela, the Allegheny, and the Ohio Rivers form the borders of the Golden Triangle at their confluence near the Three Rivers Stadium in the city of Pittsburgh. In the summer Pittsburgers attend the Three Rivers Arts Festival and the Three Rivers Shakespeare Festival. It's all so triangular. So neat and three-sided. And its all wrong.

You see there's a fourth side to the equation, a fourth river that no one has ever seen, even though every day thousands of us bathe in its waters and drink from its depths. This massive body of water flows along under the Allegheny and Ohio Rivers from a spot north of Warren, Pennsylvania, until it surfaces again in the Ohio River near Beaver, Pennsylvania.

The underground river consists of a river bed, largely of gravel, brought to its present location by the Wisconsin Glacier, a million years or so ago. It is actually a homogenous layer of coarse sand and fist-sized round stones, very porous, with loads of space for water to flow between the stones. It is constantly replenished by water from the upper Allegheny River.

Pittsburgh's "underground river" is what geologists call an "aquifer," but it differs from other aquifers, most of which are irregular and widespread and do not follow a channel. The regularity of our underground river's flow makes it more like a true river than other aquifers.

Geologists will tell you that the Allegheny and the Ohio are really one river, and that the difference in names is largely for convenience of identification. Pittsburgh's underground river roughly follows the course of the

Allegheny and the Ohio, but not totally so; in some places it lies entirely to one side or the other of the surface channel.

Exactly where is this underground river in relationship to the Golden Triangle? Some of Pittsburgh's largest buildings are built on top of it, and its existence gave special problems in the construction of the Pittsburgh subway. All told, at least one third of the Golden Triangle lies directly over this "river."

The earliest recorded use of water from the underground river was by the Economites (Harmony Society) at Ambridge, who tapped into it by digging wells. By 1900, at least 15 buildings in downtown Pittsburgh were using its waters. Today, it is estimated that more than 300 Pittsburgh buildings use it for one purpose or another. Hornes's Department Store uses approximately 1,500 gallons of water per minute from the underground river to run its air conditioning system. PPG Place drilled eight wells while its complex was under construction, and uses 2,500 gallons of water per hour for various purposes. And the West View Water Company, using several wells on Davis and Neville Islands in the Ohio River, pulls more than 14,000,000 gallons a day from this same source to help service its water customers.

In 1982, the underground river made its presence felt in a most concrete manner. While constructing the subway in Gateway Center, workers found themselves mired in mud and water. Contractors had to stop construction until 11 wells were driven into the sandstone and silt-stone bedrock under the Golden Triangle. Using electric pumps, they removed water at the rate of 500 gallons per minute from each well. This lowered the surface of the underground river enough to permit the further excavation needed. The underground river follows the subway route along Liberty Avenue and up 6th Street as far as Wood Street. The water table beneath the Golden Triangle is normally 703 feet above sea level and the bottom of the "subway box" is 700 feet, making it necessary to lower the level of the underground river temporarily.

Aquifers are not rare; they exist all over the world. In fact, the Ogallala aquifer, which underlies eight states from southern South Dakota to northwestern Texas, is largely responsible for making the American Midwest an agricultural marvel. Extensive use of this aquifer began in the 1940s, but in the 1990s water tables under these lands have dropped so far that pumping has become uneconomical. It is said that the water table has been dropping at the rate of three feet per year, and that by the year 2000 it is predicted that 3,000,000 acres of Texas farmland will be without aquifer water.

Many scientists are now beginning to believe that the traditional approach of building dams, trapping and storing surface run-off, and diverting rivers to redistribute water is self-defeating. They strongly urge massive conservation programs which will control the use of both surface and aquifer sources, with most efforts directed towards replenishment of underground sources by artificially recharging their aquifers. California has been using this approach since the 1920s, apparently with significant success.

A million years or so ago, the Allegheny River channel ran up present French Creek valley, emptied into Lake Erie, and finally out through the St. Lawrence Seaway to the Atlantic. Along came the Illinoian and the Wisconsin glaciers which choked the Allegheny valley with drift, and changed the flow of the river southward so that now it empties into the Mississippi and the Gulf of Mexico.

After the Wisconsin Glacier, the Allegheny and the Ohio never cut down deeply into this glacial drift, but flowed above it, creating the two rivers. There is said to be a similar drift underneath the Monongahela River, but it is so full of mud and clay that there is little water flow there.

The underground river seems to be remarkably separate from the surface waters of the two rivers. They differ markedly in temperature, in purity, and in chemical content. The waters in the underground river are coldest in the summer time, which is a definite advantage for those buildings using its water for their air conditioning systems. The use of the underground river water seems to have no effect on water levels in the surface rivers. In Allegheny County, this underground river varies from less than half a mile to over one mile in width and in depth from 15 to 35 feet. At no spot does its bottom lie more than 85 feet below the regular river banks.

By far the most visible evidence of Pittsburgh's fourth river is the great Point Park fountain, which uses water pumped to the surface by specially designed pumps housed in two buildings at left and right of the fountain.

When the Point area was totally rehabilitated in Pittsburgh's Renaissance I, the architectural firm of Stotz, Hess, McLachlan and Foster was commissioned to design and build a fountain which would become the focal point for Pittsburgh's rebirth. The result was the largest fountain in the Americas. They constructed 130 caissons, which went down to a depth of 60 feet. These were filled with concrete, and were used as the conduits through which water from the underground river was pumped to the surface. These caissons acted as a root system, and served to anchor the fountain, since the chief logistical problem was to keep it from being pushed up out of the ground by the water pressure from below.

Two 250 horsepower pumps push more than 6,000 gallons of water a minute to a height of up to 200 feet. (The quantity of water pumped into the air is equivalent to 2,000 home water spigots turned on full at one time.) Twenty-four white and gold quartz iodine lights illuminate the fountain, and more than 30,000 cobblestones, called "Belgium Blocks" saved from old road surfaces at the Point, were used to pave the area around the fountain. Computers are used to correlate the height of the fountain with current wind conditions, thus keeping the water within the 200-foot diameter of its basin.

What has its existence meant to the city of Pittsbugh? It is certainly impossible to put its value into dollars. One can be fairly certain that Pittsburgh will never have the kind of water shortage problems that are beginning to plague certain areas of the South, the Southwest, and the West. Pittsburgh's citizens have benefitted from this plentiful source of cool, pure water in countless direct and indirect ways.

Bill Shane, former Chairman of the Pennsylvania Public Utility Commission, said recently, "I have been saying for some time that I expect to see many of the lemmings who migrated to the Sun Belt in the latter half of the 20th century return to the northeastern United States in the 21st century, primarily because the northeastern United States has abundant water resources and the Sun Belt is already bumping up against severe water limits."

Can you imagine how much Phoenix or Los Angeles would be willing to give to have a bountiful water source detoured to flow under their cities? The Pittsburgh area is heir to one of nature's greatest blessings; it must learn to appreciate and protect it.

For Sale in Pittsburgh—Slaves (1780-1865)

FOR SALE—to any person residing in the country—a negro wench. She is an excellent cook and can do any kind of work in or out of doors. Produce will be taken or cattle of any kind. Inquire of Col. Gibson, Fort Pitt, May 23, 1787.

By virtue of a writ of fieri facias to me directed, will be exposed to public sale in Pittsburg (sic), on Tuesday, the 16th day of June, horses, cows, sheep, stills, Negroes, and household furniture. Property of John McKee. To be sold by William Lerry, Sheriff.

These advertisements, taken verbatim from old copies of the *Pittsburgh Gazette*, are shocking. Pittsburgh has always been thought of as a Northern city and has probably never been associated in peoples' minds with the scourge of slavery. But we need to be reminded that human beings were bought and sold as possessions in this city; in fact Pittsburgh was the earliest slave holding community west of the Appalachian Mountains.

Most of the first residents of Pittsburgh and vicinity, who were wealthy enough to afford it, were owners of slaves, and as early as 1780 slaves were common in the area. William Penn, the founder of Pennsylvania, was a slave owner, as were several of Pittsburgh's most famous early citizens, including Gen. George Neville, Col. Presley Neville, Adamson Tannehill, Gen. James O'Hara, and John Gibson.

The history of slavery in Pennsylvania was centered in the city of Philadelphia, all of whose affluent citizens owned slaves; in fact, many of Philadelphia's richest citizens made their fortunes as slave merchants. They outfitted slave ships and brought ship loads of slaves into the port of Philadelphia to be transported all along the Eastern seaboard. Before Pennsylvania's 10th birthday, there were at least 10 slave ships plying their trade from the West Indies and West Africa. Most ships would sail to the West Indies to bring back cargoes of sugar, rum, and molasses—and typically about 20 black slaves who were sold to any interested party at an average price of between 25 and 70 British pounds.

West Indian slaves were widely believed to be of inferior quality, while West African slaves were more highly prized. Slave owners of the day believed that West Indian slaves were less able to stand the rigorous Pennsylvania winters.

By 1800 there were over 500 slaves in Pennsylvania, most of them in the Philadelphia area. Allegheny County had only 64. One way in which wealthier citizens along the East Coast could demonstrate their social importance was by owning slaves. Pennsylvania was not considered to be a prime market for slaves, particularly since the state never had large agricultural plantations which depended on cheap labor to harvest their crops. Pittsburgh and all of Western Pennsylvania, settled a century later than Eastern Pennsylvania, was an especially poor market. The economy around Pittsburgh was for a long time a frontier one; farms were small and depended upon diversified crops for their income. The lack of social caste made the need for ostentatious display a minor concern. Also, Calvinism, the chief religious persuasion in Western Pennsylvania, always frowned on slavery as being non-Christian.

Obviously, one of the reasons for the slow growth of slavery in the North was the fact that it did not have the plantation system. Some social historians, however, have suggested that if Bessemer, Carnegie and Westinghouse had developed their specialties at the same time as Whitney invented his cotton gin, slavery might have become an important social phenomenon in the North as well. Most historians do agree that slaves in Pennsylvania were treated better than in most other states, that most had adequate food and clothing, and that there were fewer instances of physical mistreatment, but it was slavery nevertheless.

Slavery never flourished in Western Pennsylvania, more because of economic reasons than as a result of moral scruples. Boucher, one of Pittsburgh's earliest historians, noted the absence of abolitionist conscience, "Early in the nineteenth century at least half a dozen ministers in Pittsburgh and most of the elders and officials of the churches owned slaves." Hugh Henry Brackenridge also observed, "Many men in the Pittsburgh district would not for a fine cow shave their beards on Sunday, but they held and abused slaves."

A growing number of Pittsburghers, however, were opposed to slavery, and strong anti-slavery sentiment came from some of the pulpits, the press, and the speaking platform. As early as March 1, 1780, Pennsylvania passed a law stating that no person born after that date could be a slave for life; he could only be held until he was 28 years old. In the decades before the Civil War, strong Abolitionist and Black Colonization Societies became active in Pittsburgh. A clear division of public opinion resulted. Most Abolitionists believed that slavery was sinful and had to be removed from the face of the earth. Colonization Societies, however, did not want to offend the South, were afraid of the dissolution of the Union, and did not believe that slavery violated the United States Constitution. Colonization Societies generally favored the solution of herding ex-slaves together and shipping them back to Africa to "their own kind."

Opposition to slavery gradually grew in intensity. Professor Greene of the Western Pennsylvania Theological Seminary brought his slaves with him to Pittsburgh in 1840, but received much good publicity when he voluntarily freed them in 1841. In the years just prior to 1850 a number of freed slaves were living in Pittsburgh. However, many of them were living in cellars and shanties, and every winter some of them froze to death in the severe weather. Laws in Pennsylvania denied blacks admission to "tippling houses," did not permit them to carry arms, and denied them the right to assemble in groups.

In 1850 the infamous Fugitive Slave Law was passed, requiring authorities to seize and return escaped slaves to their original masters. Federal judges and United States marshals worked hard to show "slave hunters" that the North was on their side, and attractive financial rewards for the return of missing slaves became commonplace. These actions led to the strengthening of the Colonization Societies who tried to assemble former slaves and ship them back to Africa rather then return them to their former owners. It was this movement that resulted in the colonization of Liberia in West Africa.

The growing opposition to slavery in the decades before the Civil War was marked in Pittsburgh by a series of incidents which reflected the city's Northern roots. In April of 1847, the owner of four slaves, passing through Pittsburgh, was waylaid by anti-slavery elements and a group of blacks, who rescued and freed three of his slaves. In July of 1846 a runaway slave from Virginia, who had resided in Pittsburgh for several years and had married here, was induced by another black man to take a buggy ride. They were accosted by his former master and captured. However, the former slave raised such an outcry that a crowd gathered and freed him. His master was told by the city authorities that it was impossible to prevent such rescues in Pittsburgh, and that he should know better than to bring slaves to the city. In March of 1850, a slave held by a Mr. Bagolt of New Orleans, while on a river steamer in Pittsburgh, escaped with the aid of friends and was never recaptured.

These stories of the Pittsburgh citizenry's abolitionist tendencies, should be contrasted with other incidents. In September of 1850, after the passage of the Fugitive Slave Law, blacks living in Pittsburgh who had escaped from Southern masters, fearing a return to bondage, began to leave in large numbers for Canada. On September 24, 1850, 35 black men who lived in the Third Ward of Allegheny, now Pittsburgh's North Side, left for Canada in one group.

In March of 1855, Leonard Boyd, accompanied by his wife and a black slave nurse, stopped at the St. Charles Hotel in Pittsburgh. Servants at the hotel made two attempts to free the girl, but were turned away by the hostile crowd and the police who had gathered outside the hotel. Mr. Boyd left the city in haste, fearing the loss of his "property." The papers harshly responded to the rescue attempt rather than its failure,

This attempt for boldness and success has not been surpassed in Pittsburgh. Pittsburgh's business has suffered severely enough from other causes without adding the curse and disgrace of Negro riots. We hope that the next riot of the kind will be met with plenty of well-charged revolvers in ready and resolute hands.

184

Opposition to slavery finally culminated in Pittsburgh's becoming the most active station on the renowned Underground Railroad. The Underground Railroad was neither a railroad, nor was it underground. It was an elaborate system of routes and aid stations where Abolitionists hid fugitive slaves. Many of the stations were private homes; some were church basements. Pittsburgh was a logical center for such activity because of its advantageous location on the rivers, and because its wooded hills and deep ravines made capture more difficult. Pittsburgh developed such an anti-slavery reputation that slave catchers and owners feared to enter its boundaries. Escaped slaves began to feel that if they could get to the city, they were generally safe. Slaves who used this route to freedom proceeded by rail to Cleveland, or followed the Allegheny or the Ohio rivers northward.

Among the best known "stations" in Pittsburgh were the Avery Memorial AME Zion Church on the North Side and the former St. Mary's Hall on the campus of Duquesne University. During the middle of the nineteenth century, St. Mary's Hall was a red brick hospital at the corner of Cooper and Bluff Streets in the Hill District which was operated by Dr. Albert G. Walker. No records exist of how many slaves stopped to hide and rest there. St. Mary's Hall was finally demolished in 1972 to make way for a parking lot. Philanthropist Charles Avery, who founded the AME Zion Church, was a strong Abolitionist. Records show that hundreds of escaping slaves spent some time in the damp dark basement of the church before being directed north to Canada and freedom.

The Civil War finally settled the slavery question in the United States and in 1870 black people voted for the first time in Allegheny County. It is hard to believe that it took so long to finally resolve this sad page in American history.

When Pittsburghers Rode the Planks Rather Than Walked Them! (1848-1899)

Plank roads shaped a significant chapter in the early history of transportation in America and especially in Pennsylvania. Plank roads were distinctive to the United States, and became common wherever lumber was cheap.

Their popularity reached a zenith in 1850, and by 1865 there were 2,106 miles of plank roads in the United States. The country was a "wooden country"; plank roads were inexpensive; they could be built for less than $2,000 per mile. As lumber became more expensive and other road surfaces proved more practical, their importance faded rapidly and they eventually disappeared. But for 30 or 40 years, they were an important and colorful part of the area's growth and development.

With today's four lane superhighways and hundreds of thousands of miles of improved roadways, it is hard to believe that within the present century, travel by road was a hazardous undertaking. A traveler today would be shocked to read the *Pittsburgh Gazette Times* issue of Sunday, March 19, 1911:

> There is one thing that is a crying necessity in this improved road business that the county should be given the power to care for and improve county roads through boroughs. For reasons incomprehensible to most mortals many of the boroughs seem to take not the slightest care of stretches of roads within their limits. Among the offenders is the town of Carrick in the South Hills. The

Liberty road in this boro…is simply a half mile or so of morass, miniature lakes and mud of the most sticky variety. There is no sidewalk, but simply planks thrown around in unbeautiful confusion whereon pedestrians risk life and limb performing feats of gymnastics.

The same article referred to West Liberty Avenue as, "a stretch of horrible mud and unlovely pools in inclement weather," and described the Banksville Road as, "an inexcusable river of mud."

As early as 1848 writers were complaining about the sad state of roads in the United States. William Gillespie, Professor of Civil Engineering at Union College, New York State, was widely quoted in the press when he said that, "The common roads of the United States are inferior to those of any other civilized country in the world."

As urban centers grew all over Allegheny County, it became increasingly important for farmers to carry their crops into the towns and cities to feed the people. Toll roads were the first solution to the problem of keeping roads passable. The money collected from users of the roads was supposed to be used to improve the roadways, but little money or effort was expended for this purpose, and for much of the year, the roads were nearly impassable. The era of plank roads began.

In the decade following 1845, the plank road came into its own. Plank roads were properly named—heavy planks were laid across parallel lines of stringers. By today's standards plank roads were crude indeed. As built originally, split logs were smoothed with handaxes and laid lengthwise in two parallel tracks similar to a railroad track to provide a firm surface for the wheels of wagons. Where the terrain was especially difficult, the roads were completely covered with the planks and were called corduroy roads. Well drained areas used the plank rails; wet, swampy spots, which became mud holes in wet weather, were "corduroyed."

The planks were made of logs split by hand and smoothed with handaxes. They were usually three inches thick, eight feet long, and varied in width depending on the logs from which they were hewn. A pedestrian traveling the road in wet weather was apt to have a stream of water squirt up the leg when a plank was stepped on.

Usually, only the left side of the roadway was planked so that vehicles coming into the city had the right of way on the planked road. Frequent "turn-offs" were provided so that vehicles heading out of the city could leave the planked side and yield the right of way to the incoming wagons. Later some of the busier roads were planked on both sides.

Hemlock and white pine were the most commonly used woods, but they were loose grained and knotty and did not hold up well in bad weather. Later, hard woods were used on the more permanent installations. A ditch, two feet deep, normally paralleled the road to provide for necessary drainage. It took almost 32,000 board feet of planks for one mile of roadway.

Supporters of plank roads touted them as cheap, smooth, and usable in all kinds of weather, and a few misguided enthusiasts even considered them serious rivals to the railroads. Their supporters were very vocal. W. Kingsford, a strong supporter of plank roads, published a treatise on plank roads in 1851, and said, among other claims, that, "Plank roads may be made extensively and highly instrumental in the advancement of the value of lands, the growth of towns, and the progress of the arts, which is but another word for the progress of civilization itself." He was carried away when he claimed that with the advent of plank roads, "people dressed better, their manners improved, and the wives and daughters of American farmers are not the same people that they were before the era of plank roads."

Supporters alleged that land values increased 10 to 50% when plank roads were built nearby. They declared that the wear and tear on horses was cut in half and that horseshoes lasted twice as long. They liked to point out that getting the farmers out of the mud, made Sunday church attendance greater, medical help more available, and opened up the whole wide outside world to people unable to experience it before.

Pittsburgh had a dozen or so of these plank roads, which radiated like spokes from a hub and led out of the city in all directions. One newspaper reporter said that they were too crooked and circuitous to be called spokes and referred to them instead as "drunken spokes."

Plank roads were first built in Russia, but the first plank road in North America was said to have been opened in Toronto, Canada, in 1835, built by Darcy Boulton. The first plank road in the United States was opened from Syracuse, N.Y., north to Oneida Lake in 1846. Within the next 10 years thousands of miles of these roads were built in Pennsylvania and in other neighboring Eastern States.

In 1848 a group of farsighted Pittsburghers, recognizing the need for a good all weather road from Pittsburgh to Butler and the opportunity to open a lucrative business, borrowed $30,000 to finance the Allegheny and Butler Plank Road Company. The road was authorized and chartered by the Pennsylvania State Legislature in 1849.

With quite a celebration, ground was broken for the road on July 16, 1851. Built by Judge Braden and Thomas Wilson Shaw, with John H. Miller as chief engineer, it was completed and in use by 1852. The road began on the North Side, then Allegheny City, and roughly followed an old Indian trail. In the beginning about 10 miles of the road in Allegheny County was paved with flagstones quarried at Undercliff in Shaler Township, but this proved unsuccessful because of the softness of the stone, and later planks were utilized for its entire length.

Several tollgates—spaced about five miles apart—were built to collect the fares for its use. The first one was in Allegheny City, the second, at the intersection with Evergreen Road in Millvale, the third, in Etna, and the fourth, at the bridge crossing Pine Creek in Glenshaw. In the beginning a stage coach used the Plank Road on a 14 hour one–way schedule between Pittsburgh and Butler. But in 1864, a railroad connected the two cities and spelled the end of the stage coach era between Pittsburgh and Butler.

The use of tolls proved to be financially sound. In 1855, $9,030.04 was collected; in 1856, $13,069.55; and in 1857, $10,801.32. In each of these years receipts exceeded expenses for the company. Fees were as follows: 12¢ for a wagon and 2 horses, 3¢ for a horse and rider, 5¢ for 20 sheep or swine, 10¢ for 20 cattle. Workmen employed to build the Butler Plank Road were paid 61 1/2¢ a day.

Contemporary accounts of the Butler Plank Road give some interesting insights into the daily life of the area. Before the arrival of the gasoline age, scores of farmers from Glade Mills, Cooperstown, and Bakerstown used the Plank Road to fill the haymows of Allegheny City and Pittsburgh. It was said that one of the sights of the 1890s and early 1900s was to see 20 to 30 loads of hay moving down the Plank Road to be weighed at the Etna General Store owned by Spang Chalfont Company and then to proceed to the old Haymarket located in the heart of Allegheny City.

Some of the hayraisers lived too far north of the city to make the trip one day with horse transportation. Most of them spent the night near the Cut where there were two hotels near the intersection of what is now Middle Road, Saxonburg Boulevard and Route 8. Both hotels afforded stables and haysheds of sufficient height to admit a load of hay and furnish shelter in case of rain. Each shed was large enough to accommodate eight or ten loads of hay. The hotels had seven bedrooms in addition to a bar and a dining room where meals were served "family style for 25¢ each." The Cut was a famous landmark between Etna and Wildwood. A solid barrier of rock 150 feet long and 30 feet high had to be removed to build the Plank Road. The Cut was near the present intersection of Route 8 and Saxonburg Boulevard.

For many years the Plank Road was one lane wide and at intervals places were identified where wagons would pull off and allow a traveler in the opposite direction to pass. When two vehicles would approach one another, one of the drivers was required to pull off at the wide spot to allow the other to pass. The tollgate consisted of a long tapered pole, mounted in a slot on a post. The butt of the pole extended some distance past the post and was so balanced that a woman or a child could easily raise the gate. When the gate was closed the pole rested in the slot of another post.

The tollkeeper lived in a house near the gate. In the 1880s it was fashionable for a young man to take his lady for a buggy ride to Butler; the fee was $1.35 round trip. A common practice was to use the Plank Road at night hoping that the tollkeeper would be asleep and thus avoid paying. Most of the tollgates were thrown open at 10 p.m. because it would not pay the turnpike company to hire an extra man to collect fees after that hour. If the keeper chose to stay open he could do so at his own profit. In that case he would close the gate, hang a lantern on it and go to bed, and perhaps be called several times during the night to open the gate. Drivers had a grudge against what they called, "after ten gate keepers."

Local users objected strenuously to paying for short distances, and finally exemptions were granted to those going to and from public worship, funerals, farmers who used it for short distances, and those going to and from grist mills. Many users of the roads learned to avoid tollkeepers by using "shunpikes," little detours around toll gates. It was not uncommon for groups to appear at the gates on Sundays, with each member of the party waving prayer books, even though the next stop was a tavern.

For a time plank roads were considered to be good investments and desirable kinds of roads, but soon sun and water would warp the timbers, and in the end plank roads were looked upon as a thing of scorn—the worst kind of road surface. As planks rotted or split apart they were pulled out and thrown to the side of the road.

The Butler Plank Road operated for over 50 years; it was finally sold to the Allegheny County Commissioners in 1905 for $65,000. At this time it was recognized as the oldest plank road in the nation and was considered to be one of the best maintained. In about 1906 the road was macadamized and became one of the first paved roads in Allegheny County. All remains of the old plank road have completely disappeared, but it is said that portions of the toll road paved with stone continued to be uncovered from time to time in Allison Park and Glenshaw.

There were at least a dozen plank roads into and out of the city of Pittsburgh. The Perrysville Plank Road is probably the second best known. It was seven miles long, began at the north end of Federal Street in Allegheny City and wound around the hill west of that street, following the present course of Perrysville Avenue, and heading north toward Erie. This plank road was intentionally made longer and curvier by its shrewd builder to enable him to collect more money. Automobiles traveling Perrysville Avenue today note that it winds in interminable fashion through the hills, ravines, and lowlands of the area.

The Perrysville Plank Road was also the site of a famous story. Thomas M. Marshall, (Glorious Old Tom), Pittsburgh's famous criminal attorney, habitually drove this plank road to and from his home to the city. Thomas Marshall was said to have cleared more men of murder, or saved them from the gallows, than any other lawyer in the history of Pittsburgh. In 1868 the road was in a wretched condition, planks being two and three feet apart, and in between, the mud being three feet deep.

One winter day, after a thaw, Mr. Marshall came along in his buggy. Just as the horse and driver were about to pass through the barrier, the gate suddenly dropped. The tollkeeper came out to collect his toll. Mr. Marshall refused to pay and promised to return the next day with an ax to cut down the gate. Sure enough, the gate was closed on him the next day and he proceeded to demolish the tollgate and pass through to the amazement of the gatekeeper.

The road company sent him two years of bills, but he never responded. When they finally threatened to sue, Mr. Marshall told them to go ahead, that he would have the court revoke their charter for not complying with provisions to keep the road in good repair. The end of the story was that they cancelled the bill for toll in exchange for his giving them some legal advice "now and then."

One of the features of this plank road was the famous Keating Tavern in West View, where Joe Keating was the tavernkeeper and where sleighing parties from the city stopped for chicken and waffle dinners. The ride by moonlight out this road was said to be one of the finest in the state, the scenery said to be, "beautiful and inspiring."

Other plank roads in the area were: Temperanceville Plank Road, Noblesville Plank Road, Allegheny and Franklin, East Liberty and Moon Township, Lawrenceville and Sharpsville, Allegheny and New Brighton, Allegheny and Manchester. None of them, however, were as successful or as long-lived as the Butler or Perrysville ones.

The Allegheny and Manchester Plank Road was renowned because it carried travelers to Mrs. Hartman's famous tavern on the east side of Beaver Road. Travelers began their journeys in front of the St. Clair Hotel, at the southeast corner of Penn and St. Clair Streets. The route then followed the Plank Road through Manchester to the inn in Reserve Township. The inn was surrounded by five or six acres of land abundantly supplied with trees and shrubbery. Contemporary accounts describe the ride to the tavern as delightful, with ponds glistening through the trees and bushes, and to the west, the Ohio River "shimmered in the sunlight." In summer Mrs. Hartman's guests sat under the grape arbors or the trees and sipped her homemade wine, or partook of such other refreshments as their appetites craved. In winter jolly parties went to her cheerful rooms and danced the night away.

The plank roads were at their peak in the 1850s. The appearance of the railroads proved to be the death knell for both the plank roads and the canals. But in spite of that, some of the plank roads stayed in existence until the turn of the century. The stress of heavy traffic and most of all, decay, made repairs continually necessary, and if not made, users and their horses were often seriously injured. In the end it was found that plank roads had to be completely rebuilt every five years, and reasonable tolls could not meet this need. The planks rapidly vanished and the roads regressed to their original mud or were macadamized.

It is easy to over romanticize elements of our history, but there is something very attractive about moonlit sleigh rides and leisurely trips to warm, cozy inns in the suburbs. The era of plank roads is gone forever; no one could imagine a return to muddy, rough rides over sometimes impassable roads, but they do symbolize a chapter in the history of transportation that should not be forgotten.

The Glasshouse Boys of Pittsburgh (1850-1910)

The glasshouse boys of Pittsburgh were a unique breed. They played a substantial role in the history of the city, of the glass industry, and of the child labor movement in the United States. Although not a secret chapter of history, their part in the development of Pittsburgh has never been fully documented nor appreciated.

The glasshouse boys were the approximately 10,000 boys under the age of 14 who were employed in the early glass factories of Pittsburgh. In 1899 the United States Bureau of Labor Statistics reported that 7,116 boys under 16 were then employed in the glass industry, and it was common knowledge that glass factories used every trick in the book to avoid reporting numbers of child employees. The U.S. Census of 1900 reported that 675,342 boys and 391,982 girls between the ages of 10 and 14 were employed in factories, mines, and sweatshops in the United States. Clearly, the glass house boys were a small minority of the total child labor problem, but the terrible conditions of their employment made them a focus for the attacks on child labor at the beginning of the 20th century.

The use of boys in the glass industry had a long history. The first glass factories in Pittsburgh made their appearance around the beginning of the 19th century, and the common use of boys as a cheap labor supply for the glass industry continued for over 100 years. Even into the 1900s over half of the states had no minimum age requirements for workers. The largest concentrations of child laborers were in the Southern textile industries, the anthracite coal fields of Northeastern Pennsylvania, and the glass industry of Pittsburgh.

It was estimated that the anthracite coal industry employed over 18,000 boys as coal pickers, but pitiful as their working conditions might have been, the plight of the glasshouse boys aroused more public attention.

The glass industry has one of the longest and most exotic histories of any industry. On a sandy beach on the Mediterranean, long before the Christian era, a group of Tyrian sailors, hungry and tired, landed their little craft and went ashore. Kettles were filled and a fire built on the sand. Lumps of sodium salt used as ballast in their ships were used to prop the kettles over the fire. The sailors ate, packed up their belongings and prepared to move on. Then, in the embers of the fire they found a hard, smooth, substance—the first glass known to man.

The fire had accidentally fused together the sand on the beach and the sodium salt to develop a product for a new industry, one that has proven to be of great benefit to mankind. That is presumed to be the beginning of man's manufacture of glass. Glass has been called "the handmaiden of the arts and minister to every science." Its various applications include stained glass in all its forms, the valuable lenses used in so many branches of science, the mirrors employed in photography and astronomy, the windows utilized in modern architecture, and the countless other uses in our everyday lives.

The glass industry came to Pittsburgh in 1797 when General James O'Hara opened his first glass plant opposite the Point on the South Side. The industry came to Pittsburgh for several reasons. In the early days, it required comparatively little capital to start a factory. The opening of the West, and Pittsburgh's location as the gateway to western expansion also played a large role. Shipping from the East Coast was difficult and expensive. The raw materials—sand, soda, ash, clay, limestone, salt cake and charcoal—were readily available in Western Pennsylvania and were not subject to wide fluctuations in value. Glass had one other great advantage— once manufactured, there was almost no loss due to obsolescence or depreciation.

For more than 100 years the manufacture of glass was centered in and around the city of Pittsburgh. The first glass made west of the Allegheny Mountains was made at New Geneva on the Monongahela River near the

West Virginia border, but the industry soon moved to the Pittsburgh area were markets and transportation facilities were more available. The industry rapidly expanded on the South Side of the city on the flat lands along the Monongahela River. Coal was readily available from Coal Hill (now known as Mt. Washington), and General James O'Hara's first glasshouse was soon followed by many others. By 1931 there were over 100 factories making table, decorative, or window glass in the Pittsburgh area.

The most informative description of Pittsburgh and its glass industry came from the pen of Anne Royall, one of America's great eccentrics and one of its first travel writers. In 1829 she visited Pittsburgh and gave us a vivid, first–hand account of the city and its people.

There is no city in the Union I was more anxious to see, than Pittsburg.(sic) For though I had spent some years of my childhood in Westmoreland, the adjoining county, I had never seen it… Everything pursued in other towns is thrown into the shade by Pittsburgh; even in the building of steam boats, it excels by a long way our great city, New York. You see nothing but columns of smoke rolling out of these manufactories in every part of the city, and in every street. Go to the river Monongahela and you see nothing but steam boats, two stories high, many of them, and two tiers of windows, precisely like a house, and with gable ends.

Anne was most impressed by the glass industry, particularly by Bakewell's plant on the South Side. She wrote several pages praising the skill of the glass blowers. She referred to the glasshouse boys employed there, but seemed not to be concerned by their ages or treatment. She described the glass workers as, "the finest looking men in Pittsburgh, neatly dressed, sometimes leaning back and then erect, ease and inimitable grace accompanying their movements with fine countenances and soft black eyes, all bedecked with smiles of ineffable sweetness." She claimed to be "riveted to the spot," concluding that, "The proprietor had a good right to be proud of these men; they must be worth their weight in gold."

The industry itself shared Royall's high opinion of the glass factories. The glass manufacturers were the rich men of Pittsburgh, and the skilled glass workers were the master craftsmen of the day. They thought that they were the elite of American workmen; they drew larger wages than any other skilled laborers. The *Pittsburgh Gazette* reported that when they dressed up on Saturday afternoon, "with fine clothes. a clean undershirt open at the front and showing their bulging chests, they attracted more attention than any other workers." The skill of the glassworker was widely recognized. In most states they were exempt from military service except in times of invasion or civil insurrection.

Not all references to their characters were as full of accolades as Anne Royall's. O'Hara and Craig, owners of one of the largest glass plants, saw ordinary glass workers as " dissipated, undependable, rebellious, and migratory." Owners longed for virtuous qualities in their workmen, and often asked agents to find and send them "sober, industrious Germans." Contracts were made as early as the 1830s providing for bonuses for those who worked complete days or entire weeks without absences from their jobs.

The glasshouse boys became a vital element in the growing glass industry, but they were especially notorious for frequent turnover; few of them stayed on their jobs long, perhaps for good reasons. No modern industry, with the possible exception of silk-throwing and cotton manufacturing, made a stronger demand for child labor than the manufacture of glass. *The Bitter Cry of the Children,* written by John Spargo, gives a vivid picture of the glasshouse boys at work.

> I shall never forget my first visit to a glass factory at night. It was a big, wooden structure, so loosely built that it afforded little protection from draughts, surrounded by a high fence with several rows of barbed wire stretched across the top. I went with the foreman to the plant and he explained the reason for the stockade-like fence. 'It keeps the young imps inside once we've got 'em for the night shift,' he said. The young imps were of course the boys employed, about forty in number, at least ten of whom were less than twelve years of age. The hours of labor for the night shift were from 5:30 p.m. to 3:30 a.m. I stayed and watched the boys at work for several hours, and when their tasks were done saw them disappear into the darkness and storm of the night. For the first time, I realized the tragic significance of cheap bottles.

John Spargo was appalled at the working conditions and the ages of the boys employed in the glass industry, and wrote several articles pointing out what a high price he felt that society was paying in order to get "cheap bottles." After describing in detail the skilled work of the glass bottle blowers, he then vividly described the duties of the glasshouse boys:

> By the side of each mold sat a "take-out boy," who with tongs took the half-finished bottles (not yet provided with necks) out of the molds. Then other boys, called "snapper ups," took these bodies of bottles in their tongs and put the small ends into gas-heated molds till they were red hot. Then the boys took them with almost incredible quickness and passed them to other men, finishers, who shaped the necks of the bottles into final form. The "carrying in boys," sometimes called "carrier pigeons," took the red hot bottles from the benches, three or four at a time, upon big asbestos shovels to the annealing oven, where they are gradually cooled off to ensure even contraction and to prevent breaking. The work of these "carrying in boys," several of whom were less than twelve years old, was by far the hardest of all. They were kept on a slow run all the time from the benches to the annealing oven and back again. I was told that it was difficult to get men to do this work because men cannot stand the pace and get tired too quickly.

> The distance to the annealing oven in the factory was one hundred feet and the boys made seventy-two trips per hour, making the distance traveled in eight hours nearly twenty-two miles. Over half of this distance the boys were carrying their hot loads to the ovens.

The best description in the literature of the actual work done by the glasshouse boys is Spargo's book, *The Bitter Cry of the Children*, was instrumental in focusing public attention on child labor in the glass industry:

> The effects of the employment of young boys in glass factories, especially at night, are injurious from every possible point of view.

The constant facing of the glare of the furnaces and the red hot bottle causes serious injury to the sight—accidents from burning are common. Lack of proper rest, added to the strain and heat of their work, produces nervous dyspepsia. From working in draughty sheds, where one boy said, 'burning on the side against the furnace, and pretty near freezing on the other' makes them subject to rheumatism…they fall ready victims to pneumonia.

Adult glass workers rarely took their own children into the glass houses. Not only were working conditions horrible, but the moral influences surrounding the boys in a glass factory were generally considered to be corrupting. One glass worker was quoted as saying, "I would rather send my boys straight to hell than send them to the glasshouse."

Saloons and grog shops surrounded the factories; many factories permitted liquor on the job; and many of the glasshouse boys were expected to bring the liquor to the work site. So great was the demand for boys, however, that it was possible for a boy at any time to get employment for a single night. These "one shifters" as they were called greatly increased the number of boys who attended school all day and worked all night. In New Jersey, shortages of glasshouse boys resulted in importing boys from orphanages and reformatories, boarding them with laborers' families, and deducting their board from their minuscule wages. Thus a system of child slavery developed. Boys over 16 were commonly perceived as too slow, clumsy, and inefficient to work in the glass houses. By the time a boy was sixteen he knew that he had almost no chance of becoming an apprentice and therefore tried to find more promising employment.

Many of the glasshouse boys came from families where the father was dead or had deserted the family, and the boys' meager wages kept food on the tables for those families. Although an apprenticeship program existed, few glasshouse boys ever became apprentices.

Wages of the glasshouse boys varied widely by time and place. Typical wage rates, however, were: $1.35 weekly for "carrying in boys," 95¢ for "mold boys," 90¢ for "cleaning off boys," and 75¢ for "snapping off and gathering bits boys."

The temperature of molten glass is 2500 degrees Fahrenheit. Even though most glass houses closed their doors during the hottest months of

July and August, the average indoor temperature of the glass factory over the working year varied between 100 and 130 degrees. Stiff necks and colds were considered endemic to glasshouse boys. Respiratory diseases were common among the "carrying in boys" since they were constantly running between the heat of the glass furnaces through the drafty sheds to the finishers.

The mixing operations necessary for the preparation of the batch maintained a constantly high dust content. Another problem resulted from the "blow-over," the silicate cloud caused by the breaking of the thin bubbles between the punty and the mold. The "blow-over" was injurious to the eyes and tracheal passages, and was also a frequent cause of skin irritations. Floors were always littered with broken glass, which caused frequent injuries, given the natural inclination of boys to play around.

Public outrage against the use of children in industrial workshops gradually crystallized. Although children were widely used in factories, mines, and mills, it was principally the use of children in the glass industry which finally molded public opinion and resulted in child labor laws. The concentration of the industry in a large city and the resulting attention of the news media finally produced restrictive child labor laws. They were only partially successful. Some glass factories accumulated long lists of injunctions for violations of such laws, but often the injunctions were ignored and the government did not take additional legal action.

In response to growing public protest, the industry formulated several defenses of its use of children in the glasshouses. The glass manufacturers insisted that the glass industry could not be profitable without the employment of cheap child labor. The owners argued that the "labor of these little hands" was necessary to relieve the poverty of their families, and that it would be cruel of society to deprive the poor of that income. Another argument, so inhuman as to defy belief, was that most of the young immigrant boys were uneducable; to paraphrase a common attitude—they are what they are, and will always remain what they are. One manufacturer was quoted as saying, "These Slav boys are mentally irredeemable, so fast asleep intellectually that they cannot be awakened; designed by nature to be hewers of wood and drawers of water." Some contended that employment in the glass factories and cotton mills was a blessing in disguise. Working in the mills and factories was better than existence in an unsanitary dwelling. Others claimed that work indoors was preferable to "roaming the streets; late hours, evil associates, cigarettes, and other excesses which will fill the jails, and kill thousands and thousands while work kills none.

These statements appear ludicrous, but it must be pointed out that such claims delayed the passage of many child labor laws in numerous states, and even after their passage frequently effected the enforcement of their provisions. The stronger the protests from the media and the public, the more the industry defended its actions. Some of America's best known personalities led the battle against the use of children as laborers, including Dr. Felix Adler, Elbert Hubbard, Edwin Markham, and Gustavus Myers.

There were several reasons for the gradual disappearance of the glass house boys. Child labor laws were certainly responsible in part, but in fairness, it should be pointed out that other less obvious causes were present. New technical developments in the glass industry greatly reduced the need for child laborers; more and more of the glass manufacturing process became a machine operation. The use of gas as an energy source in the industry resulted in the movement of more and more plants to areas where natural gas was available and away from the city of Pittsburgh. The greater availability of public schools and the public's growing respect for education also contributed in some degree.

The glass industry, which once flourished on the South Side of Pittsburgh, is gone. Most of the old glasshouses have either been torn down or used by other types of manufacturing plants. At one time practically all the oil lamp chimneys used in this country were made on the South Side, and the glass industry payroll even in the early 20th century amounted to millions of dollars yearly. There were 31 glass factories on the South Side in 1931; today there are none.

The glass house boys of Pittsburgh now live only in legend. Not all was dreary in the glass houses. The boys were a high-spirited group; contemporary accounts say that there was constant singing and shouting, sometimes so loud at night that employers tried to muffle the boys' enthusiasm because the establishments were close to residences. *The Pittsburgh Survey* pointed out that,

It was easy to understand the lure of the glassworks, the undefinable magic that chains to the entrance way groups of small boys who have failed to be taken on for the night. The molten wax-like glass in the furnace, the skillful hands of the glass worker who turns it into a bottle, the speed with which the wax bubble is made into a thing of use, the white light, the red glare, the shifting shadows, the dexterity of the bare-armed men all combined to give the glass works a romantic aura.

The glasshouse boys played a central role in the development of the glass industry that helped make Pittsburgh an industrial giant. They also were instrumental in focusing public anger on the use of child labor, resulting in the evolution of the most stringent child labor laws in the world. They are now only a remnant from the past, though there are probably some men alive today who could tell us fascinating stories about their days as glasshouse boys.

Are Pittsburgh's Summers Getting Warmer? (1816-1991)

Recently we have been bombarded with news stories reminding us that the summers of 1988 and 1991 have been unusually hot and dry. We have been repeatedly told how many days had highs above 90° and how many days have gone by with little or no precipitation.

These two summers have been hot, but just to help us keep such statistics in perspective, it might be interesting to look back at other summers which were quite different. Two summers stand out in stark contrast to the summers of 1988 and 1991.

The year 1816 is infamous in the history of weather. It was called, "the year without a summer," "poverty year," and "eighteen hundred and froze to death." In fact Aldino Brockett, who lived in New England in 1816 and is widely regarded as one of America's earliest weather observers, wrote that, "This past summer and fall have been so cold and miserable that I have from despair kept no account of the weather."

From May to September an amazing number of cold fronts chilled the northeastern United States and Canada causing a late spring, a cold summer, and a very early fall. There was deep snow in June, frosts in July and August. Farm crops were repeatedly frozen, and the fear of widespread famine was common.

The unusual summer of 1816 is well documented in the literature. Benjamin Harrison, a farmer in Bennington, Vermont, said it was, "the most gloomy and extraordinary weather ever seen." Chauncey Jerome of

Plymouth, Connecticut, recalled, "On the seventh of June my hands got so cold that I was obliged to lay down my tools and put on a pair of mittens. On the tenth of June my wife brought in some clothes that had been spread on the ground the night before, which were frozen stiff as boards. On the Fourth of July I watched men pitching quoits with their overcoats on." In the small community of De Ruyter, Madison County, New York, it was recorded: "There was a frost every month of the year; the meager harvest of grains was nowhere sufficient to meet peoples' needs. Families were brought to the verge of starvation. Some farmers dug up potatoes they had planted to provide a single meal per day for their families. Many families went months without bread; their chief food being milk."

Spring was very late in 1816. Late frosts retarded spring plantings. Fruit trees were blasted by frosts at the end of May. Warm weather came in early June, but crops quickly planted by optimistic farmers were immediately killed by frosts which arrived from June 6 to June 9 and covered the entire area from Canada to Viginia. In northern Vermont ice one inch thick formed on standing ponds. Newly shorn sheep perished and thousands of birds froze to death. On June 6 light snow fell all over New England and into New York's Catskill Mountains. In Danville, Virginia, snow drifts were reported to be 20 inches deep.

After four weeks of milder weather, a new cold front hit on the first week of July, killing corn, beans, cucumbers, and squash all over New England. On August 20, August 30, and September 11, additional cold spells arrived effectively destroying what crops still remained. Then finally on September 27, a widespread and killing frost effectively closed out a dismal growing season. Frost was recorded in every month of that year in the every state of the Northeast.

It was not coincidental that the first major migration of people from New England to the Middle West occurred the following summer. There was a mass exodus to the Middle West, most immigrants coming from Maine, New Hampshire, and Vermont. Weather records for that year show that abnormal weather was widespread throughout the Northern Hemisphere. It was almost as cold in England, and famines occurred in France and Germany.

Another year, 1859, was also an abnormal year in the weather annals of the eastern United States. Great frosts, quite to the surprise of all weather pundits, hit the Northeast with terrible results. A history of Indiana County in Western Pennsylvania records the event as follows:

> The wheat and rye were just in blossom, and there was every prospect of a bountiful harvest. But the great frosts of June 5 and 12 smote the fields as with the 'besom' of destruction. The evening before nature smiled like Eden almost, with beauty and the prospect of plenty, but on the Sabbath morning the fields were blasted, as though the breath of the Sirocco had swept over them. A deep and heavy gloom settled over the community.

A history of Somerset County, Pennsylvania, gives the following account of the same unusual weather.

> On the night of June 4th there was a heavy frost which destroyed the crops and all the vegetation in nearly every part of the county. All fruit was killed. Rye, wheat, and corn were entirely destroyed. Even hay was badly damaged. Sugar and maple trees shed their leaves like the approach of winter. Farmers were panic stricken. Visions of famine loomed before the eyes of many. The price of flour rose from seven to eighteen dollars a barrel over night.

The Pennsylvania School Report for the year 1860 reported: "Owing to the injury to the crops by the summer frosts of 1859, many districts in the northern and western counties determined to close their schools for the year. All districts in the rural areas shortened their terms and reduced teachers' salaries." Allegheny County recorded that although not one school was discontinued, many districts shortened the school year and most reduced teachers' salaries.

Beaver County reported that June frosts caused severe results on the schools. They reported with pride that, "All schools in the county had at least four months of school." Clarion County recorded that, "The school year just closed was commenced with great discouragement and under many disadvantages by the people of Clarion County. A visitation of Providence had destroyed our hopes of harvest and caused much doubt and same despondency on the part of school officers."

Fayette County reported, "The June frosts exercised an injurious influence. In eight townships the public schools were suspended for the year. No doubt but that education has here received a retrograde action." The annual school report for Indiana County for that same year described it as follows:

> The frost of June 4, 1859, killed our schools as it did our wheat, rye, corn, and potatoes, but whilst the warm sunshine and fruitful showers to a great extent replenished the granaries of our farmers, a parsimonious policy, both ill timed and ill placed, visited our schools with a season of dearth and in some districts causing schools which were in healthy condition to languish for the lack of competent instructors, the wages being so low that qualified teachers could not be obtained for some districts.

No one knows why such abnormal weather patterns occur. Several theories for cold summers have been advanced. One theory claims that periods of abnormally cold weather follow major volcanic eruptions occurring in some part of the world. The rationale is that these eruptions spew so much dust, ash, and cinder into the earth's atmosphere that they generate a veil of volcanic dust which interferes with the surface temperatures of the Earth. The theory is that the dust partially shields the Earth from the Sun's rays, but permits heat to escape from the Earth, thus lowering the temperature.

It is true that three major volcanic eruptions occurred just prior to the cold summer of 1816. Soufriere on St. Vincent Island erupted in 1812; Mayon in the Philippines erupted in 1814, and Tambora on the island of Sumbawa in Indonesia erupted in 1815. The worst of the three was Tamboro, a 13,000 foot volcano which belched out 100 cubic miles of dust, ashes, and cinders, generating a globe girdling veil of volcanic dust. This thesis was espoused by Benjamin Franklin, but it was not original with him. References to it can be found in the literature long before Franklin.

Others conjecture that sun spots reduce the amount of solar radiation emitted from the sun and thus cause lower temperatures on the Earth. The year of 1816 was said to be a year of low sun spot activity.

Today's theories about abnormal weather patterns are linked to that buzzword of the 1990s—"The greenhouse effect." There is little mystery about this phenomenon. The principal cause is attributed to a massive buildup of pollutants in the Earth's atmosphere. This buildup is not recent in origin; in fact it is the cumulative effect of the industrialization of the Western Hemisphere over several centuries. These gases or pollutants surround the Earth with an insulating layer and act somewhat like an ordinary greenhouse. The insulation traps the sun's infra red radiation and keeps it from being reflected back up into space.

Six of the hottest years in the last hundred years were: 1980, 1983, 1986, 1987, 1988, and 1991. During 1988 we witnessed terrible droughts in the United States and China, and wholesale flooding in Sudan, Ethiopia, and Bangladesh. Whether these are cyclical weather phenomena or a developing weather pattern with great significance to the future of this planet only time will tell. Many weather observers still believe that the hot summers of the past several years are little more than "blips" on the ongoing history of weather.

Is Pittsburgh's climate getting milder, or are we just the lucky recipients of a cyclical phenomenon which will balance out for succeeding years? Only several years of weather observations can hope to answer that question. Evidence is conflicting and rarely definitive. Many oldtimers can tell interesting stories about extremes of weather which they experienced many years ago. This is usually inconclusive since all of us tend to remember best those unusual periods of weather and ignore those which are considered normal.

The newest culprit is the "hole in the ozone layer." It is being blamed for weather inconsistencies and for hazards to the health of earth's inhabitants. As we know more about it, it will be interesting to see whether it becomes a real threat to the planet's environment, or fades away before a new threat yet unidentified.

The cold and snowy winter of 1993-1994 has given another dimension to the story. Pittsburgh citizens are now asking, "Are our winters getting colder?" Only many years of record-keeping can definitely answer such questions.

Part V
The City

25

Pittsburgh—Progress and Prophecies (1877-1928-1989)

It is said that prophets are without honor in their own countries, and it is true that few prophets have managed to retain their reputations long. The Old Testament prophets are among the few to have stood the test of time. Anyone trying to foresee the future or to predict events is participating in a very precarious activity.

There have been numerous recorded instances of failed prophecy, including that of Napoleon. In 1807 a young Pennsylvanian, Robert Fulton, traveled to Paris and offered to give Napoleon his new invention, the steamboat. He was turned away as a half-mad dreamer. Napoleon later said that it was one of the greatest mistakes of his life; he said that if he had given Fulton the opportunity to demonstrate his invention, he might have used it to wrest domination of the seas from England and could have turned his downfall in 1815 into a world–wide victory.

When George Westinghouse invented the air brake, he could find no one interested. Most of those who saw or heard about the invention, considered it worthless. It was quite a while before he could find anyone impressed enough to consider its potential.

Thomas Edison is widely revered for inventing the electric light. Yet few realize how widely the invention was ridiculed. John T. Sprague, a well known Londoner, delivered a speech which was widely quoted. He said that, "Neither Mr. Edison nor anyone else can over-ride the well known laws of nature, and when Edison says that the same wire which brings you light will also bring you power and heat, there is no difficulty in seeing that more is promised than can be performed. The talk about cooking food by heat derived from electricity is positively absurd."

In 1913 T. Commerford Martin reporting for the Committee on Progress at the National Electric Light Association Convention, declared, "The truth will emerge clearly in this period on which we are now entering, that water power, as such is of no use to anybody, that its development is as risky a business as mine prospecting and as unprofitable. All the capital invested in hydro-electrical power would be better spent in any other business."

When alternating current was invented in Pittsburgh, most engineers pronounced it as visionary, impractical, and dangerous. One of the outstanding engineers of the day said that, "Alternating current's only useful application would be in the operation of the electric chair."

Today only readers of Tarot cards and tea cups, and TV evangelists work very hard at predicting the future. Most of us are wary of those who profess to be able to see or to describe what lies ahead.

Is it any wonder, when very reputable scientists warn us of the dangers inherent in our pollution of the planet, or talk about the "greenhouse effect" and describe the vast ozone holes in the stratosphere, that we take such warnings with vast grains of salt? Prophecy is not a highly regarded profession in our modern society.

To appreciate the development of a great city, we must first know what its past was like. In 1877 Pittsburgh was a rather primitive place. There was no urban development beyond East Liberty. Nothing existed beyond Allegheny, now the North Side. Five story buildings were skyscrapers; the Monongahela House was the city's only hotel. Cobblestones were used to pave all the streets. Penn Avenue, the city's major thoroughfare, known to all as "The Pike," was paved with wooden blocks and was intercepted by several toll houses. The trolley cars were all pulled by horses. Steam railroads were just making their appearance, and electric lighting had not yet been invented. Gas lamps were used for street lighting, but candles and oil lamps were still used in most homes because gas was too expensive. Telephones were just making their first appearance. An acre of grass between Grant and Ross Streets was the only park in the city. Five railroads did service the city, but river traffic flourished and was by far the most important type of transportation.

In 1928, 50 years later, Pittsburgh had changed dramatically. It had grown into one of America's most important commercial cities and appeared to be at its peak in industrial might. It was widely recognized as the heart of America's industrial greatness. It sat in the midst of the richest coal beds in the nation. It had an unlimited supply of electrical power, and as a result had the lowest electrical rates in the nation. It claimed to have the greatest per capita wealth in the United States, and it led the nation in individual buying power.

The city was flexing its muscles and felt justified in establishing its bragging rights. In 1928 the Pittsburgh Chamber of Commerce sponsored a series of meetings where its most renowned citizens were invited to speak and to describe for the world the tremendous advances made in the City of Pittsburgh.

At the end of this series of lectures, all of which were compiled and published in a 400–page hardback volume, A. L. Humphrey was invited to bring the series to a logical conclusion by lecturing on the topic, "Pittsburgh Fifty Years Hence." Mr. Humphrey was President of the Westinghouse Air Brake Co., the Union Switch and Signal Company, the Keystone Clay Products Co., and The American Brake Co. In addition he was a member of the Board of Directors of several other well known Pittsburgh corporations.

At any rate, Mr. Humphrey took his crystal ball in hand and tried to predict what Pittsburgh would be like 50 years from the time of his speech in 1928. It is fascinating to look at his predictions and square them against the Pittsburgh of the 1980s.

He first predicted that there would be one municipal government for all of Allegheny County. Mr. Humphrey considered this prediction a sure one. Legislation had been introduced in the state capitol in Harrisburg to do just that. Pittsburgh and Allegheny County were to become one metropolitan city in the same manner as had happened to Philadelphia and Philadelphia County. He gloried in the fact that such a merger would eliminate waste and encourage efficient coordination of services in the 124 independent municipalities. He said that such a merger, "Seems as certain as anything human can be." He talked of the prestige that would come from a city of 1,500,000 people, and of the new trade, new industry, and new cultural advantages that would accrue from such a city. He pointed out how community improvements of county-wide proportions could be accomplished, improvements which would otherwise have been impossible because of the difficulty in achieving the necessary concerted action from 124 separate ruling bodies.

It is hard to fault his reasoning, but his ability to prophesy was suspect. What would be his reaction today if he could return to his beloved city and to see how 60 years later, no progress in this direction has occurred. Today we still face this issue. Much wrangling goes on over whether county residents should be taxed to help support numerous city facilities such as the zoo, the conservatory, the aviary, etc. We can only speculate how such a merged municipality if it became a reality 70 years ago, might have influenced the development of this city.

His second prophecy was that Pittsburgh would become the center of the entire nation's water transportation facilities. He said that Pittsburgh was at the head of the world's greatest waterway system and that it was inevitable that Pittsburgh would experience enormous expansion of trade and would become the nation's greatest center of water transportation. He said that large ships from New Orleans and Mexico would be docked at the foot of the Golden Triangle.

Unfortunately this development never happened. Dams on the Ohio River helped flood control, but the massive development of the nation's railroads and the rise of the great trucking industry pushed river transportation into the background. River traffic is still of some importance locally in transporting raw materials to industrial plants on the river banks, but very little tonnage is transported from any distance and certainly large ships from Mexico and New Orleans have never docked at the Monongahela Wharf.

The third prophecy was closely related to the second. Mr. Humphrey predicted that the Ohio River and Lake Erie Canal would become a reality, making Pittsburgh a lake port. Thus, it became possible to transport by water vast quantities of natural resources to the Nation's heartland and to its southern states, without carrying cargo out through the St. Lawrence Waterway and then by a long and dangerous route down the Atlantic Seaboard. He felt that the need for such a canal made its construction inevitable, and that the result would be that Pittsburgh's industrial development would be limitless and Pittsburgh's river tonnage would be many times greater than it was in 1928.

The Canal was never built; Pittsburgh did not become a great lake port, and water tonnage continues to work its way through the St. Lawrence Seaway to the Atlantic Ocean. The "great fleets of vessels from the Great Lakes and the Gulf of Mexico" never materialized.

Mr. Humphrey anticipated that all of Pittsburgh's railroads would be electrified; that the use of coal in steam locomotives would be totally eliminated within just a few years. Steam locomotives did finally become obsolete, but it took a long time and when it did happen, the power which was utilized to drive them was not usually electricity.

His fifth prophecy was that 50 years from 1928 would find Pittsburgh in the midst of the "airplane era." He felt sure that every able-bodied "man" would be licensed to fly a plane, and that the principal means of commuting to and from one's employment would be by airplane. He specifically said that workers would think nothing of flying to and from their places of employment from distances well "over 100 miles one way." The difficulty of landing the planes would be solved by new planes which could land in small areas and would prove to be amazingly economical to operate. The helicopter does need limited space to land, but we have never managed to produce a plane cheap enough to seriously challenge the automobile or to entice many people to adopt it as a commuting possibility.

Mr. Humphrey flatly stated that the city of Pittsburgh would have a population of over 2,000,000 people by 1970. The 1980 Census gives Allegheny County a population of 1,450,195. Actually this is one of the brighter spots in his series of predictions. The figures are quite reasonable if the city had been merged with Allegheny County. Instead we selfishly pursued our separate ways and identities, created innumerable confusions and overlapping of services, and in 1980, the City of Pittsburgh had a population of 423,759.

Our favorite seer thought that Pittsburgh 50 years from 1928 would experience unlimited industrial diversification, even though "iron and steel would retain its unequaled supremacy." Pittsburgh in the 1980s does pride itself on its new found diversification, but iron and steel have certainly failed to "retain its unequaled supremacy."

Mr. Humphrey's percentage of accuracy was not high; prophets nearly always suffer this malady. At any rate in 1928 he was a tremendous public relations representative for the city. It is hard to imagine how he could have been more laudatory. "Pittsburgh," he said, "was where there was more thrift and industry than in any other city in the world." He further claimed that "Pittsburgh had the greatest per capita wealth in 1928 of any city in the nation." If true, Pittsburgh was really quite a city; one could not help but be proud of being one of its citizens.

In spite of this lack of success in foretelling the future, we continually try to do just that. All of us are fascinated by the uncertainty of the future and we love to hear what others think will happen even though we are well aware that most predictions are very suspect.

On October 24, 1989, the *Pittsburgh Post Gazette* attempted to presage what Pittsburgh might be like in the year 2000. Among many prophecies, great and small, were the following:

- The major growth of the city will occur in Oakland.
- At least one new hotel and several new office towers will be built in the Golden Triangle.
- There will be a computer in every household.
- Fax machines will replace the telephone as the major communication tool.
- Public school teachers will become highly paid professionals with top salaries over $90,000 per year.
- Kitchens in homes will be designed as entertainment centers.
- Most food will be shelf-stable and will require no refrigeration.
- Debit cards will automatically deduct the cost of food products in supermarkets from your bank accounts.
- Your family car will be designed to become your breakfast nook of the 21st century.
- We will have a woman president.
- Professional sports will have global conferences.
- Magnetic levitation will be the next high tech industry.
- Movie theaters will have roomier seating, automated concession stands, wider menus of real food, satellite systems which deliver movies from studios directly to theaters, and will be used as tele-conference centers during the day.

There have been many other predictions made by a variety of prophets. How many of these prophecies will fall by the wayside only the next decade will tell. But regardless of their validity or the lack of it, prophets will continue to try to look into their crystal balls and predict that enchanting future.

The rate of societal change has increased so dramatically that these predictions seem much more attainable than the list from 1928. In 1990, Pittsburgh dropped from first to third among the hundreds of cities ranked in Rand McNally's list of America's most livable cities. In 1993, it dropped to fifth place, but it still represents a most respectable performance. Where will Pittsburgh rank in the year 2000?

Pittsburgh: As Others Saw Us (1754-1989)

Pittsburgh—What kind of a city is it?

A heavy industrial metropolis, capital of the rust belt, giant corporate headquarters, pollution center of the Ohio valley, America's most livable city, a fading center of heavy manufacturing, a delightful confluence of three of America's great rivers, one of the dirtiest cities in America, one of America's cultural centers, a city fading with the demise of the iron and steel industry, a sports town whose Steeler, Pirate, and Penquin fans are unequaled, an automobile driver's nightmare, a city whose striking skyline as one exits the Fort Pitt Tunnels is unmatched, a city that has never joined the two party political system of its state and nation, a city made up of numerous small ethnic neighborhoods, a city where stealing cars has become a metropolitan hobby, a city with one of the nation's lower violent crime rates, a parking problem whose common solution involves two folding chairs placed on the street in front of a private dwelling, a city where perfect strangers smile, speak, and wish each other a good day, a congested downtown area which defies the stranger to find his way in a maze of one-way streets, a downtown area where one can walk to any desired destination, a city whose government is often subject to citizen ridicule and a city council often referred to as "the circus," but which at election time usually re-elects its incumbents, a city beginning to capitalize on its three rivers with regattas, river-front development, marinas, and restaurants, a city doomed to second class status in state government, always trailing behind the political might of Philadelphia, a photographer's paradise, with hills, hillside homes, skylines, and rivers.

Yes, Pittsburgh is a bit of all of these. Non-Pittsburghers listen, smile, and find it hard to believe Rand McNally's designation of the city as "the most livable in the United States" in 1985. They dismiss most of it as Madison Avenue purple prose and keep in their memory pictures of a dirty city taken during and after World War II when it frequently turned on its lights at midday. True Pittsburghers smile, go on loving their city, and are secretly a little happy that not too many people believe all the propaganda. They want Pittsburgh to thrive, but they do not want it to change too dramatically.

It is fascinating to read what others have said about Pittsburgh through the years—some derogatory, some laudatory, and some indifferent. All of them were probably sincere; all were affected by conditions at the time they made their statements. The most reassuring fact is that current assessments are on the positive side; Pittsburgh is gaining ground in terms of the public's perceptions, but it has a lot of its past to live down. Here are some descriptions of the city of Pittsburgh as seen by many different observers, some famous, others unknown, from 1754 to the present.

Pittsburgh

1754   George Washington, from his Williamsburg Journal

As I got down before the canoe, I spent some time in viewing the rivers, and the land in the Fork. which I think is extremely well situated for a fort, as it has the absolute command of both rivers. The land at the "Point" is 20 or 25 feet above the common surface of the water; and a considerable bottom of flat, well-timbered land all around it, very convenient for building. The rivers are each a quarter of a mile or more across, and run very near at right angles. The Allegheny bearing NE and the Monongahela SE. The former of the two is very rapid and swift running water; the other deep and still, without any perceptible fall.

November 19 to 21, 1781   James Kenny's Journal

A young man was ordered by Colonel Bouquet to number all ye
dwelling houses without ye fort and records that there were above
one hundred houses. Colonel Bouquet's papers give the number of
houses as 160 and the number of people living in Pittsburgh as
332...

Kenny predicted that "if ye place continues to increase near this
manner it must soon be very large which seems likely to me."

1783   Dr. Johann Schoepf, a German doctor and early city visitor

The town consisted of perhaps sixty wooden houses and cabins in
which live something more than 100 families. The buildings were
neither elaborate nor were they beautiful; they were simple
structures made of unsquared logs. The streets before them were
unpaved, dirty, littered with refuse, with dogs and hogs roaming
through the mire. On rainy days one waded through the mud; in dry
weather the dust rose in clouds.

People in Pittsburgh. who gained their living hitherto by farming
and trafficking in skins and furs appeared not only idle; so much so
that they are recalcitrant when given work and an opportunity to
earn money, for which, however they hanker. People here do not
grow rich by industry and fair prices but prefer rather to deal
extortionately with strangers and travelers; and shunning work
charge the more for it, their comfortable sloth being interrupted.

May, 1784   Thomas Vickroy, an assistant to surveyor George Woods
          of Bedford

The first thing we did was to circumscribe the ground where we
intend to lay out the town. We began where Grant Street now is, on
the bank of the Monongahela, and proceeded down the
Monongahela, according to the meanderings of the river, to its
junction with the Allegheny River. Up to Washington St. than to
Grant's Hill, thence along the hill to the place of its beginning.

December 17, 1784   *Arthur Lee, a member of a celebrated*
                            Virginia family, and one of three
                            commissioners sent to Fort McIntosh to
                            negotiate a treaty with the Indians

Pittsburgh is inhabited almost entirely by Scots and Irish, who live in paltry log houses, and are as dirty as in the north of Ireland or even Scotland. There is a great deal of small trade carried on; the goods being brought at the vast expense of 45 shillings per cwt. from Philadelphia and Baltimore. They take in the shops, money, wheat, flour, and skins. There are in the town four attorneys, two doctors, and not a priest of any persuasion, nor church, nor chapel so that they are likely to be damned without benefit of clergy. The place, I believe, will never be considerable.

About 1765   *John Wilkins, later one of the city's foremost*
                      citizens

"In Pittsburgh all sort of wickedness was carried on to excess and there was no morality or regular order."

August 19, 1786   *Hugh Henry Brackenridge, Princeton-educated*
                           lawyer

As I pass along, I may remark that this new country is in general highly prolific; whether it is that the vegetable air, if I may so express it, constantly perfumed with aromatic flavor, and impregnated with salts drawn from the fresh soil, is more favorable to the production of men and other animals than decayed grounds. There is not a more delightful spot under the heaven to spend any of the summer months than at this place. Nor is the winter season enjoyed with less festivity than in more populous and cultivated towns. The buildings warm, fuel abundant, consisting of the finest coals from the neighboring hills, or of ash, hickory, or oak brought down in rafts from the river. In the meantime, the climate is less severe at this place than on the other side of the mountain.

It may be observed that at the junction of these two rivers, until 8 o'clock of summer mornings a light fog is usually incumbent; but it is of a salutary nature, inasmuch as it consists of vapor, not exhaled from stagnant water but which the sun of the preceding day had extracted from trees and flowers, and in the evening had sent back in dew, with it rising from a second sun in fog, and becoming of aromatic quality, it is experienced to be helpful.

This town in future time will be the place of great manufactory, indeed the greatest on the continent or perhaps in the world. Our distance from either of the oceans will make the importation of heavy articles very expensive. The manufacture of them will become more an object here than elsewhere. It is prospect of this that men of reflection which renders the soil of this place so valuable.

February 19, 1788   *David Reddick, who laid out the future town of Allegheny, in a letter to Benjamin Franklin*

On Tuesday last I went with several other gentlemen to fix on the spot for laying out the town opposite Pittsburgh, and at the same time took a general view of the tract, and found it inferior to expectations, although I had been no stranger to it. There is some pretty low ground on the rivers Ohio and Alleghenia (sic) but there is but a small proportion of it dry land which appears anyway valuable, either for timber or soil; but especially for soil, it abounds with high hills and deep hollows, almost inaccessible to a surveyor. I'm of the opinion that if the inhabitants of the Moon are capable of receiving the same advantages from the earth as we do from their world, I say if it be so, this same far-famed tract of land would afford them a variety of lunar spots, not unworthy the eye of a philosopher. I cannot think that 10 acre lots on such pits and hills will profitably meet with purchasers, unless, like a pig in a poke, it be kept out of view.

1807   The Stranger in America, *a book published in London*

"Pittsburgh is a well built town, has a swanky appearance, and contains about five hundred houses."

1816   *David Thomas, a traveler through the Western country in his journal*

Pittsburgh is gloomy, because dark, dense smoke rises from every part, and a hovering cloud of vapor obscures the view. Wooden buildings, interspersed with those of brick, mar the beauty of its streets; and as few of these are paved, mud in showery weather becomes abundant.

1817   Cramer's Navigator

Life in Pittsburgh is drab; the character of the people is that of enterprising and persevering industry; every man to his business is the prevailing maxim, there is therefore little time devoted to amusements or to the cultivation of refined social pleasures. Luxury, pomp, and parade are scarcely seen, there are, perhaps, not more than one or two carriages in the place. There is a public academy, but not in a flourishing state, where the Latin and Greek classics are taught. The amusements of these industrious people are not numerous, a few balls during the winter season; there is also a small theater where a company from the Eastern cities sometimes performs.

1818   Darby's Emigrants Guide for 1818

"Pittsburgh is by no means a pleasant city to a stranger. The constant volume of smoke preserve the atmosphere in a continued cloud of coal dust."

1828   *Hall's* Letters from the West

"The city lay beneath me enveloped in smoke; the clang of hammers resounded from its numerous manufactories; yet behind me were all of the silent, soft attractions of rural sweetness."

1828   *Anne Royall, after her first visit to Pittsburgh, America's first woman travel writer*

Pittsburgh filled me with dread. Volumes of smoke, fires, thundering steam factories, and the fumes of furnaces. All the houses are colored quite black with the smoke; the interior of the houses are still worse; carpets, chairs, walls, furniture—all black with smoke. No such thing as wearing white; the ladies mostly dress in black with a cap or white ruff. Put on clean in the morning, ruffs are tinged black by bed-time; the ladies are continually washing their faces. The smoke is most annoying to the eyes, and everything has a very gloomy, doleful appearance. Soon after I arrived, the town's water pipes burst and mud covered the paved sidewalks. Walking was slippery and arduous, too great for a female, especially one of years and lame. But during the whole of my visit to the factories, I never saw an instance of intoxication.

March 20, 1842   *Charles Dickens,* American Notes

Our boat passed through a long aqueduct across the Allegheny River, and we emerged upon that ugly confusion of the backs of buildings and crazy galleries and stairs, which always abuts on water, whether it be river, sea, canal, or ditch, and were in Pittsburgh.

1860   *Washington Roebling, a son of John Roebling, builder of several of Pittsburgh's bridges*

"The city is making improvements with feverish haste; every day someone commences to tear down an old house and put up a new one with an iron front."

1860   *An unknown newspaper editor in the city*

"Life in Pittsburgh is of a social, genial cast, the stiffness and formality of larger cities not being felt in our more hospitable community. Our people resemble, in some respects, more those of a borough than a city."

1861   *J. Ernest Wright, an early American writer*

"...the blackest, dirtiest, grimiest city in the United States."

1862   *Anthony Trollope, English writer*

Blackest place I ever saw. At my hotel everything was black; not black to the eye, for the eye teaches itself to discriminate colors even when loaded with dirt, but black to the touch. On coming out of a tub of water my foot took an impress from the carpet exactly as it would have done had I trod bare footed on a path laid with soot. I thought that I was turning negro upwards, until I put my wet hand upon the carpet, and found that the result was the same. And yet the carpet was green to the eye—a dull, dingy green—but still green.

1868   *James Parton, an American biographer*

"Every street appears to end in a big, black cloud. Pittsburgh is smoke, smoke, smoke—everywhere smoke—by night, it was Hell with the lid taken off."

1871   *A reporter for* Harper's Weekly

Pittsburgh—the dense volumes of black smoke pouring from the hundreds of furnaces, the copious showers of soot, the constant rumbling of ponderous machinery, the clatter of wagons laden with iron—the fiery lights stream forth, looking angrily and fiercely up toward the heavens.

1883   *Willard Glazier*

"Pittsburgh is a smokey, dismal city at its best; at its worst nothing darker, dingier, or more dispiriting can be imagined."

1890   *Andrew Carnegie in a letter to William Gladstone, Queen Victoria's Prime Minister, shortly after he had given Carnegie Institute to the city*

Pittsburgh is the smokiest place in the world; your Sheffield is clean by comparison. It has never been anything but a center of materialism; it has never had a fine hall for music, nor a museum, nor an art gallery, nor public library, and yet the result proves that there has been lying dormant the capacity to enjoy all of these.

1892   *Hamlin Garland, a noted American writer*

"...horrible streets, poor buildings, soot and dirt; its saloons are many and its club and reading rooms few."

1896   *Harry Castle—while delivering the keynote speech at the National Convention of the Prohibition Party, meeting in Pittsburgh at Exposition Hall*

"I know of no other city with darker skies and brighter men and women, with dirtier hands and cleaner hearts, with narrow crookeder streets, and broader straighter hospitality."

1906   *From a publication of the Russell Sage Foundation, Homestead*

One third of all who die in Pittsburgh die without having anything to say about it. That is, they die under five years of age. One fourth of all who die, die without having anything to say about anything. That is, they die under one year of age. Most of these deaths are preventable, being the outcome of conditions which, humanly speaking, have no right to exist.

1908   Researcher for Russell Sage Foundation

The common laborer in and around the mills works seventy-two hours a week...The congested condition of most of the plants in Pittsburgh adds to the physical discomforts for an out-of-doors people; while their ignorance of language and of modern machinery increases the risk. How many of the Slavs, Lithuanians, and Italians are injured in Pittsburgh in one year is not known. No reliable statistics are compiled; in their absence people guess. When I mentioned a plant that had a bad reputation to a priest, he said, "Oh, that is a slaughterhouse; they kill them there every day." I quote him not for accuracy, but to show how the rumors circulate and are real to the people themselves.

1908   Willa Cather, a renowned American novelist

"Pittsburgh was even more vital, more creative, more hungry for culture than New York. Pittsburgh was the birthplace of my writing."

1910   Herbert Spencer, an English philosopher

"A month in Pittsburgh would justify anyone in committing suicide."

1917   President Theodore Roosevelt

There is no more typical American city than Pittsburgh. And Pittsburgh, by its Americanism, gives a lesson to the entire United States. Pittsburgh has not been built up by talking about it; your tremendous concerns were built by men who actually did the work. You make Pittsburgh ace high when it could have been deuce high—There is not a Pittsburgh man who did not earn his success through his deeds.

1920   *Henry L. Mencken—an American writer and critic*

Here was the very heart of industrial America, the center of its most lucrative and characteristic activity, the boast and pride of the richest and grandest nation ever seen on earth—and here was a scene so dreadfully hideous, so intolerably bleak and forlorn that it reduced the whole aspiration of man to a macabre and depressing joke. Here was wealth beyond computation, almost beyond imagination, and here were human habitations so abominable that they would have disgraced a race of alley cats. I am not speaking of mere filth. One expects steel towns to be dirty. What I allude to is the unbroken and agonizing ugliness, the sheer revolting monstrousness of every house in sight.

1926   *Hervey Allen, a Pittsburgh poet and novelist*

"When I left Pittsburgh about ten years ago, I recall they were discussing a subway. I see they are still talking it, and are no nearer bringing it about. Good old Pittsburgh; hasn't changed much." (The PAT subway opened in the late 1980s.)

1920s   *Mary Roberts Rinehart, American novelist who lived in Pittsburgh and made the city the setting for her novels*

"I have wonderful memories of Pittsburgh, of learning to ride horseback, of skating on the pond in a North Side park. Of wagons clattering on cobblestone streets, of the high walls of the penitentiary near my home."

1935   *Haniel Long was a teacher at Carnegie–Mellon University. In 1935, Long was forced to move to Santa Fe because of the smoke of the city.*

There is something very moving, emotionally, about Pittsburgh. This is true and explains why Pittsburgh is a creative place. It is par excellence the city of effort and suffering and hope. It is strange that

I espouse a city that I cannot love; I suppose my love is for the people who have been caught in her meshes, and the people who are trying to make her better.

1940s   *Marcia Davenport, the author of* Valley of Decision, *one of the best known novels whose setting is the city of Pittsburgh, whose descriptions of steel making are considered among the best in American literature.*

"All the mill whistles used to blow together in one raucous, ear-splitting blast at midnight on New Year's Eve, filling the valleys of the two rivers with echoes that could be heard all over Pittsburgh."

1940s   *Frank Lloyd Wright, renowned American architect*

When asked by the city fathers how he would improve the place, he snapped, "Abandon it."

1960s   *Johnny Carson, a host of the NBC "Tonight Show"*

"Pittsburgh is kind of like Newark without the cultural advantages."

1983   *Samuel R. Ohler, a Pittsburgh historian*

Pittsburgh has certain characteristics common to all cities. It contains slums, semi-deserted areas, beautiful residential neighborhoods, other neighborhoods on the way up or down, suburbs as diversified as the intercity, beautiful parks, activities too numerous to mention, bad air sometimes, dirty streets, and potholes in the spring. Pittsburgh was and is a bona fide "melting pot"…most citizens are a friendly lot and take pride in their homes and neighborhoods. Our climate is usually very moderate and many days are enjoyed by thousands. It would seem that Pittsburgh has "everything" except salt air and a beach.

| 1986 | *Franklin Tokar, an architectural and urban historian in* Pittsburgh, An Urban Portrait |

The chief distinction of Pittsburgh is not smoke, and it never was. There has been no major smoke in Pittsburgh for thirty years, and even when smoke hung thick over the city for a century it was accepted stoically and almost affectionately as the life-sign of its prosperity. Instead, the chief distinction of Pittsburgh is work. As surely as Paris represents glamour, Dallas wealth and Rome the "dolce vita," so Pittsburgh stands for industry and production.

It gave the world its first mass-produced oil, steel, aluminum, and glass; it created the world's first hygienically packaged food, and supplied AC electricity to supplement DC in every corner of the globe. The list of notables in science and the arts include: Stephen Foster, John Roebling, Mary Cassatt, Gertrude Stein, Mary Roberts Rinehart, George S. Kaufmann, Rachel Carson, Willa Cather, Martha Graham, Gene Kelly, Jonas Salk, "Mister Rogers," and Andy Warhol. It gave the world Andrew Carnegie's several thousand public libraries, Jonas Salk's polio vaccine, George Ferris's ferris wheels, Stephen Foster's songs, Heinz's ketchup, and Rockwell's space shuttle.

...one of the delightful cities in America, with a setting of three rivers and a score of hills that rivals the topography of San Francisco. Cohesiveness is the key to Pittsburgh's social life as well as its economic endeavors. It has one of the highest rates of owner-occupied homes in the nation, a conservative work ethic, a still more conservative family life, a low crime rate, and a passion for sports. It has spawned fine quarterbacks—Namath, Unitas, Montana, and Marino; fine musicians—Oscar Levant, Lena Horne, Henry Mancini, Billy Eckstine, Errol Garner, Art Blakey, Perry Como, Byron Janis, and Lorin Maazel.

1985   *Rand McNally's* Places Rated Almanac

Pittsburgh, Pennsylvania, which ranked fourth in the first edition of *Places Rated Almanac*, has climbed to the top of the list in this second edition. Many people who perhaps have a stereotyped and outdated image of a smoky, noisy, blast furnace of a city may be surprised at this. But Pittsburgh shows great strength in the social indicators and is remarkably like a small town in many respects. despite its great size. Values are traditional and simple, neighborhoods tight but friendly.

Pittsburgh's strengths lie as much in what it doesn't have as in what it does...Pluses—across the board strength in nearly all categories; excellent rankings in education, health care, and the arts. Minuses—middling rankings for housing costs and economic indicators.

January 9, 1989   *Brenden Gill, the columnist of "The Sky Line," in* The New Yorker

If Pittsburgh were situated somewhere in the heart of Europe, tourists would eagerly journey hundreds of miles out of their way to visit it. Its setting is spectacular; between high bluffs, where the Monongahela River and the Allegheny River meet to form the Ohio. Driving in from the airport, one gains a first startling glimpse of the city at the end of a highway tunnel through Mt. Washington; a conventionally pretty rural landscape suddenly gives way to the whole sweep of the city, with its bridges and skyscrapers.

Over two centuries Pittsburgh forged its vigorous and not uncantankerous personality little by little out of the sum of a score of separate neighborhoods. Settled by generations of immigrants of disparate ethnic backgrounds, (Poles, Czechs, Italians, Irish, Germans), these neighborhoods managed to create a city that could be perceived at once as a closely knit, inimitable American presence....Indeed, the ideal population of a city today is about that of Pittsburgh, and the ideal area of a city is—again like that of Pittsburgh, which is fifty-five square miles—comparatively small.... What a New Yorker especially responds to in Pittsburgh is a sense of the city as an organism whose many parts have been made to function as they were designed to. The note struck in Pittsburgh is not one of hysteria but one of equilibrium. Pittsburgh is psychically an open city, one that people walk about in without dread.

November 26, 1989　　　　　*Vince Rause, "Pittsburgh Cleans Up Its Act" in* The New York Times Sunday Magazine

In the late 70s and early 80s the steel industry...virtually disappeared...90,000 jobs were lost..unemployment soared to over 14%... economic collapse seemed imminent. But the collapse never came. Instead, in a swift and dramatic economic restructuring, the city managed to sidestep catastrophe.

Today its unemployment rate has dipped to 5%; it has sustained a quality of life that gained national recognition in 1985 when Rand McNally's *Places Rated Almanac* named it "America's Most Livable City."...It is now one of America's most promising post-industrial experiments. Pittsburgh is the home of America's first public television station; it produced a dazzling array of jazz talent; it boasts of a 71–year–old grandmother Mayor; it has a thriving cultural life, with highly regarded museums of art and natural history, a world class symphony orchestra, strong opera and ballet companies, and a profusion of smaller galleries and performing arts companies.

It is by far the safest, most affordable city in the nation. Its median housing price is the lowest of twenty-five metropolitan areas; today it is clean and attractive. One Midwestern columnist wrote that, "The Pittsburgh waterways, the mountains, the trees reminded me of a cross between Venice and San Francisco.

November 26, 1989   *Harvey Adams, Jr., the President of the*
                                       Pittsburgh Branch of the National
                                       Association for the Advancement of
                                       Colored People, as quoted in The New
                                       York Times

"Pittsburgh is not a healthy environment for blacks. We are being destroyed here. We are an endangered species."

November 26, 1989   *Byrd Brown, a defeated candidate for*
                                       mayor of Pittsburgh

The unemployment rate in black communities is catastrophic; we have areas that have been devastated by crime and drugs and the city's neglect. Racial conflict is not outspoken; it's a very subtle thing. But its there. When I was campaigning everywhere I went, people were very polite and gracious. I'd give a speech in a white area and sometimes I'd get more applause than the white candidates. And I did very well in approval polls; I think I even won a couple of them, but when you check the election results, you'll see that in one white district, out of about 14,000 votes, I got 241. This statistic shows that no matter how subtle we are about it, we're just as racially polarized as any other city. Look, I love Pittsburgh, but if you love something, you've got to realize when its sick. The fact of the matter is that the black community is not sharing in the white community's success. The disparity is truly unacceptable and its got to change.

1980   *Mayor Sophie Masloff*

Pittsburgh works because we cooperate—the neighborhoods, the government, the universities, the corporations. I can call up the president of PPG or USX—these vast financial empires—and say, "Look,this is what I want to do. What do you think? Let's do this." We work together, and it gets done.

These quotations are not intended to be definitive. They were selected from a wide variety of sources. Some will irritate; some will please; but all of them represent someone's impression of the city of Pittsburgh. True Pittsburghers will take pride in the advances made by their city and will learn from past mistakes. Non-Pittsburghers need only come and judge the city for what it is today. The sources for the quotations are listed in the bibliographies for the various articles in the book.

Appendix A

Memories of an Old Resident: The Early 1900s

by Herbert Steinbrink as recorded by S. Trevor Hadley

The following is a transcript of a tape-recoded interview conducted with Herbert Steinbrink in the summer of 1987. Mr. Steinbrink was born on December 17, 1898, in the Hill District of the city of Pittsburgh. He was the son of Frank Steinbrink and Mary Reitz Steinbrink. Early in life his family moved to Mt. Washington in Pittsburgh. Mr. Steinbrink married Jean Herring of Shadyside, Pittsburgh. Mr. Steinbrink was a salesman for trucking and trailer companies. He lived in Minneapolis, Philadelphia, and New York City and later retired to Stonybrook, Long Island. In 1988, Mr. Steinbrink died in a tragic accident at his home. He always spoke with love of his boyhood home in Pittsburgh. This interview was conducted at his home in Stonybrook in the summer of 1987.

Trevor Hadley and his wife, Olive, were both present during the taping. Mr. Steinbrink was a cousin of Olive Hadley's, so frequently his responses were directed to her. The following is a transcript of the questions and the answers as given by Mr. Steinbrink.

Remember you told us about going down to old Exposition Park?

Yes, that was down at the end of Carson Street at the West End right near the Duquesne Heights Incline.

That was right down near the Ohio River?

It was just about opposite the Point. They had a beautiful building there. That's where Goldman and Sousa came with their bands, and people came from all over the state. Everytime Sousa or Goldman came, the place was crowded.

Was that on the south side of the Ohio River?

It was on the south side of the Ohio right near the base of the incline, where they came down. (This is an inaccurate memory of its location. The Exposition Buildings were opposite the Point, but they were first located on the North Side of the Allegheny River and later on the Point itself.)

What did they have there?

It was like a little Smithsonian Institution; they had a lot of things. They had shows and an iron building there. The New York City Fire Department had a display featuring the saving of peoples' lives in a burning building. It was all steel. They would set off a flame inside and the flames would be coming out all over the building, and the horses—regular big fire horses— would come in with the steam pumper up and pump water into the windows. They would get out a net, and people would jump into the net. It actually happened; they had it there for years. During one show, a girl was badly injured when she jumped from the building too soon, and the net was not properly placed to catch her.

When you were a boy, were most of the streets in downtown Pittsburgh paved?

Yes, downtown they were all paved. A trolley ran down there—a West End trolley. When I was a youngster, Grandview Avenue on Mt. Washington was not paved. I was a very narrow road; it had ditches in the road and only room for one carriage. If another carriage came from the opposite direction, you had to pull over into one of the niches in the road and let the other carriage pass. The only way we got to town was by the West End trolley. It started over at the top of the Castle Shannon incline; it came down on to Carson Street about a mile up from the Monongahela Incline. It came out on Bailey Avenue in Mr. Washington. It had a little coach arrangement for passengers, but it was primarily for commercial use.

When you were a boy, where there many automobiles in downtown Pittsburgh?

I can remember when there were no cars on the roads. There might have been one or two automobiles in the city. The first ones had a tiller, no steering wheel or gears.

How old were you then, Herbert?

Oh, about six or seven. I wanted to mention more about the West End car line. It went down to the end of Merrimac Street, down to Woodville Avenue, and than came out at the West End.

You mean Woodville Avenue which is now Route 51?

I think they changed it to Woodruff Street later. It was little more than a cowpath then. The Wabash Railroad came through there; there was an old tunnel there. I don't know what it is used for now.

Is that the tunnel they are using for the new Subway?

No, the Wabash tunnels were closed up. At one time they talked about using the tunnel, but they never did. I remember very distinctly we had a dentist in the West End; all of our activity at that time was in the West End. That trolley did finally get over to the Old Wabash Building in the city. It came up Carson Street and crossed a bridge into the city. I don't remember which bridge it used, but it ended up near the Wabash building; that's how we always got to the downtown. The Mt. Washington car line had not started yet.

Who lived in the Hill District when you were born?

Well, on Centre Avenue my father's brother had a store there. My father had a store there too. My mother and my uncle's mother would attend the store. My father would buy a whole carload of watermelons for Saturday night. They would sell them under a big canopy stretched over the sidewalk with a gaslight.

Was this all on Centre Avenue?

Yes, 1810 Centre. That was originally my grandmother's place. My dad bought the property and started a store there. He was very well known; he had all those German customers from all over the Hill District—it was known as the "Hill District Grocery Store." Many years later when I became a salesman for a motor truck company—working as a salesman—I ran into many people who knew my father. They would ask if I was any relation to Frank Steinbrink, who had the Hill District store. And I would say, "Yes, that was my father," and that would always start a conversation.

Who was the funeral director in the Hill District at the time, was that a relation?

That was William Reitz, my grandfather's brother. That was much earlier. You probably don't remember Flannary's Funeral Home—that was a big funeral home.

Herbert, were you born in Mt. Washington?

No, I was born on Center Avenue, over the store. My brother Carl was born there too. My sister, Ruth, was born after we moved to Mt. Washington. I don't remember just when we moved to Mr. Washington; I was just a kid.

How long did your father have the store on the Hill after you moved to Mt. Washington?

About five or six years.

Were the streets in the Hill District paved at that time?

Yes, all brick—a cable car ran up Wylie Avenue from Fifth Avenue; It finished up at Center Avenue. The Wylie Avenue car went in one direction, and the Center Avenue one the other. There were really two separate car lines.

When did your father get out of the grocery business?

I'm not sure, but I think the insurance company he sold for read the riot act to him and told him to get rid of the grocery business or get out of the insurance business. He decided to give up the grocery business. He never said why; I don't know why.

Did our grandparents move to Mt. Washington before your mother and father did?

Oh, yes. I think my father bought that land in Mr. Washington from grandfather. There was quite a family deal when my father built those five houses there. He built them next to my grandfather's and built them higher than grandpap's house, and that made him mad. They were at sword's ends for a while according to my mother.

How old were your parents when they moved to Mt. Washington?

I don't know; I was too young then to remember.

When our grandfather came from Germany, he worked as a cabinetmaker which was his trade in Germany; later according to the Pittsburgh Directories, he worked as a clerk. When he moved to the Hill, he opened a dairy and a store. Do you remember that?

I never knew where the store was located. My mother never mentioned where it was; she always talked about how hard she had it. She was the oldest in the family and was always in the store as a youngster waiting on trade. She worked in the store from early morning to late at night for many years.

They lived in the same building as the store, didn't they?

Yes. Uncle Bill's family lived in the back of the store on Center Avenue; they lived there for many years after our grandparents moved out. My mother lived there too; that's when I was born there. The day after I was born, the doctor who brought me into the world was killed in a buggy accident. I never got a birth certificate until many years later.

The people who lived on the Hill were pretty prosperous people then, weren't they?

The business section of the Hill was a very busy place in those days.

Where they lived – is that where the Civic Arena is now?

I don't know where the Civic Arena is; they lived five stores up from Roberts Street on Center Avenue.

Where did they get the milk for the dairy?

From farmers all over the area; milk wasn't pasteurized then.

How did they treat the milk?

They didn't; they just sold it raw—no tuberculin tests at that time. They just put it in five or ten gallon containers, and just used a dipper to fill the bottles. They then delivered milk all over the Hill.

When were you born, Herbert?

I was born in 1898 on the Hill. When we moved to Mt. Washington I remember that our house had a sign in the gable, saying "1889." When my father bought the house, that was the first thing he did—he took that sign out of there.

When you were a boy, were there many theaters downtown?

There was one movie house, the first in the United States, on Smithfield Street. The first movie I saw there was, "Tarred and Feathered," an Indian story. They had a fellow there with a player piano, and a fellow there knocking blocks together for the sound of hooves. People would clap like the dickens.

Were there a lot of stage shows then?

Yes, the old Opera House, the Lyceum, the Alvin—all the New York shows came then.

Was the Davis theater there then?

No, that came years later.

What about the Nixon?

It was there.

Where was it?

It was on 6th Avenue right around the corner from the Lutheran Church. Samson's had a beautiful building right there also—a funeral establishment. It was almost next door to the Nixon Theater. There was the Bijou, the Alvin; they all had shows.

Where was the Grand Opera House?

On Fifth Avenue; it ran from 5th to Diamond Streets. My father used to take us for ten cents to "peanut heaven" to see the vaudeville shows. The Opera House was on 5th, between Smithfield and Wood Streets—not quite the middle of the block.

Where was the Hotel Henry?

On Fifth Avenue, directly across from Kaufmann's. The Nixon was on Sixth, almost back back to back with the Hotel Henry. The thing that very few people talk about is the cutting of The Hump.

Tell us about that.

That was a great big mountain like at Grant and 6th. I remember it vividly; the first steam shovels I ever saw worked there and then they built the William Penn Hotel. The Hump was about 30 feet high up there and it extended from the William Penn Hotel to the old jail—you know where the jail is. There was a steep hill up from Smithfield Street; it was then cut down to where it is now. After it was cut, the William Penn was built.

My father told me that when they built some of those buildings, they ran into rivers. Is that right?

Yes, they had to pile many of them because of the water.

Did they ever drain that water out?

I don't know whatever became of it.

They claim there is still an underground river under the Point; that's supposed to supply the water for the fountains at the Point. That Hump you talk about, was it mainly soil or rock?

Mostly dirt.

What did they do with it?

They hauled it by horse and wagon for fill along the river, most of it to the North Side.

Were the street cars pulled by horses then?

No, not in my day. Horse cars had been gone for several years. They had trolley cars. Oh, I wanted to show you something in McCrory's Five and Ten in the Mall here in Stonybrook. There is a great big mural there as large as that wall of a Pittsburgh trolley car—you should see that. We'll have to make a special trip up there. It's the dirtiest thing, taken in the winter time—what a sight. Why they put up such a picture, I don't understand. Why would McCrory's do that?

Well, the McCrory family had Pittsburgh roots; I imagine that explains the connection. What else is in the picture?

The trolley cars had no glass in front then; the driver stood right out on an open platform—even in the winter time. They had great big coats; their faces were always so red. We'll have to make a special trip out there to see that. It's funny.

Where was Child's Restaurant?

It was catty-cornered from Kaufmann's. Campbell's Store was just a couple of stores down from that on the same side of the street. That's were Uncle John worked.

Was Frank and Seder's there then?

No, it was on Smithfield Street right where the first movie theater was—the first in the world. There is still a placard there for the first movie house. The Warner brothers who worked in Kaufmann's watched men from New Castle going in and out of the movie house, and decided to open one in New Castle. That's how they got started in the movie business. I don't know who started the first movie house in Pittsburgh; everyone thought it would be a flop. No one would invest any money in it; there weren't any movies to show then.

You were talking about department stores—

Frank and Seder's wasn't there then. McCreary's was there on the corner of Wood and Sixth. Gimbels wasn't there. There was Ike and Edgar Kaufmann's; there was another Kaufmann who left and started the Kaufmann and Baer Store where Gimbels was located for many years. They built a nice store—they broke away from Kaufmann's and had a store there for several years. In fact, I have a watch my mother gave me that she bought there. Horne's is an old store; it was there then and Boggs and Buhl was on the North Side. Pittsburgh was known for its department stores; it had a nationwide reputation for its department stores.

Were the rivers busy then?

Yes—very busy. A river captain lived right next door to us. He plied between Pittsburgh and New Orleans. He would be gone for about six weeks at a time. They lived in the middle house that my father built.

Were most boats excursion or commercial boats?

Both – they would take passengers and cargo. At the wharf they would have a long runway—30 feet long—where horse and buggies could disembark; they had a big crane there. I remember we went to get a pony that was shipped in by boat. It was a big white one and had to be blinded to get it off the boat. It was a nice pony, but kind of old. My friend's uncle shipped him the pony from Wellsburg, Ohio. They built a stable for it.

How old were you when you moved to Mt. Washington?

I was a baby. My father was building the houses then. One Easter they came up to see how the project was going. They had a horse and buggy. My father had just bought a house on Grandview Avenue. There was a picture in the paper recently of this same house that some doctor had just bought. It was an Easter Sunday, and while my mother and father were looking at the houses, there was a big windstorm that blew the steeple off the Catholic Church just up the street from the house he had bought. The storm also blew down some trees. My mother said she would never live in that house because it sat right on the brink of the hill. It is located right where McArdle Roadway starts down the hillside. My father could not convince her that it was safe; he couldn't change her mind, so they sold that house and later moved into one they were building.

The one they sold was a beautiful house; It had two living rooms, a big central hall, overlooking the city—a glass enclosure in the back. I used to play with a boy who lived in that house; I practically lived in that house as a kid. Today that view is priceless, but in those days you got so used to looking at that view, that you never looked at it. You never had any idea that it was such a marvelous scene from that hilltop there. You got sick of looking at it; the river and the buildings were so dirty.

There was a blast furnace right at the base of the hill. It was on Carson Street right below the house I am talking about. I don't know the name of the mill. We used to watch them pouring ingots out of the blast furnace; you could see it from Grandview Avenue. It was a great big mill; a large tonnage of pig iron came out of there everyday about 4 o'clock in the afternoon.

The neighbors used to run around shouting, "They're pouring down there; hurry and get your clothes in; close the windows. Everybody would run and close all their windows. The wind would blow that dirt up the hill; it was terrible—yellow dirt and smoke. People breathed that stuff every day —it's a wonder they didn't die early of black lung or something—but they seemed to live to a pretty ripe age.

What other relatives lived on Mt. Washington?

Uncle John lived up there for 12 or 15 years at least. Uncle Charlie lived on Merimac Street, then moved to Belonda Street.It was a popular street at that time; that's where Charlie lived when he had the hardware store. There was a man by the name of Shannon who made pipe elbows for Bindley's Hardware. They built a big shed on the corner in back of the little house on Amabel Street. They sold all their stove pipe to Bindley's Hardware in downtown Pittsburgh. Uncle Charlie made a deal to make all the elbows for Bindley's Hardware and hired Shannon to make them. Uncle Charlie and your dad built the shed.

Do you remember my Dad's store?

Oh—sure—they both worked in the store for several years, then your Dad began to do roofing business on the side. They operated the store for ten years.

My father then worked for the Pennsylvania Railroad; they fired my father for organizing a union. My father had a little old typewriter, called a Molle, which he said was the only thing he ever got out of the railroad. Do you remember that?

I remember that your Dad worked for the railroad; I was about ten years old. I remember that Carl's wagon axle broke and your Dad took it to the railroad shop to fix it. Every week we would ask him about it, and he would say that they were not allowed to do such work anymore at the shop, and he was afraid to bring it home. He said he would put it down his pant leg some day and bring it home, and that is what he did. Uncle Charlie also worked at the railroad; they had a hard time then because they ran out of money. Charlie got early retirement because he got a piece of steel in his eye. I guess he didn't really retire early; they just gave him an easier job.

What was my Dad's store in Mt. Washington like?

It was a nice long store with about 3,000 square feet of floor space— two nice front windows. It was all renovated before they moved in—all up to date—a modern cash register with a big crank—it kept account of every sale by category. They built a balcony in the back and had an office girl there for several years. Her name was Skerball, a very nice girl, who took care of all the books. Then your Dad started to contract roofing jobs and Charlie took care of the store. Your Dad did the outside work; they had quite a business.

How far did Pittsburgh extend out into the South Hills in those days?

It went to Sheradan on one side; Carrick was a separate borough then. At that time Pittsburgh tried to bring all of Allegheny County into the city just as Philadelphia did with its area, but it never worked because they saw what was happening in New York City. New York was taking in all its boroughs, Bronx, Staten Island, etc. People had voted it in thinking that they were getting a better deal, but it turned out they were just used. The New York boroughs did not do as well as when they were separate. That discouraged the citizens of Allegheny County form approving it. Everybody at the time thought it was going to be approved, but they were fooled. When the people saw what had happened in New York and Philadelphia, they refused to be caught in the same mess.

Where did your grandfather have his greenhouse?

Right in the back of the house; it was a nice one too. It was just a hobby, not a business. He gave geraniums away; he grew beautiful geraniums. On Memorial Day he would give them to the schools to take to the cemeteries for the Civil War veterans. George Durcker on Amabel St. would deliver them to the schools for him. He would wrap them all in paper with soil still on the roots. They would pack them in boxes and take them to Prospect School and to Duquesne Heights School. The school kids would take them and plant them at the cemeteries.

How about this stovepipe business?

That's when they got into the stovepipe business. They would make hundreds of them; wire them together in groups of four; then a wagon would come and deliver them to the Bindley Hardware.

Where was the Bindley Hardware?

It was downtown near 7th Avenue—took in half a block. Five or six blocks from Liberty Street—right downtown not too far from Union Station. That reminds me of a true story—A friend of a fellow on the South Side told this fellow where he could get a job. He went to the place and talked to the owner about working for him. The owner asked him if he belonged to the union. "No" he said, "I don't belong to the union." The owner said, "Well, you'll have to join the union; everyone here goes to the union." The fellow reported to work, worked only about an hour and disappeared; they missed him. Finally, an hour later, he came back. They asked him where he had been. He said that, "I had to go to the bathroom so I was told that I had to go to the Union Station."

The Bindley Hardware was originally up in the Hill. It was a builders' hardware and a wholesale hardware. They did a tremenduous business. They had an electric truck, one of the first in Pittsburgh. It didn't go very fast, no faster than you could walk. It was a great big truck.

Where did the Pirates play baseball then?

Over on the North Side—Exposition Park—near where the Three
Rivers Stadium is now. People used to line up on Mt. Washington with
telescopes; there would be a line of people there every day. They could see
who was at bat; this was the days of Honus Wagner, the same people every
day with field glasses and telescopes. They would rest them on the fence
and they would announce the score. The Pirates were one of the charter
teams in the National League—started about 1860.

What else do you remember about Mt. Washington?

There is no Mt. Washington carline now; they run buses now. I was in
school when the first trolley car went by; they let us all go up to the
windows to watch the first trolley. They had a fancy car for the use of the
executives—a beautiful looking car—it always seemed to have a lot of
politicians in it. All the inclines were operating then; they were there long
before the trolleys. Everybody used them; we always used them because we
could get to town much faster than by trolley. We always used the
Monongahela Incline. It cost 2 $1/2$¢ a ride; you could ride 60 times for a
$1.25. You paid a nickel if you didn't have a ticket. If you forgot your
ticket, the conductor would say bring it tomorrow and next day he would
take two tickets out of it. Dewalt, who was the superintendent of the
Inclined Plane Co., was a member of our church. He fought the plans for
the McArdle Roadway and urged me to vote against its construction. He
said it would never work; that they would never be able to build a roadway
there. It was opened in 1928.

When did they build the trolley tunnels?

About 1906. The Liberty Tubes were built about 1924 or 1925.

How much property did our grandfather own up on the Hill?

All those buildings they owned ran together, with common walls—a
stable behind it and a house behind it also. They had a dairy in the store and
later they lived in a separate house. After grandfather moved to Mt.
Washington, Uncle Will lived in the house. Uncle Will Steinbrink was a
watchmaker who went into business with my father. My father owned a lot
of property on the Hill, most of it was taken when they built the Project. He
had properties on Kirkpatrick St., Wylie Avenue, Shaffer Street, Sola

250

Street —some looked down over Baum Boulevard. He had a nice brick house on Wylie Avenue, another house on Wylie, four houses on Shaffer, a house near where Uncle Will lived, and a house on Duff right behind it. Then he bought all the properties up on Mt. Washington.

In those days did everyone pay cash for everything in the department stores?

Everything was cash; there was no credit. They had cash boys in the stores. When you bought something you went to a counter. The clerk would put it in a tube and it would go to the cashier. In many stores they used cash boys who would carry your money over to the cashier, and then they would run the change back to your clerk. The only store that offered credit was Pickerings Department Store—they had a special deal—they had a slogan, "Let Pickerings Feather Your Nest."

Where was Pickerings?

Not in the heart of the city—somewhere near Union Station—quite a big store, the only store I knew that would sell on credit. For under $100 they would sell you a carpet and all the furniture needed for one room.

What were the street lamps like?

They were gas lights; a guy would come around with a ladder and light them every night with a gasoline blow torch. Arc lights were installed later. A fellow would come along with a big bag of cylinders—each about eight inches long—they had to renew the lamps about every eight months. He would drop the globe and replace the carbon cylinders. Then the incandescent bulb came along. That was a big saving—they didn't have to replace the carbon filament.

Do you remember the first radio broadcast in Pittsburgh?

Oh—yes, Elizabeth Graff, your cousin, was one of the first people to sing on the radio. KDKA used to go get her when she lived in Bellevue, and bring her by Model T Ford to the studio in East Pittsburgh. She sang there for three or four months, one of the first to do so.

When you were a boy, was East Liberty a thriving section of the city?

Very nice—Highland and Penn Avenues were important streets. The business section was all nice stores; Shadyside was a nice section with nice homes. The main line of the railroad ran through there; now it is the East

251

Busway. Jean lived near the Graham mansion. Her family opened a cleaning establishment. They had two acres of ground, a big stable, five horses—her father had a small interest in the business. The owner was a conductor on the Pennsylvania Railroad. He met one of the Arbuthnots, a daughter, on the train and eventually married her. The family was very wealthy. They were in the high society crowd, very snobbish. The family disowned her for a while, but finally accepted the marriage. Arbuthnot and Stevens owned a big store in Pittsburgh; later they were bought out by Horne's.

Some time later they went on a world tour. They had three children— a daughter and two boys—one later became president of the Colonial Trust Co. On the world tour, the wife died in Egypt of some disease. The Arbuthnot family took the children and the husband was left alone with lots of money. He had horses up at Schenley Oval; he had a couple of sulkies— a Scotsman—he spent a lot of time at the Oval. He began spending too much money, playing the horses, and finally went broke. He had a hard time for a while. They had a good cleaning business—big fiber boxes for the clothes—800 clients—they would press, clean, and repair—replace buttons, etc.—it was thriving business.

What was Grandfather Reitz like?

Grandfather Reitz didn't like chilren very well. He had a beautiful grape arbor behind the house and a beautiful garden. People used to come from miles around to look at it. I remember Tom, my friend, and I decided to get some grapes after school. I crawled up and began handing them down to Tom. Grandpa grabbed my pants and pulled me down. Grandma saw him and bawled him out something terrible. I knew Grandma's house as well as I knew my own. It had a large porch, with windows down to the floor. The first thing my father did was take those windows out and remove the date sign on the gable.

Selected Sources

Chapter 1: Whatever Happened to Grant's Hill and The Hump?

Alberts, Robert C. *The Shaping of the Point*. Pittsburgh: University of Pittsburgh Press, 1980.

Baldwin, Leland D. *Pittsburgh: The History of a City*. Pittsburgh: University of Pittsburgh Press, 1938.

Brackenridge, Hugh Henry. *Recollections of Persons and Places in the West*. Pittsburgh, 1868.

Dahlinger, Charles W. *Pittsburgh: A Sketch of the Early Social Life*. New York: G. P. Putnam, 1916.

Grant's Hill: Center of the Pittsburgh Dream. Pittsburgh: Union Savings Bank, 1939.

Grant's Hill in Indian Days. Pittsburgh: Union Savings Bank, 1936.

Picturesque Pittsburgh and Allegheny. Pittsburgh: 1898.

Pittsburgh Dispatch. August 1899; May 6, 1912; May 7, 1912.

Pittsburgh Post. April 5, 1912; April 6, 1912; March 26, 1912; October 12, 1916; April 8, 1909; January 1, 1914.

Pittsburgh Post Gazette. August 20, 1961.

Pittsburgh Press. December 4, 1966.

Tokar, Franklin. *Pittsburgh: An Urban Portrait*. State College: Penn State University Press, 1986.

Chapter 2: Pittsburgh's Great Expositions

Baldwin, Leland D. *Pittsburgh: History of a City*. Pittsburgh: University of Pittsburgh Press, 1938.

Greater Pittsburgh. February, April, June, 1952.

Ohler, Samuel R. *PittsburGraphics*. Pittsburgh: S. R. Ohler, 1983.

Pittsburgh Dispatch. January 6, 1915.

Pittsburgh Post. July 23, 1913; August 17, 1913; August 30, 1913; January 7, 1914; January 9, 1914.

Pittsburgh Post Gazette. November 9, 1932; November 9, 1932.

Pittsburgh Press. January 7, 1912; January 19, 1915; December 20, 1929; April 11, 1934.

Pittsburgh Sun Telegraph. August 20, 1913; April 22, 1932.

Programs of the Annual Expositions. Pittsburgh: Pennsylvania Historical Society Library.

Story of Old Allegheny City. Pittsburgh: Western Pennsylvania Historical Society. 1941.

Tokar, Franklin. *Pittsburgh: An Urban Portrait.* State College: Penn State University Press, 1986.

Wilson, Erasmus. *Standard History of Pittsburgh, Pennsylvania.* Pittsburgh, 1898.

Chapter 3: Inclined to Disaster

Pittsburgh Press. April 6, 1909; April 7, 1909; April 8, 1909; February 15, 1929; February 17, 1930; October 7, 1953; November 29, 1953.

Chapter 4: The Great Pittsburgh Poetry Hoax

Bynner, Witter. "The Spectric Poets." *The New Republic.* November 18, 1916.

Hay, Sara Henderson. "The Spectric Hoax." *Carnegie Tech Quarterly.* 1961.

Kenner, Hugh. *The Poetry of Ezra Pound.* Norfolk: New Directions, 1951.

Morgan, Emanuel and Anne Knish. *Spectra: A Book of Poetic Experiments.* New York: Mitchell Kennerley, 1916.

Smith, William Jay. *The Spectra Hoax.* Middletown: Wesleyan University Press, 1961.

Smith, William Jay. "The Spectral Poets of Pittsburgh." *Horizon.* May 5, 1960.

Stein, Herbert G. "Hoax of Poetry School Recalled in New Book." *Pittsburgh Post Gazette The Forum.* Pittsburgh, 1916.

Williams, William Carlos. *Imaginations.* New York: New Directions Books, 1970.

Chapter 5: The Day the Pittsburgh Symphony Almost Went to Jail

Pittsburgh Post Gazette. April 21, 1927; April 22, 1927; April 23, 1927; April 24, 1927; April 25, 1927; April 26, 1927; April 29, 1927; May 2, 1927; May 3, 1927; May 10, 1927; May 11, 1927; May 12, 1927; November 10, 1927; November 11, 1927; November 26, 1927; November 30, 1927.

Chapter 6: Washington's Landing, Another Lost Opportunity?

Baldwin, Leland D. *Pittsburgh: The Story of a City.* Pittsburgh: University of Pittsburgh Press, 1938.

Church, Samuel H. *A Short History of Pittsburgh.* New York: DeVinne Press, 1908.

Conomikes, John D. TV Editorial by Station Manager. WTAE-TV, September 4–7, 1970.

Dahlinger, Charles W. "Old Allegheny." *Western Pennsylvania Historical Magazine.* 1918.

Herr, Fred R. "Herr's Island." *Western Pennsylvania Historical Magazine.* 1970.

Pittsburgh Post Gazette. May 17, 1973; October 23, 1975; December 10, 1980; December 11, 1980; December 10, 1981; February 19, 1983; October 13, 1983; October 24, 1983; September 10, 1986; September 24; 1986; October 14, 1986; October 24, 1987.

Pittsburgh Press. July 10, 1969; October 24, 1974; January 25, 1976; April 7, 1976; March 9, 1979; April 18, 1980; November 18, 1983; April 7, 1985; June 10, 1986; September 28, 1986; November 27, 1986; December 9, 1986; April 7, 1988.

Chapter 7: Pittsburgh's Forgotten Islands

Boucher, John N. *Century and a Half of Pittsburgh and Her People.* Pittsburgh: Lewis, 1908.

Fleming, George T. *History of Pittsburgh and Environs.* New York: American Historical Society, 1922.

Grant, B. A. "Missing Isle." *Pittsburgh Post Gazette*, n.d.

History of Allegheny County. Pittsburgh: 1889.

Kulamar, John. "Kilbuck Island." KDKA radio script. Pittsburgh: Pittsburgh Album, October 11, 1962.

Lorant, Stefan. *Pittsburgh: The Story of an American City.* Garden City: Doubleday, 1964.

Pittsburgh Post Gazette. October 15, 1927; December 8, 1949; December 17, 1949.

Pittsburgh Press. December 8, 1936.

Story of an American City. Pittsburgh: WPA Writer's Project, Allegheny Centennial Commission, 1941.

Wiley, George. *The Monongahela: The River and Its Region.* Butler, Pa.: Zeigler, 1937.

Chapter 8: The Strip and Its Colorful Personalities

McCabe, Adelaide Hunter. "The Strip: A District in Transition." *The Federator.* December 1940.

Pittsburgh Press. March 18, 1979; October 1, 1985; August 31, 1986.

Seibert, P. W. Address. Western Pennsylvania Historical Society, January 27, 1924. Western Pennsylvania Historical Society, 1926.

The Strip: A Socio-Religious Survey of a Typical Problem Section of Pittsburgh. Pittsburgh: Christian Social Service Union, July-September 1915.

Tokar, Franklin. *Pittsburgh: An Urban Portrait.* State College: Penn State University Press, 1986.

Chapter 9: Pittsburgh's Canal

Baldwin, Leland. *Pittsburgh: The Story of an American City.* New York: Doubleday, 1964.

Harper, Frank S. *Pittsburgh: Forge of the Universe.* New York: Doubleday, 1957.

Ilisevich, Robert D. and Carl K. Burkett, Jr. "The Canal Through Pittsburgh: Its Development and Physical Character." *Western Pennsylvania Historical Magazine.* 1985.

Killekelly, Sarah. *History of Pittsburgh: Its Rise and Progress.* Pittsburgh: Gordon Montgomery, 1906.

Klein, Theodore B. *The Canals of Pittsburgh and the System of Internal Improvement.* Harrisburg, Pa.: Harrisburg Press, 1901.

McCullough, Robert and Walter Leuba. *The Pennsylvania Main Line Canal.* Philadelphia, 1958.

Ohler, Samuel P. *PittsburGraphics.* Pittsburgh: S. R. Ohler, 1983.

Pittsburgh and the Pittsburgh Spirit. Addresses. Pittsburgh: Chamber of Commerce, 1928.

Pittsburgh Dispatch. August 16, 1911; August 27, 1911; May 16, 1915.

Pittsburgh Sun. November 21, 1916.

Reiser, Catherine. Pittsburgh, *Pittsburgh's Commercial Development.* 1951.

Shank, William H. *The Amazing Pennsylvania Canals.* York, 1960.

Wilson, Erasmus. *Standard History of Pittsburgh.* Pittsburgh, 1908.

Chapter 10: What Do You Think This Is, The Monongahela House?

Baldwin, Leland. *Pittsburgh: The Story of a City.* Pittsburgh: University of Pittsburgh Press, 1938.

Evans, Henry Oliver. *Iron Pioneer: Henry W. Oliver.* New York: E. F. Dutton, 1942.

Howard, John Tasker. *Ethelbert Nevin.* New York: Thomas Y. Crowell, 1935.

Killekelly, Sarah H. *History of Pittsburgh: Its Rise and Progress.* Pittsburgh: Gordon Montgomery, 1906.

Lorant, Stefan. *Pittsburgh: The Story of an American City.* New York: Doubleday, 1964.

Pittsburgh First. February 26, 1921.

Pittsburgh Gazette. April 21, 1941; February 14, 1961; February 15, 1961; May 17, 1980.

Pittsburgh Post. April 25, 1851; April 26, 1951.

Pittsburgh Press. January 23, 1920; October 17, 1920; March 8, 1938; September 10, 1936; October 4, 1969.

Pittsburgh Sun Telegraph. April 12, 1935; April 13, 1935; April 14, 1935; April 28, 1935; June 2, 1935.

Chapter 11: Central High School: Pittsburgh's First

Elkus, Leonora R., Ed. *Famous Men and Women of Pittsburgh.* Pittsburgh, 1981.

Fleming. George T. *Flem's Fancies: My High School Days.* Pittsburgh, 1904.

Fleming. George T. "The Old Central High School." *Gazette Times.* June 13, 1920.

"A Gals Day of a Half Century Ago." *Gazette Times.* October 10, 1920.

Kelly, G.H. *Handbook of Greater Pittsburgh.* 1895.

McCoy, W.D. *Educational Bulletin.* Pittsburgh Public Schools Publication, 1959.

"Old Central High School Building in Process of Being Razed." *Pittsburgh Teachers Bulletin.* November 8, 1946.

Class Reunion Programs for Central High School. Pittsburgh: Historical Society of Western Pennsylvania Archives.

Chapter 12: Controversy on The Mon—Was the Smithfield Street Bridge Too Low?

Bissell, Richard. *The Monongahela.* New York: Rinehart, 1949.

Havighurst, Walter. *Voices on the River.* New York: Macmillan, 1964.

Herbertson, E.T. *Pittsburgh Bridges.* Pittsburgh, 1924.

"Mr. Wiley, Grand Old Man of Journalism, Dies at 98." *Pittsburgh Post Gazette.* January 12, 1955.

"Newsman Celebrates 97th Birthday." *Pittsburgh Press.* January 25, 1955.

Pittsburgh Commercial Gazette. March 6, 1982; March 14, 1982.

Pittsburgh Sun Telegraph. April 24, 1940.

Seabright, Thomas B. *The Old Pike.* Orange: Green Tree Press, 1971.

Wiley, George T. *Monongahela: The River and Its Regions.* Butler: Zeigler, 1937.

Chapter 13: That Fabulous Nixon Theater

Gardner, Dorothea B. *History of the Nixon Theater.* Dissertation Thesis. Pittsburgh: University of Pittsburgh, 1959.

Lorant, Stefan. *Pittsburgh: The Story of An American City.* New York: Doubleday, 1964.

Pittsburgh Post Gazette. March 7, 1939; October 3, 1939; May 8, 1950.

Pittsburgh Press. July 16, 1941; April 17, 1950; February 29, 1976.

Pittsburgh Sun Telegraph. January 14, 1936; July 16, 1941; February 27, 1945; September 13, 1949; April 23, 1950; May 3, 1950.

Walszak, Ann Irene. "The World's Perfect Playhouse." *Carnegie Magazine.* March 1960.

Chapter 14: The Wabash Tunnel—To Nowhere or to Somewhere?

Beachler, Edwin. "Last Train Out of Wabash Tunnel Breaks Final Link into City's Traffic Gold Mine." *Pittsburgh Press.* February 8, 1948.

Hritz, Thomas. "Wabash Tunnel Nicely Done but Useless." *Pittsburgh Post Gazette.* October 3, 1974.

Miller, Anne Clark. "Old Houses and Estates in Pittsburgh." *Western Pennsylvania Historical Magazine.* April 1926.

Pittsburgh Press. April 3, 1947; May 13, 1947; July 16–21, 1947; August 4, 1975.

Walsh, Regis. "Wabash Tunnel Entombs Gould Jinx." *Pittsburgh Press.* April 14, 1958.

Chapter 15: John Ormsby: Pittsburgh's First Aristocrat

Coleberry, Harvey. "Unwritten History and Romance." Clipping file. Pittsburgh: Carnegie Library.

"History of the South Side." Clipping file. Pittsburgh: Carnegie Library.

Kamprad, Walter D. "John Ormsby; Pittsburgh's Original Citizen." *Western Pennsylvania Historical Magazine.* December 1940.

"Life of Pittsburg (sic) Pioneer Forms Subject Before D.A.R." *Pittsburgh Post.* December 20, 1908.

"Ormsby." Clipping file. Pittsburgh: Carnegie Library.

Ormsby, John. "Portion of Narrative of the Life of John Ormsby." Clipping file. Pittsburgh: Carnegie Library.

"The Romantic Life of John Ormsby." *Pittsburgh Dispatch.* August 8, 1908.

White, William. "Ormsby's Struggle." Clipping file. Pittsburgh: Carnegie Library.

Chapter 16: Anne Royall: America's First Feminist

Gazette Times. Pittsburgh: March 19, 1911.

History of Allegheny County, Pennsylvania. Chicago, 1889.

Jackson, George S. *Uncommon Scold: The Story of Anne Royall.* Boston: B. Humphries, 1937.

Porter, Sarah Harvey. *The Life and Times of Anne Royall.* Cedar Rapids, Ia.: Torch Press Book Shop, 1908.

Royall, Anne. *The Black Book, or a Continuation of Travels in the United States.* Washington, 1827.

Royall, Anne. *Pennsylvania, or Travels Continued in the United States.* Washington, 1829.

Royall, Anne. *Sketches of History, Life and Manners in the United States, by a Traveler.* New Haven, 1826.

Chapter 17: Martin R. Delaney: Pittsburgh's First Human Rights Hero

Afro-American Encyclopedia. North Miami: Educational Book Publishers, 1952.

Baldwin, Leland. *Pittsburgh: The Story of an American City.* Pittsburgh: University of Pittsburgh Press, 1937.

Brawley, Benjamin. *Negro Builders and Heroes.* Chapel Hill: University of North Carolina Press, 1937.

Delaney, Martin R. *Blake, or the Huts of America.* Boston: Beacon Press, 1970.

Delaney, Martin R. and Robert Campbell. *Search for a Place: Black Separatism and Africa.* Ann Arbor: University of Michigan Press, 1969.

Greene, Robert Ewall. *Black Defenders of America.* Chicago: Johnson, 1974.

Killekelly, Sarah. *History of Pittsburgh: Its Rise and Progress.* Pittsburgh: Gordon Montgomery, 1906.

Ploski, Harry A. and James Williams, Eds. *Negro Almanac.* 5th Edition. Detroit: Gale Research, 1987.

Sterling, Dorothy. *The Making of an Afro-American: Martin Robison Delaney, 1812–1885.* Garden City, NJ: Doubleday, 1971.

Turner, Edward. *The Negro in Pennsylvania.* New York: American Historical Association, 1911.

Chapter 18: John Brashear: Pittsburgh's Forgotten Hero

Brashear Association Scrapbook. Pittsburgh: Archives of Hillman Library. Special Collections Room. University of Pittsburgh.

Brashear, John A. "Get Interested in Something." *American Magazine.* July 1916.

Brashear, John A. *A Man Who Loved the Stars.* Pittsburgh: University of Pittsburgh Press, 1924.

Crowell, Merle. "John A. Brashear." *American Magazine.* July 1916.

Gaul, Harriet A. and John Eiseman. *Alfred Brashear: Scientist and Humanitarian.* Philadelphia: University of Pennsylvania Press, 1940.

Gazette Times. March 1, 1918.

"John Brashear." *Pitt Magazine.* Winter 1956.

Pittsburgh Post Gazette. November 24, 1916; March 1, 1918.

Pittsburgh Press. December 12, 1951.

Starrett, Agnes Lynch. *Henry C. Frick Educational Commission.* Pittsburgh: Board of Trustees Annual Report, 1975.

The Story of John Alfred Brashear: A Man Who Loved the Stars. Pittsburgh: Brashear Association.

Chapter 19: Billy Sunday: Professional Baseball Player and Evangelist

Brown, Elijah P. D. D. *The Real Billy Sunday.* New York: Fleming H. Revell, 1914.

Collins, Joseph M. "Revivals, Past and Present." *Harpers.* November 1917.

Ellis, William T. *Billy Sunday: The Man and His Message.* Philadelphia: L. T. Myers, 1914.

McLaughlin, Jr., Wm. G. *Billy Sunday Was His Real Name.* Chicago: University of Chicago Press, 1955.

National Encyclopedia of American Biography. New York: James T. White, 1921.

Odell, Joseph H. "Mechanics of Survivalism." *Atlantic Monthly.* May 1915.

Chapter 20: Deep Waters Run Still: The Underground River

"The Fountain." *Carnegie Magazine.* Summer 1975.

Ohler, S. R. *PittsburgGraphics.* Pittsburgh: S. R. Ohler, 1983.

Pittsburgh Post Gazette. June 8, 1982.

Pittsburgh Press. August 22, 1965; September 5, 1965; June 21, 1982.

Shane, William. "It's Your PUC." Press Release. Harrisburg: Pennsylvania Public Utility Commission, 1988.

Zielkowski, Heide. "Groundwater: Our Unseen Resource." *Calypso Log.* February 1988.

Chapter 21: For Sale in Pittsburgh—Slaves

Baldwin, Leland D. *Pittsburgh: The Story of A City.* Pittsburgh: University of Pittsburgh Press, 1938.

Blackson, Charles L. *The Underground Railroad in Pennsylvania.* Jacksonville, Fl.: Flame International, 1981.

Brewster, Robert W. "The Rise of the Anti-Slavery Movement in Pennsylvania." *Western Pennsylvania Historical Magazine.* March 1939.

Bulletin Index. February 9, 1939.

Carnegie, Andrew. "The Negro in America." Address. Edinburgh: The Philosophical Institute of Edinburgh, October 10, 1907.

Dahlinger, Charles W. *Pittsburgh: A Sketch of Its Early Life.* New York: G. P. Putman, 1916.

Pittsburgh Dispatch. February 1919.

Pittsburgh Post Gazette. January 12, 1957.

Pittsburgh Press. August 20, 1978.

Proceedings of the Anti-Slavery Convention of American Women. Philadelphia: Merrihew and Gunn, 1838-1839.

Turner, Edward R. *The Negro in Pennsylvania.* Washington: American History Association, 1912.

Wax, Donald D. *Negro Stave Trade in Colonial Pennsylvania.* Ph.D. Dissertation. University of Washington, 1962.

Wilson, Erasmus. *Standard History of Pittsburgh, Pennsylvania.* Chicago: H. R. Cornell, 1898.

Chapter 22: When Pittsburghers Rode the Planks Rather Than Walked Them!

"Allegheny County and Good Roads." *Pittsburgh Post.* November 29, 1921.

Hulbert, Archer Butler. *Historic Highways.* Cleveland: Arthur H. Clark, 1904.

Hulbert, Archer Butler. *Pioneer Roads.* Cleveland: Arthur H. Clark, 1904.

Jones, Fred. "You Didn't Walk Plank, You Rode It." *Pittsburgh Press.* December 13, 1959.

Kingsford, W. *History, Structure, and Statistics of Plank Roads in the U.S. and Canada.* Philadelphia: A. Hart, 1951.

Lorant, Stefan. *Pittsburgh: The Story of an American City.* Garden City, NJ: Doubleday, 1964.

Murphy, Julius W. "The Butler Plank Road." *Glenshaw Glass Letter.* July 1969.

"Old Toll Gates About Pittsburgh." *Western Pennsylvania Historical Magazine.* April 3, 1920.

Phelps, Hartley M. "Allegheny County Leads in Improved Roads." *Gazette Times.* March 19, 1911.

Chapter 23: The Glasshouse Boys of Pittsburgh

Cosmopolitan Magazine. Editorial. November 1906.

"Glass Making." *Pittsburgh Gazette Times.* March 19, 1911.

"Glass Not the Leader in Pittsburgh Manufactures." *Pittsburgh Gazette.* September 27, 1908.

Innes, Lowell. *Pittsburgh Glass.* New York: Houghton Mifflin, 1976.

Larner, John William. "The Glasshouse Boys." *Western Pennsylvania Historical Society Magazine.* October 1965.

Markham, Edwin. "Child Wrecking in the Glass Factories." *Cosmopolitan Magazine.* October 1906.

Markham, Edwin. "The Hoe Man in the Making." *Cosmopolitan Magazine.* November 1906.

Spargo, John. *The Bitter Cry of the Children.* New York: Macmillan, 1907.

"The Tragic Significance of Cheap Bottles." New York: Current Literature, 1908.

White, William A. "Tyrian Mariners Discovered Glass Manufacture by Accident." *Pittsburgh Press.* January 24, 1931.

Chapter 24: Are Pittsburgh's Summers Getting Warmer?

Hughes, Patrick. *American Weather Stories.* Washington: U.S. Department of Commerce, 1976.

Hughes, Patrick. *Low Temperatures, Snow and Frost.* Washington: Weatherwise, June 1979.

Kimble, George H. T. *Our American Weather.* New York: Doubleday, 1955.

Koontz, William H. and William H. Welfley, Eds. *History of Bedford and Somerset Counties.* New York: Lewis, 1986.

Pennsylvania School Report of 1860. Harrisburg, Pa.: Department of Education, Commonwealth of Pennsylvania, 1861.

Stewart, J. T. *Indiana County, Pennsylvania: Her People Past and Present.* Indiana, Pa: 1921.

Chapter 25: Pittsburgh—Progress and Prophecies

Humphrey, A. L. "Pittsburgh Fifty Years Hence." *Pittsburgh and the Pittsburgh Spirit.* Pittsburgh: Chamber of Commerce, 1929.

"Pittsburgh in the Year 2000." *Pittsburgh Post Gazette.* October 24, 1989.

Chapter 26: Pittsburgh: As Others See Us

Carnegie, Andrew. *Autobiography.* ed. John C. Van Kyck. Pittsburgh, 1920.

Dickens, Charles. *American Notes.* London, 1842.

Gill, Brenden. "The Sky Line." *The New Yorker.* January 9, 1989.

Hodges, Margaret. "Pittsburgh: Seven Authors, Seven Views." *Western Pennsylvania Historical Magazine.* July 1973.

Kenny, James. "Journal." *Pennsylvania Magazine of History and Biography,* 1913.

Lee, Richard Henry. *Life of Arthur Lee.* Virginia, 1829.

Lorant, Stefan. *Pittsburgh: The Story of An American City.* Garden City: Doubleday, 1964.

Mencken, Henry L. *Prejudices.* New York: Vintage Books. 1958.

New York Times. November 26, 1989.

Ohler, Samuel R. *PittsburGraphics.* Pittsburgh: S. R. Ohler, 1983.

Rause, Vince. "Pittsburgh Cleans Up Its Act." *New York Times Magazine.* November 26, 1989.

Schoepf, Johann David. *Travels in the Confederation, 1783-42.* 1911.

Tokar, Franklin. *Pittsburgh: An Urban Portrait.* State College: Penn State University Press, 1986.

Washington, George. *The Journal of Major George Washington, to the Commandant of the French Forces on Ohio.* Williamsburg and London, 1754.